CU00802973

Simulations, genetics and
human prehistory

Simulations conference delegates (left to right): (Back row) Henry Harpending, Felix Riede, Charles Higham, Daniel Falush, Maru Mormina, David Phillipson, John Terrell, Ian Wilson, Paul Mellars, Pedro Soares, Stephen Shennan, Colin Renfrew, Chris Tyler-Smith, Mark Beaumont, Phillip Endicott, Christopher Gillson, Laurent Excoffier, Mark Thomas, Anthony Edwards, Stephen Oppenheimer; (Third row) Bill Amos, Yali Xue, Denise Carvalho-Silva, Tatiana Zerjal; (Second row) Nicolas Ray, Andrea Manica, Robert Griffiths, Naruya Saitou; (Front row) Rosalind Harding, Erika Hagelberg, Shuichi Matsumura, Bryndis Yngvadottir, Peter Forster.

MᴄDONALD INSTITUTE MONOGRAPHS

Simulations, genetics and human prehistory

Edited by
Shuichi Matsumura, Peter Forster & Colin Renfrew

Published with the aid of a grant from the
ALFRED P. SLOAN FOUNDATION

Published by:

McDonald Institute for Archaeological Research
University of Cambridge
Downing Street
Cambridge, UK
CB2 3ER
(0)(1223) 339336
(0)(1223) 333538 (General Office)
(0)(1223) 333536 (FAX)
dak12@cam.ac.uk
www.mcdonald.cam.ac.uk

Distributed by Oxbow Books
 United Kingdom: Oxbow Books, 10 Hythe Bridge Street, Oxford, OX1 2EW, UK.
  Tel: (0)(1865) 241249; Fax: (0)(1865) 794449; www.oxbowbooks.com
 USA: The David Brown Book Company, P.O. Box 511, Oakville, CT 06779, USA.
  Tel: 860-945-9329; Fax: 860-945-9468

ISBN: 978-1-902937-45-8
ISSN: 1363-1349 (McDonald Institute)

© 2008 McDonald Institute for Archaeological Research

All rights reserved. No parts of this publication may be
reproduced, stored in a retrieval system, or transmitted, in any
form or by any means, electronic, mechanical, photocopying,
recording or otherwise, without the prior permission of the
McDonald Institute for Archaeological Research.

Edited for the Institute by Graeme Barker, James Barrett (*Series Editors*) and Dora A. Kemp (*Production Editor*).

Cover illustration: *Outrigger canoe on the beach at Katsepe, northwest Madagascar.*
(Photograph: Alison F. Richard.)

Printed and bound by Short Run Press, Bittern Rd, Sowton Industrial Estate, Exeter, EX2 7LW, UK.

CONTENTS

On CD

Simulated data sets produced by Henry Harpending for the conference workshop

Contributors

WILLIAM AMOS
Department of Zoology, University of Cambridge, Downing Street, Cambridge, CB2 3EJ, UK.
Email: wa100@hermes.cam.ac.uk

FRANÇOIS BALLOUX
Theoretical and Molecular Population Genetics Group, Department of Genetics, University of Cambridge, Downing Street, Cambridge, CB2 3EH, UK.
Email: fb255@mole.bio.cam.ac.uk

WEIDONG BAO
State Key Laboratory of Plant Genomics and Center for Plant Gene Research, Institute of Genetics and Developmental Biology, The Chinese Academy of Sciences, Beijing 100101, China.
Email: baoweidong@hotmail.com

MARK BEAUMONT
School of Biological Sciences, The University of Reading, Whiteknights, PO Box 68, Reading, RG6 6BX, UK.
Email: m.a.beaumont@reading.ac.uk

PETYA BELINDA BLUMBACH
50 Draycott Park, #27-02, Singapore 259396.
Email: petyablumbach@gmail.com

NIGEL BURROUGHS
Mathematics Institute, University of Warwick, Coventry, CV4 7AL, UK.
Email: N.J.Burroughs@warwick.ac.uk

MATHIAS CURRAT
AGP, Department of Anthropology & Ecology, University of Geneva, 12, rue Gustave-Revilliod, 1227 Geneva, Switzerland.
Email: mathias.currat@anthro.unige.ch

ROBERT DEWAR
McDonald Institute for Archaeological Research, University of Cambridge, Downing Street, Cambridge, CB2 3ER, UK.
Email: red30@cam.ac.uk

RUOFU DU
Institute of Genetics, Chinese Academy of Sciences, Beijing, 100101, China.
Email: zhchen0217@yahoo.com

LAURENT EXCOFFIER
CMPG, Zoological Institute, University of Bern, Baltzerstrasse 6, 3012 Bern, Switzerland.
Email: laurent.excoffier@zoo.unibe.ch

DANIEL FALUSH
Environmental Research Institute, University College Cork, Lee Road, Cork, Ireland.
Email: d.falush@ucc.ie

PETER FORSTER
Department of Life Sciences, Anglia Ruskin University, East Road, Cambridge, CB1 1PT, UK.
Email: peter.forster@anglia.ac.uk

SONGBIN FU
Department of Medical Biology, Harbin Medical University, Harbin, 150086, China.
Email: fusb@ems.hrbmu.edu.cn

GARY GERMAN
English Department, Faculté des Lettres et Sciences Sociales, University of Brest, France.
Email: german@mailhost.univ-brest.fr

ROBERT C. GRIFFITHS
Department of Statistics, University of Oxford, 1 South Parks Road, Oxford, OX1 3TG, UK.
Email: griff@stats.ox.ac.uk

YVONNE J. GRIFFITHS
St Hilda's College, University of Oxford, Cowley Place, Oxford, OX4 1DY, UK.
Email: yvonne.griffiths@st-hildas.ox.ac.uk

HEINRICH HÄRKE
Visiting Research Fellow, Department of Archaeology, The University of Reading, Whiteknights, Reading, RG6 6AB, UK.
Email: h.g.h.harke@reading.ac.uk

HENRY HARPENDING
Department of Anthropology University of Utah, 270 South 1440 East, Room 102, Salt Lake City, UT 84112-0060, USA.
Email: henry.harpending@anthro.utah.edu

CHARLES HIGHAM
Anthropology Department, University of Otago, P.O. Box 56, Dunedin, New Zealand.
Email: charles.higham@otago.ac.nz

MATTHEW E. HURLES
The Wellcome Trust Sanger Institute, Wellcome
Trust Genome Campus, Hinxton, Cambridge, CB10
1SA, UK.
Email: meh@sanger.ac.uk

HOWSUN JOW
Mathematics Institute, University of Warwick,
Coventry, CV4 7AL, UK.

PU LI
Department of Medical Biology, Harbin Medical
University, Harbin, 150086, China.
Email: lipu@ems.hrbmu.edu.cn

HUA LIU
Theoretical and Molecular Population Genetics
Group, Department of Genetics, University of
Cambridge, Downing Street, Cambridge, CB2 3EH,
UK.
Email: h.liu@gen.cam.ac.uk

ANDREA MANICA
Evolutionary Ecology Group, Department of
Zoology, University of Cambridge, Downing Street,
Cambridge, CB2 3EJ, UK.
Email: am315@cam.ac.uk

SHUICHI MATSUMURA
Evolution and Ecology Program, International
Institute for Applied Systems Analysis, Laxenburg,
A-2361, Austria.
Email: matsumur@iiasa.ac.at

RASMUS NIELSEN
Center for Bioinformatics, University of Copenhagen,
Universitetsparken 15, 2100 Kbh Ø, Denmark.
Email: rasmus@binf.ku.dk

STEPHEN OPPENHEIMER
School of Anthropology, Oxford University, 51
Banbury Road, OX2 6PE, UK.
Email: stephen.oppenheimer@ntlworld.com

FRANCK PRUGNOLLE
Laboratoire Génétique et Evolution des Maladies
Infectieuses, UMR 2724 CNRS-IRD-UMI, IRD
Montpellier, 911 Av. Agropolis, 34394 Montpellier,
Cedex 5, France
Email: franck.prugnolle@mpl.ird.fr

NICOLAS RAY
CMPG, Zoological Institute, University of Bern,
Baltzerstrasse 6, 3012 Bern, Switzerland.
Email: nicolas.ray@zoo.unibe.ch

COLIN RENFREW
McDonald Institute for Archaeological Research,
University of Cambridge, Downing Street,
Cambridge, CB2 3ER, UK.
Email: mcdrenf@hermes.cam.ac.uk

SAITOU NARUYA
Division of Population Genetics, National Institute
of Genetics, Mishima, 411-8540, Japan.
Email: saitounr@lab.nig.ac.jp

STEPHEN SHENNAN
Institute of Archaeology, University College
London, 31–34 Gordon Square, London, WC1H 0PY,
UK.
Email: s.shennan@ucl.ac.uk

QUNFANG SHU
Institute of Genetics, Chinese Academy of Sciences,
Beijing, 100101, China.

JAMES STEELE
AHRC Centre for the Evolution of Cultural
Diversity, Institute of Archaeology, University
College London, 31–34 Gordon Square, London,
WC1H 0PY, UK.
Email: tcrnjst@ucl.ac.uk

MICHAEL P.H. STUMPF
Centre for Bioinformatics, Division of Molecular
Biosciences, Imperial College London, Wolfson
Building, South Kensington Campus, SW7 2AZ
London, UK.
Email: m.stumpf@imperial.ac.uk

MARK G. THOMAS
Research Department of Genetics, Evolution and
Environment, University College London, Wolfson
House, 4 Stephenson Way, London, NW1 2HE, UK.
Email: m.thomas@ucl.ac.uk

CHRIS TYLER-SMITH
The Wellcome Trust Sanger Institute, Wellcome
Trust Genome Campus, Hinxton, Cambs., CB10
1SA, UK.
Email: cts@sanger.ac.uk

Introduction

Shuichi Matsumura & Peter Forster

What is simulation? Why do we need it?

Consider a system which we are keen to understand. The system could be mechanical (e.g. an airplane), biological (e.g. a circulatory system), ecological (an ecosystem), or economic (e.g. a stock market). An important tool in modern science to understand the behaviour of a system is experimentation. We usually manipulate one of the variables involved while keeping the others constant, and then see what happens. In many cases, however, we find it quite difficult or impossible to carry out experiments on the real system. For example, we cannot manipulate a human brain or a distant galaxy to understand how it works. An alternative is to consider a model of the system instead of the system itself and conduct experiments on it.

The model could be a substitute in the real world, for example, a miniature airplane or a rat brain. Or the model might be located in a virtual world — a mathematical model. In the latter case, problems are represented mathematically and answers are obtained by solving equations. In many complicated models, however, analytical solutions are unachievable. This is the situation where we often use computer simulation. Computer simulation is an experiment based on mathematical models in the virtual world where we can manipulate variables easily. The outcome of the simulation gives us useful insights into the real system if the model reflects its features appropriately.

Historical processes are typical examples for which we often cannot obtain answers by real experiment. We are basically unable to manipulate an event in the past to elucidate what kinds of processes or factors were really responsible for the event. However, we may be able to repeat the historical process by simulating a world. This will give us an insight into the process. Simulation now plays an important role in studies of human evolution and population histories.

Computer simulation and human prehistory studies

Computer simulation has developed in parallel with the rise of computers. Projects during World War II, in particular the development of atomic bombs and ballistic missiles, are thought to have played a critical role in the emergence of computer simulation. However, simulation itself has its own long history. Some types of simulations have been carried out for centuries by hand or by using various types of calculators. A famous example is Buffon's needle experiment in the eighteenth century. Buffon obtained an approximate value of π by throwing a needle repeatedly onto a table, where parallel lines were drawn, and by calculating the probability of the needle's crossing the lines. One might say that Buffon's experiment is not a simulation in the sense described above because it did not aim to understand a particular system. However, it clearly contains an important element of Monte Carlo simulation — stochasticity or randomness. Sometimes the needle crosses the lines, and sometimes it does not. If the trials are repeated numerous times, the proportion of the trials when the needle crosses the lines approaches a constant value.

The paper by Kunstadter and colleagues (1963) has been recognized as the first study which used computer simulation in anthropology. They investigated the effect of demographic parameters, such as birth rate, death rate and age-specific marriage rates, on the frequency of cross-cousin marriage in a society. Even when cross-cousin marriage is preferred in a society, the realized proportion depends on the availability of cross-cousins, which is affected by demographic variables. For example, if all of your cross-cousins, including you, happen to be the same sex, or if you have no cross-cousin, or if the age difference is too large according to the norm of the society, you have no choice but to marry non-cousins. We can examine stochasticity in the demography factors using computer simulations. In a simulated world, virtual men and women are born, grow up, marry, have children, and die. After repeating this process for generations, we obtain a set of genealogies. If we alter demographic parameter values, we have a different set of genealogies. We can analyse these genealogies as if they were real data and identify the effect of the demographic factors.

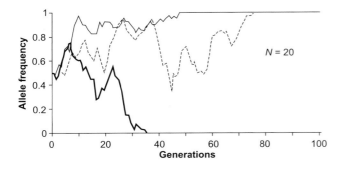

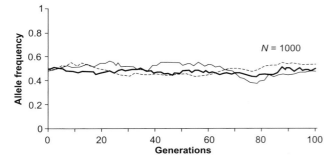

Figure I.1. *Genetic drift in large and small populations. The depicted three simulation runs show changes in allele frequencies of a binary marker in populations of size 20 (above) or 1000 (below). Each run starts from a frequency of 0.5, and the assumptions of the Wright-Fisher model, i.e. constant size, non-overlapping generations, and a random sampling from one generation to the next, are applied. (After Jobling* et al. *2004, fig. 5.5.)*

The earliest application of stochastic computer simulation to population genetics, to our knowledge, also began to be published in the early 1960s (e.g. Lewontin & Dunn 1960; Brues 1963). One of the important aims of simulations in this area was to investigate stochastic changes in allele frequencies over the generations. If a parent has alleles A and B at a genetic locus, for example, the child inherits either A or B. The probability is fifty-fifty. Does this mean that, on a population level, the allele frequencies A and B do not change over the generations? No. In actual human populations, some parents have more than 10 children, while some have none. Therefore, if parents who have the allele A happen to have considerably more offspring than the others, the frequency of A can increase. If this process happens to continue, the allele A can spread and ultimately become fixed in the population even when it has no advantage in the sense of natural selection. When the opposite happens, it vanishes from the population. Outcomes of this random process can easily be illustrated using a simple computer simulation. Again, in a simulated world virtual men and women grow up, marry, have children and die. Their children inherit alleles A or/ and B from their parents. After repeating this process for generations, we can follow the change of the allele frequencies.

Fixation and extinction of alleles are greatly influenced by the size of the population (Fig. I.1). Although random fluctuations of the allele frequencies seldom lead to fixation or extinction in a large population, they commonly occur in a small population. Polymorphism found at various loci dies out once a severe reduction of population size or a population bottleneck happens. This is one reason why we can infer past demographic histories from present genetic data. A population which shows few genetic polymorphisms is likely to have experienced a small population size in the past. It is believed that this neutral fluctuation of allele frequencies has played a major role in the evolution of the polymorphisms at a molecular level (Kimura 1983), for example, the polymorphisms in blood proteins widely seen in human populations.

The Neolithic transition in Europe has been one of the major research areas where computer simulation plays an important role. Ammerman & Cavalli-Sforza (1971) measured the speed of the spread of Neolithic culture by a careful consideration of the dates of archaeological sites. Combining this with clines in protein polymorphism seen in Europe, they proposed a model of highly fertile farmers migrating from the Middle East into Europe (demic-diffusion model). The early years following the initial proposals saw significant progress in the use of computer simulation in population genetics. Cavalli-Sforza & Bodmer (1971) and Ammerman & Cavalli-Sforza (1973) presented results of preliminary simulations illustrating the effect of diffusion. The book *The Neolithic Transition and the Genetics of Populations in Europe* by Ammerman & Cavalli-Sforza (1984) devoted a whole chapter to simulation studies. Since then, various simulation approaches to the Neolithic transition in Europe have been made (e.g. Barbujani *et al.* 1995; Fix 1999; Currat *et al.* this volume), in part stimulated by new genetic data from modern as well as ancient DNA (Haak *et al.* 2005).

An important turning point in the history of genetic inference on human demographic history came with Kingman's (1982) coalescent theory. Traditionally, population genetics places emphasis on predicting the genetic composition of a population in the future. Simulations follow all the individuals in the population forwards in time. By contrast, the coalescent is a sample-based theory. We consider a genealogy which starts from a sample (i.e. individuals from the present generation) and go backwards in time toward their common ancestors (Fig. I.2).

The popularity of coalescent simulation is reflected in this volume. All the simulations except one (see the paragraph below) employ coalescent simulation as a core component. Why has coalescent simulation become so popular? Firstly, the rapid accumulation of DNA sequence data since the late 1980s is a prerequisite for coalescent simulation. Since DNA sequences potentially contain information about their ancestral relationships, it is natural to construct a genealogical tree backward in time from individual DNA sequences as tips of the tree. Secondly, from a computational point of view, coalescent simulations are much more efficient than forward ones. As shown in Figure I.2, the former considers only a part of the population. Furthermore, Kingman's coalescent theory provides efficient algorithms to simulate samples under various demographic models.

However, coalescent simulation is not a panacea. If some haplotypes have a selective advantage over others, for example, the probability of coalescence must vary between the sequences. In this case, the construction of genealogies is not straightforward. This is why the paper by Mark Thomas and colleagues (Chapter 6), who examine the effect of differential reproductive success between the local people and immigrants on the genetic composition in British Isles, is an exceptional chapter based on forward simulation which can incorporate differential reproduction with ease.

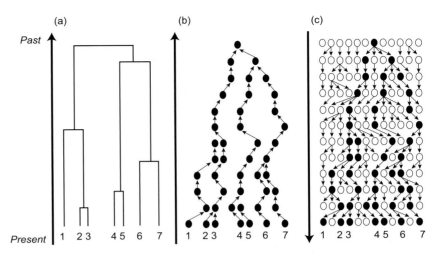

Figure I.2. *Conceptual difference between coalescent and forward simulations. (a) Genealogy of seven sampled sequences. This is an example of trees generated based on Kingman's coalescent theory. Coalescent simulation starts from the present. Each of the samples coalesces with one of the others at some time in the past (i.e. reaches their common ancestor) with a certain probability which is determined by demographic parameters, but not, initially, by genetic distances or inferred mutation events. The branch lengths represent time, and mutations may then randomly be assigned to the branches afterwards. (b) The equivalent tree in discrete-generation coalescent simulation. Simulation allows each of the sampled sequences to coalesce in each generation up to the common ancestor of all the sequences. (c) Forward simulation running from the past to the present. Arrows represent parent–offspring relationships. The genealogy (solid circles) from the common ancestor to the seven sampled sequences is the same as in the previous coalescent example. The difference is however that the forward simulation also contains some dead branches which render this method computationally cumbersome.*

Types of DNA data used in simulation studies

Although serological polymorphisms such as blood types used to be favourite data sources for studies of relationships between populations, direct investigation of polymorphisms in DNA sequences is now common in this area of research. The human genome consists of chromosomal DNA in the nucleus and mitochondrial DNA (mtDNA) in the cytoplasm (see Fig. I.3). The forty-six human chromosomes are divided into 22 pairs of autosomes, and the X and Y chromosomes. Different types of DNA have been used for different research purposes. Combining information from different molecules often results in an improved,

multi-faceted view of the history of a particular geographic region, as seen in Chapter 10 by Saitou.

MtDNA and Y-chromosomal DNA

Mitochondria are tiny but important organelles which provide energy necessary for life through complicated processes of chemical reactions. As human children do not inherit mitochondria from their father, mitochondria are passed through the maternal line only. The mutation rate of mtDNA is higher than that of other DNA, and this makes mtDNA advantageous in studies of relatively short histories such as relationships between populations within a species. Polymorphisms in the hyper-variable regions (HVS-I and HVS-II) of mtDNA have frequently been used in human population genetic studies so that information from more than 35,000 individuals is now available in data bases. Sequencing of the whole mtDNA genome has been introduced in order to obtain a higher resolution in phylogenetic investigations (e.g. Horai *et al.* 1995; Ingman *et al.* 2000).

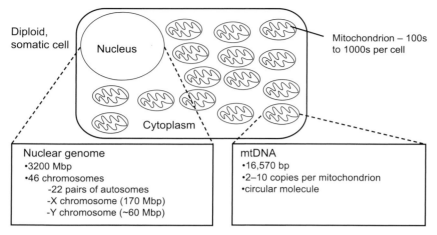

Diploid, somatic cell

Nucleus

Cytoplasm

Mitochondrion – 100s to 1000s per cell

Nuclear genome
•3200 Mbp
•46 chromosomes
  -22 pairs of autosomes
  -X chromosome (170 Mbp)
  -Y chromosome (~60 Mbp)

mtDNA
•16,570 bp
•2–10 copies per mitochondrion
•circular molecule

Figure I.3. *Overview of the human genome. The human genome consists of nuclear chromosomes and cytoplasmic mitochondrial DNA (mtDNA). Females have 22 pairs of autosomes and two X chromosomes, while males have 22 pair of autosomes and one X and one Y chromosome. Usually a single cell contains hundreds or thousands of mitochondria. Each mitochondrion has its own DNA which is about 16,570 basepairs long. (After Jobling et al. 2004, fig. 2.1.)*

Since the seminal paper by Cann *et al.* (1987), mtDNA variation has been studied intensively to understand the colonization history of humans throughout the world. As Oppenheimer (Chapter 3) describes, the construction of phylogenetic trees or networks among individual mtDNA sequences is one of the popular methods in this area. Forster and colleagues (Chapter 7) and Matsumura & Forster (Chapter 10) try to estimate the founding population sizes of Madagascar and Greenland, respectively, using modern mtDNA data from the island populations as well as mtDNA from putative source areas.

In contrast to mtDNA, Y-chromosomal DNA is passed from father to son. As a majority (>90%) of the Y chromosome avoids recombination, phylogenetic relationships of this non-recombining region can be studied using approaches similar to those in mtDNA studies. Since the size of the Y DNA is much larger and the overall mutation rate is lower than mtDNA, researchers usually concentrate on SNPs (Single Nucleotide Polymorphisms) and/or STRs (Short Tandem Repeats) instead of on continuous DNA sequences of the Y chromosome (see Fig. I.4).

Amos and colleagues (Chapter 5) focus on Y STR data and investigate the ancestral relationship and gene flow between several populations in Britain and in Europe. In Chapter 9, Tyler-Smith and colleagues test whether the popular software for coalescent simulation, 'BATWING' (Bayesian Analysis of Trees With Internal Node Generation) is able to extract traces of

population expansions in China. Thomas and colleagues (Chapter 6) carry out simulations to reconcile apparent discrepancies between Y DNA reports and archaeological studies on the number of Anglo-Saxon migrants.

There is another reason to use mtDNA for the inference of past demographic history. Successful extraction and amplification from ancient samples is much easier to achieve for mtDNA than for other types of DNA, because mtDNA is present in a much higher copy number. Hyper-variable regions of Neanderthal mtDNA have been sequenced successfully from several Neanderthal specimens, starting with Krings *et al.* (1997). The fact that we cannot find any Neanderthal mtDNA types in more than 12,000 modern European samples suggests that admixture between Neanderthals and modern humans was quite limited even if it did occur. Using spatially explicit simulations, Currat and colleagues (Chapter 4) estimate that interbreeding rates between the Neanderthals and modern humans should have been less than 0.1%.

Autosomal DNA
Archaeologists are generally interested in the prehistory of a region, instead of that of a particular gene. Owing to stochasticity, natural selection, or sexually different demographic processes, the demographic history inferred from a single locus such as mtDNA or Y DNA might not represent the regional prehistory well. Thus, inference based on many loci is desirable. The technical drawback is that a coalescent approach to many loci with potential recombination is computationally challenging.

Excoffier and colleagues (Chapter 1) and Balloux and colleagues (Chapter 2) use the same autosomal STR data set (Rosenberg *et al.* 2002) but take different approaches. In the original article, hidden structures among human populations were investigated using the software 'STRUCTURE', which is discussed in detail by Falush (Chapter 12). Balloux and colleagues rely on a rather traditional approach, calculating summary statistics for each population and examining these statistics in relation to the distance between populations. Their novelty lies in their way how to calculate the distance. By contrast, Excoffier and colleagues carry out spatially explicit coalescent simulations to look for the birthplace of modern humans.

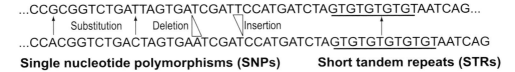

Figure I.4. *Examples of SNPs (Single Nucleotide Polymorphisms) and STRs (Short Tandem Repeats). A SNP represents a change in a nucleotide at one position in the DNA, which can be a substitution, insertion or deletion of a single nucleotide. STR loci, also known as microsatellites, consist of tandemly repeated DNA motifs, for example, (GT)(GT)(GT)...(GT) which are prone to motif insertions and deletions. (After Jobling* et al. *2004, fig. 3.2.)*

Griffiths & Griffiths (Chapter 13) and Beaumont (Chapter 14) also use basically the same data set, but select only a few populations from them. Although recently developed methods of genealogical analysis based on Markov chain Monte Carlo (MCMC) or importance sampling (IS) are quite powerful for obtaining the likelihood of demographic parameters, they are typically restricted to small data sets due to computational difficulties. All three endeavour to extend the existing methods and apply them to subdivided populations. Griffiths & Griffiths apply their IS method to several pairs of selected populations and inferred migration rates, while Beaumont extends his ABC (Approximate Bayesian Calculation) method from two to three sub-populations with gene flow between them.

There is another potential data source for demographic inference of past human populations: the HapMap data. The International HapMap Project aims to create 'a public, genome-wide database of common human sequence variation, providing information needed as a guide to genetic studies of clinical phenotypes' (The International HapMap Consortium 2005). Although it is a clinically oriented data base, the huge amount of genome-wide SNP data is a treasure trove for geneticists who seek to learn more about human prehistory. There is an urgent need to develop methods to utilize information contained in genome-wide SNP data such as the HapMap data. Both Nielsen (Chapter 15) and Wilson (Chapter 16) take up this challenging task.

Let's try to read history from genetic data: experimental workshop

We face a fundamental problem when we try to infer prehistory by applying our favourite methods to genetic data: we do not know the true history. Therefore, how can we be sure about the validity of the methods we use? Which result should we believe if we obtain different answers from different methods?

There is a way to overcome this problem. We can use computer simulation to generate a fully-documented test case which includes both the exact demographic history and the genetic outcome. Then we apply a method to this artificial genetic data, and obtain estimates on the history. By comparing our own estimates with the known simulated history, we can test the validity and limits of the method. As exemplified in the chapters by Excoffier *et al.* and Beaumont, it is actually common practice to perform such simulation experiments before applying new methods to real data.

Ideally, the researcher should not know the simulated history before applying his or her methods to the simulated test data. In other words, the test data should be created by a third party. This is why we held an experimental workshop after the symposium. Professor Henry Harpending (University of Utah) sent four sets of data generated by simulation to a variety of researchers two months before the workshop and asked them to 'read history from the data!' The details of the workshop are described in the note by the editors and the following chapter by Henry Harpending (Chapter 20).

A compact disc attached to this volume contains the simulated data sets produced by Henry Harpending as well as his original explanatory notes. We offer you a special opportunity to test your own favourite methods on Henry Harpending's tasks. Please choose your favourite methods and apply them to the data. You will then see how well your methods work. The answers ('the true histories') are described in the latter half of Henry Harpending's chapter.

References

Ammerman, A.J. & L.L. Cavalli-Sforza, 1971. Measuring the rate of spread of early farming in Europe. *Man* 6, 674–88.

Ammerman, A.J. & L.L. Cavalli-Sforza, 1973. A population model for the diffusion of early farming in Europe, in *The Explanation of Culture Change: Models in Prehistory*, ed. C. Renfrew. Pittsburgh: University of Pittsburgh Press, 343–57.

Ammerman, A.J. & L.L. Cavalli-Sforza, 1984. *The Neolithic Transition and the Genetics of Populations in Europe*. Princeton (NJ): Princeton University Press.

Barbujani, G., R.R. Sokal & N.L. Oden, 1995. Indo-European

origins: a computer-simulation test of five hypotheses. *American Journal of Physical Anthropology* 96, 109–32.

Brues, A.M., 1963. Stochastic tests of selection in the ABO blood groups. *American Journal of Physical Anthropology* 21, 287–99.

Cann, R.L., M. Stoneking & A.C. Wilson, 1987. Mitochondrial DNA and human evolution. *Nature* 325, 31–6.

Cavalli-Sforza, L.L. & W.F. Bodmer, 1971. *The Genetics of Human Populations*. San Francisco (CA): Freeman.

Currat, M. & L. Excoffier, 2004. Modern humans did not admix with Neanderthals during their range expansion into Europe. *PLoS Biology* 2, 2264–74.

Fix, A.G., 1999. *Migration and Colonization in Human Microevolution*. Cambridge: Cambridge University Press.

Haak, W., P. Forster, B. Bramanti, *et al.*, 2005. Ancient DNA from the first European farmers in 7500-year-old Neolithic sites. *Science* 310, 1016–18.

Helgason, A., S. Sigurðardóttir, J.R. Gulcher, R. Ward & K. Stefánsson, 2000. MtDNA and the origin of the Icelanders: deciphering signals of recent population history. *American Journal of Human Genetics* 66, 999–1016.

Horai, S., K. Hayasaka, R. Kondo, K. Tsugane & N. Takahata, 1995. Recent African origin of modern humans revealed by complete sequences of hominoid mitochondrial DNAs. *Proceedings of the National Academy of Sciences of the USA* 92(2), 532–6.

Ingman, M., H. Kaessmann, S. Pääbo & U. Gyllensten, 2000. Mitochondrial genome variation and the origin of modern humans. *Nature* 408, 708–13.

The International HapMap Consortium, 2005. A haplotype map of the human genome. *Nature* 437, 1299–320.

Jobling, M.A., M.E. Hurles & C. Tyler-Smith, 2004. *Human Evolutionary Genetics: Origins, Peoples & Disease*. New York (NY) & Abingdon: Garland Science.

Kimura, M., 1983. *The Neutral Theory of Molecular Evolution*. Cambridge: Cambridge University Press.

Kingman, J.F.C., 1982. The coalescent. *Stochastic Processes and Applications* 13, 235–48.

Krings, M., A. Stone, R.W. Schmitz, H. Krainitzki, M. Stoneking & S. Pääbo, 1997. Neandertal DNA sequences and the origin of modern humans. *Cell* 90, 19–30.

Kunstadter, P., R. Buhler, F.F. Stephan & C.F. Westoff, 1963. Demographic variability and preferential marriage patterns. *American Journal of Physical Anthropology* 21, 511–19.

Lewontin, R.C. & L.C. Dunn, 1960. The evolutionary dynamics of a polymorphism in the house mouse. *Genetics* 45, 705–22.

Rosenberg, N.A., J.K. Pritchard, J.L. Weber, *et al.*, 2002. Genetic structure of human populations. *Science* 298, 2381–5.

(RAO) model or one of its extensions seems the most likely evolutionary model for past human populations (Excoffier 2002), alternative models could include non-African locations for a recent and unique origin (UO) of modern humans, an incomplete replacement of *Homo erectus* individuals by modern humans, or the multiregional evolution model (ME model: see e.g. Wolpoff 1989; Wolpoff *et al.* 2000). The latter model postulates that there was a gradual and simultaneous transition from *Homo erectus* to modern forms on different continents, and that this synchronized process was possible due to continuous migrations between continents. Our main aim is to see whether the patterns of genetic diversity allow one to distinguish between UO and ME models. We thus simulate a range expansion process under the UO model from arbitrary geographic origins or a ME model assuming various continental sizes, environmental heterogeneity, and rates of exchange between continents, and we see how well we can recover them by an estimation procedure based on extensive simulations. Here we do not consider any models that incorporate interbreeding.

As there is a large uncertainty about past environments and their effect on human demography, it appears important to study the impact of various levels of environmental heterogeneity on our ability to distinguish among human evolutionary scenarios. In the present study, we extend the recent results from Ray *et al.* (2005) concerning the possibility of recovering the origin of modern humans from spatially explicit computer simulations by incorporating extra levels of environmental heterogeneity. This paper is also an attempt at evaluating the impact of various levels of environmental heterogeneity on the recovery of the geographical origin of a range expansion.

Methods

Demographic simulations
Details of the demographic simulations are reported in Ray *et al.* (2005) and in Currat *et al.* (2004), and we only summarize them in the following. We considered a simulated world subdivided into 9226 demes covering the surface of the Old World, each deme occupying an area of 100 by 100 km^2. Using the software SPLATCHE (Currat *et al.* 2004), we performed simulations of a range expansion from 25 different geographic origins, which were evenly distributed every 2000 km on the surface of the Old World, as shown in Figure 1.1. We first simulated, forward in time, a demographic and spatial expansion from an initial population of size equal to 50 diploid individuals (100 nuclear genes). We recorded, for each generation, the number of individual genes

present in a deme, as well as the number of immigrant genes coming from each of the four nearest neighbouring demes on the grid. This demographic and migration history was stored in a data base, which was then used to generate, backward in time, the genealogy and the diversity of genes sampled at given locations.

We assumed a generation time of 30 years for modern humans (Tremblay & Vezina 2000). Each generation, the occupied demes were subject to a growth phase followed by an emigration phase. The growth phase was logistic with a constant growth rate of $r = 0.3$ (Cavalli-Sforza *et al.* 1994; Steele *et al.* 1998), and a carrying capacity (K) that depended on the environment in which the deme was located (see below). The emigration phase consisted of distributing a total of $0.05 \times N_t$ emigrants among the four nearest-neighbouring demes, where N_t is the size of the deme (number of gene copies within deme) at time t. The exact number of emigrants sent to each of the neighbouring demes i (E_i) was controlled through friction values (F_i) assigned to each neighbouring deme. Friction expresses the relative difficulty of moving through a deme, and was kept within a range of 0.1 (lowest friction, easiest migration) to 1 (highest friction, most difficult migration). E_i was computed from a multinomial distribution, with directional probabilities P_i proportional to the relative frictions F_i of four neighbouring demes obtained as

$$P_i = \left(F_i \times \sum_{j=1}^{4} \frac{1}{F_j} \right)^{-1}.$$

This formula implies that the number of emigrants sent to any deme is inversely proportional to its relative friction. Seas were considered as complete barriers to migration.

For the genetic simulations, we used the sample locations and sizes of a large data set of 377 STR markers analysed in 52 human worldwide populations (Rosenberg *et al.* 2002). However, we considered only populations with a sample size of more than 20 individuals, reducing this data set to 22 population samples, referred to hereafter as the 'Rosenberg22 data set'.

We simulated 25 scenarios, each with different unique origins of early modern humans (Fig. 1.1), as well as 9 scenarios of multiregional origins (Fig. 1.2). The characteristics of each of the multiregional scenario were chosen to cover a large panel of alternative propositions. In each case, multiple origins were located in Africa, Asia and Europe, the size of the African population was related to European/Asiatic population sizes, and the migration rates between continents changed accordingly (see Ray *et al.* 2005 for details).

Table 1.1. *Carrying capacities and frictions attributed to the present-potential vegetation map.*

Vegetation category [a]	Description [a]	Carrying capacity [b]	Friction [c]
1	Tropical rainforest	1433	0.9
2	Monsoon or dry forest	1390	0.9
3	Tropical woodland	446	0.5
4	Tropical thorn scrub and scrub woodland	232	0.5
5	Tropical semi-desert	726	0.1
6	Tropical grassland	1598	0.1
7	Tropical extreme desert	25	0.9
8	Savanna	1104	0.1
9	Broadleaved temperate evergreen forest	1424	0.5
10	Montane tropical forest	1715	0.5
11	Mediterranean sclerophyll woodland or forest	1424	0.5
12	Temperate deciduous broadleaved forest	673	0.5
13	Southern taiga	501	0.1
14	Mid taiga	501	0.1
15	Open boreal woodlands	501	0.5
16	Semi-arid temperate woodland or scrub	673	0.5
17	Semi-arid temperate scrub	673	0.5
18	Tundra	501	0.1
19	Steppe-tundra	501	0.1
20	Polar and alpine desert	141	0.1
21	Temperate desert	141	0.1
22	Temperate semi-desert	141	0.1
23	Forest steppe	501	0.1
24	Forest tundra	501	0.5
25	Montane mosaic	501	0.5
26	Dry steppe	50	0.1
27	Temperate steppe grassland	443	0.1
28	Bog/swamp	0	1.0
29	Ice sheet and other permanent ice	0	1.0
30	Lakes and open water	0	1.0
31	Land bridges (Japan, Sardinia, Orcadian, Australia)	10	0.1

[a] Vegetation categories and descriptions are those from the Present Potential vegetation map of Ray and Adams (available at: http://lgb.unige.ch/~ray/ppveg/index.html). Category no. 31 has been added to the original map and represents artificial land bridges (see Fig. 1.1).
[b] Carrying capacities were derived from the population density estimates derived from present hunter-gatherer groups by Binford (2001). Links between Binford's environment types and the vegetation categories used here are given in Ray (2003, table 3.2). They are expressed in number of effective individuals per 10,000 km².

Environmental heterogeneity
We considered three levels of environmental heterogeneity: (1) *Uniform environment*: all demes have the same carrying capacity of $K = 250$ diploid effective individuals (about 0.05 individual/km², in agreement with average density estimates for Palaeolithic hunter-gatherers: see e.g. Alroy 2001; Steele *et al.* 1998), and friction was identical across the landscape; (2) *Low environmental heterogeneity*: carrying capacities and frictions were related to the type of vegetation associated with each deme (see Table 1.1); a digital map of present potential vegetation (around 4000 years ago: Ray & Adams 2002; Ray *et al.* this volume) was used in that case; (3) *High environmental heterogeneity*: similar to level (2), but with major rivers and coastlines having carrying capacity increased by a factor two, and friction decreased by the same factor. Rivers and coastlines were thus considered as migration corridors and to have a higher density of resources. See Ray *et al.* (this volume) for discussion of these landscape elements. Moreover, in this third level, topography-related friction was introduced through a topographical roughness index. For each deme, this index was computed as the standard deviation of the 10,000 altitude values given by the 1-km resolution GTOPO30 data set (USGS 1996) (see Ray *et al.* this volume). Areas with rough topography were indeed considered more difficult to cross than flatter areas. The final friction values was computed as the mean of the vegetation-related and the topography-related friction terms, corrected for the presence of streams and coastlines. The relative carrying capacity and the friction maps for the two levels of environmental heterogeneity are shown in Figure 1.3.

Assignment score for a given evolutionary scenario: the R_{90} statistic
In order to differentiate the various demographic scenarios, we simulated in a second phase the genetic diversity of the 22 worldwide samples of the Rosenberg 22 data set using a coalescent approach based on the demographic information stored into the data base, itself generated during the demographic simulation (see Ray *et al.* 2005 for details on the coalescent simulation).

If we assume that a given genetic data set is the product of a particular evolutionary scenario, one would ideally like to estimate the likelihoods of all possible scenarios compatible with the observed data, and choose the scenario with maximal likelihood. Due to the spatially explicit nature of our simulation model and the complexity of these potential scenarios, it is very difficult to compute their likelihoods. An approximation was envisioned, however, by computing a goodness-of-fit summary statistic (R_{90}) as follows:

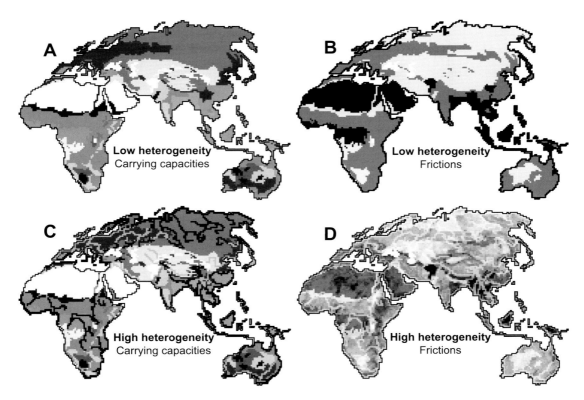

Figure 1.3. *Representation of relative carrying capacity and friction values for the two environmental scenarios 'low heterogeneity' (A and B) and 'high heterogeneity' (C and D). Darker colours indicate relatively higher carrying capacity or friction values.*

1. Compute the observed matrix D_{obs} of pairwise R_{ST} among all pairs of populations.
2. For each evolutionary scenario j ($j = 1 \ldots 34$):
   1. Simulate 10,000 genetic data sets (1, 20, or 377 STR loci) and for each of them compute $D_{sim}^{(i)}$.
   2. Compute the Pearson correlation coefficient between the observed and the simulated R_{ST} matrices $r_{ji} = corr(D_{obs}, D_{sim}^{(i)})$.
   3. From the distribution of r_{ji}, take the 90% quantile value (R_{90}) as the assignment score for the j-th evolutionary scenario.
3. Select the evolutionary scenario with the largest assignment score (largest R_{90} statistic), and thus giving the best fit between observed and simulated data.

The 90% quantile value of the distribution, the R_{90} statistic, was taken as our goodness-of-fit index based on previous experience resulting from extensive simulations (Ray 2003).

Results

Recovering the geographic origin under a UO model
In Table 1.2 we show the frequency of correct assign-

ment for 1, 20 and 377 loci for each of the environmental scenarios. This frequency is very low (between 0.129 and 0.168) when considering a single locus, but still three to four times higher than for a completely random assignment over 25 putative origins. It suggests that some information on the geographic origin of an expansion can be extracted from a single locus, despite the high stochasticity of the coalescent process. When using 20 loci, frequencies of correct assignment increase substantially (between 0.552 and 0.721), and are very high (between 0.976 and 0.989) with 377 loci. When a limited number of loci are available, frequencies of correct assignment also increase with

Table 1.2. *Proportion of simulated cases (over a total of 125,000) in which the true origin of the range expansion is correctly assigned. Standard deviations over the 25 origins are given within parentheses.*

	Environment		
	Uniform	**Low heterogeneity**	**High heterogeneity**
1 locus	0.129 (0.152)	0.149 (0.136)	0.168 (0.148)
20 loci	0.552 (0.240)	0.657 (0.230)	0.721 (0.215)
377 loci	0.976 (0.069)	0.989 (0.035)	0.988 (0.045)

Table 1.3. *Proportion of the simulations in which single origin or multiregional evolution models are correctly recovered by our approach.*

	Environment								
	Uniform			Low heterogeneity			High heterogeneity		
	Single	Mult.	Total	Single	Mult.	Total	Single	Mult.	Total
1 locus	0.878 (0.396)	0.436 (0.423)	0.761 (0.403)	0.935 (0.438)	0.388 (0.420)	0.790 (0.433)	0.931 (0.438)	0.425 (0.427)	0.797 (0.435)
20 loci	0.987 (0.859)	0.985 (0.872)	0.987 (0.863)	0.995 (0.884)	0.992 (0.877)	0.994 (0.882)	0.994 (0.880)	0.995 (0.876)	0.994 (0.879)
377 loci	1.000 (0.987)	1.000 (0.990)	1.000 (0.988)	1.000 (0.991)	1.000 (0.991)	1.000 (0.991)	1.000 (0.990)	1.000 (0.991)	1.000 (0.990)

Values within parenthesis are the mean values of the R_{90} statistic computed when the inferred origin is correctly assigned.

the level of environmental heterogeneity. This is most noticeable when using 20 STR loci, where correct assignment climbs from 55.2% to 72.1% if simulations are performed in a highly heterogeneous environment rather than in a uniform environment. This shows that homogeneous and heterogeneous environment do not lead to identical genetic signatures. Note that with 377 loci, the level of environmental heterogeneity does not matter much, since the assignment is excellent in all cases. In Table 1.3, we report the rate of correct assignment by geographic location for the 9 combinations of environmental heterogeneity and number of loci. It appears that there is a large heterogeneity in correct assignment across the different geographic origins when a few loci are available. For instance, with a single locus, the origins numbering 3, 7, 17, 20 and 23, have much larger probabilities of being correctly assigned than other origins, which may be related to their position on continental edges. With 20 loci, the contrast in probabilities for these different origins is stronger. The origins with lowest assignment success are mainly inland origins, with the exceptions of Australian origins, which seem particularly difficult to assign. Note that a closer look at the incorrect Australian assignments revealed that they were mostly in favour of a Southeast Asian origin (no. 23), suggesting that a potential exit from Australia would be difficult to distinguish from an Indonesian origin, possibly due to the occurrence of spatial bottleneck in the Indonesian peninsula. With 377 loci, all origins are well recovered, with the exception of the two sets in Australia for the reasons just mentioned.

Distinguishing UO from ME models
The same procedure aiming at finding the geographic origin of a range expansion can be used to distinguish between data sets generated under a UO or under a ME model. In this context, a data set is correctly assigned if the scenario chosen on the basis of the R_{90}

statistic belongs to the same evolutionary model as that used to generate it, regardless of the location of the origin or the type of ME scenario. In Figure 1.5, we show the assignment scores of data sets simulated under the 25 UO scenarios and those simulated under the 9 ME scenarios. 125,000 simulated data sets were generated under the UO model (over all possible geographic origins), and 45,000 data sets were generated under all considered ME scenarios. It clearly appears that the evolutionary models are extremely well discriminated. With a single locus, correct assignment increases from 76.1% to 79.7% with the level of environmental heterogeneity, but there is a sharp difference between the correct assignment of data sets generated under a single or multiple origins model, with a much lower recovery rate (less than 45%) of the ME model compared to >85% correct assignment to the UO model. With 20 loci, correct evolutionary model assignment is around 99% and reaches 100% with 377 loci.

Dealing with unknown origins and inaccurate environmental heterogeneity levels
For the demographic simulations so far, the potential geographic origins and the pattern of environmental variability were known without error. We investigate here the consequence of assuming an incorrect geographical origin of the expansion, as well as inadequate environmental information on the probability of recovering the source of a spatial expansion. The locations of 14 alternative and 'assumed true' positions for the origins of an expansion are reported in Figure 1.1 as empty squares. A series of 10,000 simulations were performed from these origins under each of the three levels of environmental heterogeneity defined earlier. The 25 potential origins defined in Figure 1.1 were simulated as actual origins and the resulting genetic data sets were compared to those generated from 'assumed true' origins, either under the same or under different environmental conditions. Since the 'assumed true' and actual origins differ, as could be the case in reality, we measured the probability of recovering the correct geographic region of origin. We partitioned the Old World into four regions according to the results of Rosenberg *et al.* (2002), and as reported in Figure 1.1. The frequencies of correct assignment per region between actual and 'assumed true' origins for different environmental conditions are shown in Table 1.4. We first note that, barring one exception, the assignment score is best when data are simulated

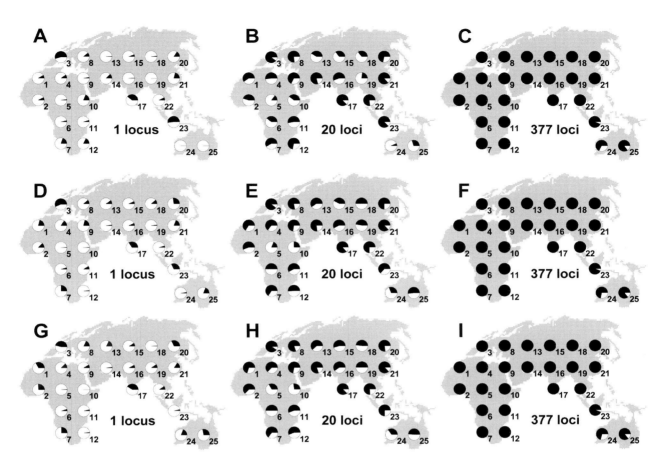

Figure 1.4. *Relative frequencies of correct assignment for 25 simulated origins under various environmental conditions and for different number of available STR loci. Level of environmental heterogeneity are uniform (A, B and C), low (D, E and F), and high (G, H and I). The black area represents the proportion of simulations for which the origin of demographic expansion was correctly recovered from the R₉₀ statistic.*

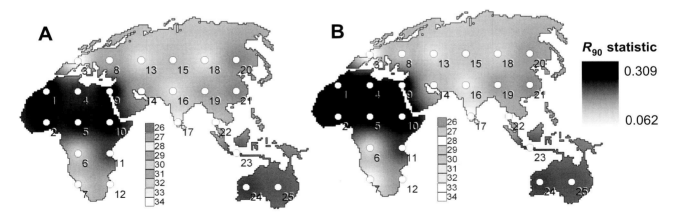

Figure 1.5. *Values of the R₉₀ statistic for 25 UO scenarios (Nos. 1–25) and 9 ME scenarios (Nos. 26–34) computed from the Rosenberg22 data set under the ascertainment bias-uncorrected (A) and ascertainment bias-corrected (B) simulated data sets. Values of the R₉₀ statistic were spatially interpolated between the 25 tested origins to facilitate visual comparison between regions (exact values of the statistic are found in Ray et al. (2005)). The lowest and highest R₉₀ values are indicated on the grey intensity scale.*

15

Table 1.4. *Proportion of the UO simulations in which geographic regions of origin were correctly assigned.*

Environments for the simulated origins	Correct assignment score at the regional level [a]	Environments for the 'true' origins [b]		
		Uniform	Low heterogeneity	High heterogeneity
20 loci				
Uniform	0.785	0.802	0.740	0.743
Low heterogeneity	0.882	0.753	0.771	0.808
High heterogeneity	0.918	0.772	0.709	0.824
377 loci				
Uniform	0.993	0.938	0.778	0.752
Low heterogeneity	0.999	0.795	0.852	0.855
High heterogeneity	1.000	0.889	0.734	0.825

[a] Correct assignment score is computed by assuming that the simulated origin is the true origin, as in Figure 1.1, but for the four regions defined in Figure 1.1.
[b] Correct assignment score obtained by comparing data sets generated from 'true' origins (Fig. 1.1) to data sets generated from simulated origins that are not at the same location. In columns 2–4, diagonal elements are obtained when the true and the simulated environments are similar, and off-diagonal elements represent cases where the true environment is different from the simulated environment.

under the same environmental conditions for the 'assumed true' origin as for the actual origin (compare diagonal elements to off-diagonal elements in columns 2–4 of Table 1.4). The assignment success also usually drops when the geographical origin of the expansion is not known exactly (compare first column to diagonal elements of columns 2–4 in Table 1.4), but to a much lesser degree when the environment is assumed to be uniform. Overall we find that the assignment scores are much lower when there are uncertainties concerning the environmental conditions and the exact origins. Increasing the number of STR loci from 20 to 377 does not lead to a vast improvement as in the case of perfectly known evolutionary conditions (Table 1.4, column 1). Unless we assume no impact of environmental heterogeneity (uniform environment) on human evolution, we see that there is about a 15–20% chance of incorrectly inferring the regional location of an expansion from the matrix of pairwise genetic distances between populations.

Application to real data
The Rosenberg22 data set was used to assign scores to the 34 different scenarios of modern human evolution (25 geographic origins under the UO model as well as 9 scenarios under the ME model) simulated under low levels of environmental heterogeneity. We only evaluated the R_{90} statistic under this low level of heterogeneity because higher levels of environmental heterogeneity imply strong assumptions about the impact of a given environment on human density and

dispersal abilities. Such strong assumptions would not be safe given the uncertainties about past climatic and cultural changes, which have probably modified the impact of environment on human demography. As it still seemed reasonable to take some environmental constraints into account, the low heterogeneity described above made a good compromise.

The R_{90} statistics computed for the 34 scenarios are reported on Figure 1.5A, and the highest is found for a unique origin in Northwest Africa ($R_{90} = 0.265$), followed by an origin in the Near East ($R_{90} = 0.260$). As more fully explained in Ray *et al.* (2005), this unexpected result prompted us to examine the possibility of ascertainment bias because these 377 STR loci were originally assessed on a CEPH panel made up of individuals of European ancestry. We then performed a new set of simulations by constructing sets of 377 STR loci chosen for their particularly high heterozygosity levels in European populations (see Ray *et al.* 2005 for details). The new results are reported in Figure 1.5B, and now ranks the highest scores first for an East African origin ($R_{90} = 0.309$) followed by a Northwest African origin ($R_{90} = 0.290$). Note that ME scenarios have much lower scores in all cases ($R_{90} = 0.153$ at best), implying that the best UO scenario explains about 4 times more of the observed genetic diversity than any ME scenario.

Discussion

Our present study complemented our recent model (Ray *et al.* 2005) by examining the effect of various levels of physical constraints to dispersion on human genetic diversity. These constraints are typically the contours of continents, but we have also envisioned scenarios where dispersal was limited in deserts and in mountainous regions, and facilitated along coastlines and major rivers. Our simulation results show that patterns of genetic diversity after a range expansion in a heterogeneous environment do depend on the geographical origin of the expansion, which is not the case in a uniform and homogeneous environment (Ray *et al.* 2003). It implies that extant patterns of genetic diversity can be used to recover the place of origin of modern humans, if one assumes that they speciated at a single and precise location. However, our results show that this location can only be well recovered provided that a large number of markers are available (Fig. 1.4), that the simulated origin is close to the true origin, and that the effect of environmental heterogeneity on past demography of the population is known to a certain extent (Table 1.4). These results underline the importance of modelling environmental data as closely as possible to reality, and of interactions between demographic and environmental parameters. An obvious but difficult extension of our approach would be to obtain a dense grid of point covering the whole world, and for each of these points the corresponding likelihood of being the origin of early modern humans.

The application of this inferential framework on the Rosenberg22 data set shows that multiregional evolution scenarios are overall much less favoured than most UO scenarios. Once ascertainment bias is taken into account, the data support a unique and East African origin for modern humans. While the environmental scenarios we have envisioned may not be fully realistic, our approach could be extended, such as to incorporate additional information about past environments, as well as their dynamics (see Ray *et al.* this volume). The fact that the dispersal abilities of early modern humans were probably deeply affected by their environment should motivate further research on their impact on early human migrations, and on the reconstruction of these palaeoenvironments, in order to refine estimates of various scenarios of human evolution.

Future improvement would also be to consider potential interactions between early modern humans and former representatives of the *Homo* genus (Currat & Excoffier 2004; Eswaran *et al.* 2005), and potentially estimate their degree of interbreeding. While mitochondrial DNA shows no evidence for interbreeding (Currat & Excoffier 2004) nuclear markers could be more sensitive for detecting some minor contribution, as suggested by Eswaran *et al.* (2005). The recent advance of Approximate Bayesian Computations (ABC methods: Beaumont *et al.* 2002), relying on massive simulations to estimate the parameters of different scenarios by comparing simulated to observed summary statistics, should enable us to compare the relative probabilities of various models, and to anchor the study of human evolution into a more statistical framework. Another advantage of such methods is that it would allow us to incorporate more information from the available data than the matrix of pairwise genetic distances we have been using here, like some aspects of genetic diversity within populations, (see e.g. Excoffier *et al.* 2005). This additional information could help us resolve not only geographic origins, but it could help establishing to which degree early humans were actually influenced by environmental heterogeneity. Some recent studies have found that nuclear heterozygosity within populations was steadily decreasing with geographic distance from eastern Africa (Prugnolle *et al.* 2005; Ramachandran *et al.* 2005). These results are compatible with the occurrence of a series of founder effects during the spread of modern humans out of Africa, and do not seem to depend on known environmental heterogeneities outside Africa. But since the environment has considerably fluctuated during the late Pleistocene, time-average environmental pressures could be quite similar for different locations, while local heterogeneities could be significant at any given time.

Acknowledgements

This work was made possible thanks to a Swiss NSF grant No. 3100A0-100800 to LE.

References

Alroy, J., 2001. A multispecies overkill simulation of the end-Pleistocene megafaunal mass extinction. *Science* 292, 1893–6.

Beaumont, M.A., W. Zhang & D.J. Balding, 2002. Approximate Bayesian computation in population genetics. *Genetics* 162, 2025–35.

Binford, L.R., 2001. *Constructing Frames of Reference: an Analytical Method for Archaeological Theory Building using Hunter-gatherer and Environmental Data Sets.* Berkeley (CA): University of California Press.

Cavalli-Sforza, L.L., P. Menozzi & A. Piazza, 1994. *The History and Geography of Human Genes.* Princeton (NJ): Princeton University Press.

Currat, M. & L. Excoffier, 2004. Modern humans did not admix with Neanderthals during their range expansion into Europe. *PLoS Biology* 2, e421.

Currat, M. & L. Excoffier, 2005. The effect of the Neolithic expansion on European molecular diversity. *Proceedings of the Royal Society London, Biological Science* 272, 679–88.

Currat, M., N. Ray & L. Excoffier, 2004. SPLATCHE: a program to simulate genetic diversity taking into account environmental heterogeneity. *Molecular Ecology Notes* 4, 139–42.

Eswaran, V., H. Harpending, & A.R. Rogers, 2005. Genomics refutes an exclusively African origin of humans. *Journal of Human Evolution* 49(1), 1–18.

Excoffier, L., 2002. Human demographic history: refining the recent African origin model. *Current Opinion in Genetics and Development* 12, 675–82.

Excoffier, L., A. Estoup & J.-M. Cornuet, 2005. Bayesian analysis of an admixture model with mutations and arbitrarily linked markers. *Genetics* 169, 1727–38.

Prugnolle, F., A. Manica & F. Balloux, 2005. Geography predicts neutral genetic diversity of human populations. *Current Biology* 15, R159–60.

Ramachandran, S., O. Deshpande, C.C. Roseman, N.A. Rosenberg, M.W. Feldman & L.L. Cavalli-Sforza,

2005. Support from the relationship of genetic and geographic distance in human populations for a serial founder effect originating in Africa. *Proceedings of the National Academy of Sciences of the USA* 102, 15,942–7.

Ray, N., 2003. Modélisation de la démographie des populations humaines préhistoriques à l'aide de données environnementales et génétiques. Thèse de doctorat, Université de Genève. Available at: http://www.unige.ch/cyberdocuments/theses2003/RayN/these.html.

Ray, N. & J. Adams, 2002. Present-potential vegetation maps of the world.

Ray, N., M. Currat & L. Excoffier, 2003. Intra-deme molecular diversity in spatially expanding populations. *Molecular Biology and Evolution* 20, 76–86.

Ray, N., M. Currat, P. Berthier & L. Excoffier, 2005. Recovering the geographic origin of early modern humans by realistic and spatially explicit simulations. *Genome Research* 15(8), 1161–7.

Rosenberg, N.A., J.K. Pritchard, J.L. Weber, *et al.*, 2002. Genetic structure of human populations. *Science* 298, 2381–5.

Steele, J., J.M. Adams & T. Sluckin, 1998. Modeling Paleoindian dispersals. *World Archaeology* 30, 286–305.

Tremblay, M. & H. Vezina, 2000. New estimates of inter-generational time intervals for the calculation of age and origins of mutations. *American Journal of Human Genetics* 66, 651–8.

USGS, 1996. GTOPO30: a global digital elevation model at 30 arc-second resolution. U.S. Geological Survey.

Wolpoff, M.H., 1989. Multiregional evolution: the fossil alternative to Eden, in *The Human Revolution: Biological perspectives in the Origins of Modern Humans*, eds. P. Mellars & C. Stringer. Princeton (NJ): Princeton University Press, 62–108.

Wolpoff, M.H., J. Hawks & R. Caspari, 2000. Multiregional, not multiple origins. *American Journal of Physical Anthropology* 112, 129–36.

Chapter 2

Worldwide Genetic Patterns in Human Population Genetics

Andrea Manica, Hua Liu, Franck Prugnolle & François Balloux

In this chapter, we discuss the extent to which human settlement history can be reconstructed by using large-scale genetic patterns in current human populations. It has been argued in the past that human colonization history has been so complex that it should be impossible to detect simple correlations between geography and genetics on a large scale. Relatively recent migration events, such as the spread of early farmers, might also obscure the genetic signature of the initial settlement history. Despite all this complexity, we show that clear simple patterns between geography and genetics can be documented. We then discuss how such trends may be used to make inferences about the details of past human settlement history.

The challenge of using genetic patterns to infer human settlement history

The current leading theory for human colonization of the world, the so called Recent African Origin (RAO) theory, postulates that the ancestors of all modern humans originated in East Africa. The wave of migration out of Africa is suggested to have occurred less than 100,000 years ago, and to have led to the subsequent colonization of the entire world, with the replacement of previously established human species such as Neanderthals in Europe (Cann *et al.* 1987; Stringer & Andrews 1988; Ray *et al.* 2005). Archaeological findings provide potential dates for the key events of RAO. The oldest remains of modern humans, presumably pinpointing the origin of our species, have been found in East and South Ethiopia and have been dated at 160,000 and 195,000 years (McDougall *et al.* 2005; White *et al.* 2003). The first evidence for modern humans outside Africa comes from Israel, and has been dated between 80,000 to 100,000 years (McDermott *et al.* 1993). This observation of modern humans in the Middle East is isolated and may represent an early offshoot that died out. The later, successful migration out of Africa is believed to have occurred some time between 55,000 and 85,000 years ago (Foster & Matsumara 2005; Macaulay *et al.* 2005). The pace of movement outside Africa varied greatly. The fastest migration route followed the Indian Ocean coastline and led to the colonization of Australia

around 50,000 years ago (Bowler *et al.* 2003). The colonization of Eurasia was slower, possibly hampered by the presence of archaic humans or by unsuitable climate (Finlayson 2005). Finally, the colonization of the Americas only occurred recently, probably dating back to the crossing of the Bering Strait less than 20,000 years ago (Hoffecker & Elias 2003).

Within the RAO framework, the simplest model for human settlement history can be viewed as a diffusion process away from the hypothetical African origin, progressively covering all suitable habitats. Such a scenario leads to two straightforward predictions. The first is that the highest genetic diversity should be found in the oldest populations in East Africa and that it should decline with geographic distance from there. The reason for this decrease lies in the sampling process inherent to a diffusion process. Whenever colonizers move from a previous settlement into previously unoccupied areas, some alleles might be lost due to stochastic sampling. The second prediction is that we should observe strong patterns of genetic isolation by distance, with geographically closer populations sharing more alleles. However, this second prediction is not unique to RAO, as strong isolation by distance might arise under several alternative scenarios of human settlement, and could be fully explained by recent migration events.

While such a simple diffusion process might seem too simplistic to capture accurately the process

Figure 2.1. *Shortest routes (dashed lines) through landmasses and specified land bridges between the 51 populations analysed (dots) and a hypothetical East African origin (white dot).*

of human settlement history, there are two lines of evidence that are compatible with the predictions of such a model. First, human populations from Africa are genetically the most diverse (Tishkoff & Kidd 2004). Second, genetic diversity of non-African populations is negatively correlated with their genetic differentiation from populations from Africa (Harpending & Rogers 2000). However, the crucial prediction from the simple model is that genetic diversity should decrease with geographic distance from eastern Africa. To test this prediction, we need a framework to generate geographic distances that are meaningful in the context of human migrations, and that can subsequently be linked to genetic quantities.

Origin of humans and genetic diversity

To test the relationship between genetic diversity and distance from the origin of the initial migration out of Africa, we must infer possible routes allowing to colonize the whole globe. Early humans were unable to cross large distances over open water, so the simplest approach is to assume that movement had to occur over landmasses. The exact routes are unknown, so we developed an algorithm based on graph theory that computes the shortest distance on land between East Africa (using Addis Ababa, in Ethiopia, as the putative centre of diversity) and any other location on earth (Prugnolle *et al.* 2005a). To allow cross-continent

movement, we added a few putative land bridges that might have existed in the past, such as the one over the Bering Strait that allows movement from Asia to America. We simulated movement on a spherical earth rather than using a geographic projection, since the latter approach is too inaccurate when dealing with routes that cross most of the globe. Our algorithm generates migration routes compatible with the ones proposed by Cavalli-Sforza and colleagues (1994), with the exception of the route to America, where the algorithm suggested a scenario with a long stretch at very high latitudes in Asia. To avoid this unrealistic northern migration path, we forced the route to first reach eastern Asia before veering to high latitudes to move through the Bering Strait (Fig. 2.1). Thus, with our algorithm, we can estimate the shortest possible distance that humans have travelled from a hypothetical origin located in East Africa to the current position of any population on earth.

Data on genetic diversity are available for 51 populations around the globe, based on 377 autosomal microsatellite loci (Rosenberg *et al.* 2002). We used the unbiased expected heterozygosity H_S following Nei (1987) as a measure of genetic diversity. As expected from the simple diffusion model based on RAO, there is a very strong, negative linear correlation between genetic diversity with geographic distances to East Africa, with populations most geographically distant from Ethiopia characterized by the lowest genetic variability. The relationship is highly significant ($p < 10^{-4}$) and geographic distance is an excellent predictor of the neutral genetic diversity of human populations, explaining 85 per cent of the observed variance at a worldwide scale. There is no obvious outlier and we could not detect any effect of the historical census size of the populations or any obvious macro-geographic pattern such as a stepwise decrease in genetic diversity corresponding for instance to a severe bottleneck following the colonization of a continent (Fig. 2.2).

Our approach also allows us to get an idea for the pace at which modern humans have colonized the world, as it provides us with a way to estimate the minimal distances travelled from East Africa. The minimal estimated pace is remarkably fast. The distance from East Africa to South America along likely migration routes through landmasses represents 30,000 km. Assuming a constant expansion that started 100,000 years ago and reached South America 10,000 years ago, and a generation time of 25 years, our ancestors would have colonized new territories at a rate of 8.3 km per generation. Obviously there is little reason to expect the process to have been constant. Dispersal along favourable habitats such as coastline or major

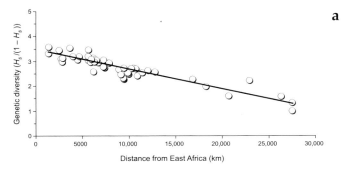

Figure 2.2. *Relationship between mean genetic diversity (transformed as $H_S/1 − H_S$) of 51 human populations computed over 377 autosomal microsatellite markers and their geographic distances in km from East Africa. The percentage of variance explained by geographic distance is $R^2 = 0.85$ ($p < 10^{-4}$).*

rivers might have been fast (Macaulay *et al.* 2005). On the other hand unsuitable habitat such as desert or jungle might have slowed the diffusion process. It is also important to remember that the climatic conditions have varied dramatically over the last 100,000 years. Periods of favourable weather have alternated with glaciations, possibly forcing humans to retreat to refugia. Over the same period, the level of the sea has been fluctuating by 130 m, thus dramatically altering habitat suitability. This suggests that, on more than one occasion, our ancestors are likely to have covered legs of over several tens of kilometres during a single generation.

Differentiation between human populations (F_{ST})

The simple diffusion model based on RAO also predicts clear patterns of isolation by distance, with geographically closer population sharing more alleles. The pioneering work by Cavalli-Sforza and colleagues suggested that differentiation between human populations was largely clinal (Cavalli-Sforza *et al.* 1994). However, over the recent years a near consensus has emerged that all humans cluster into five or genetic clusters, roughly corresponding to continents (Jorde & Wooding 2004; Risch *et al.* 2002; Rosenberg *et al.* 2002; Tishkoff & Kidd 2004; Zhivotovsky *et al.* 2003). While there is disagreement over how marked those clusters are, their existence is essentially unchallenged. One dissenting opinion has recently been raised by Serre & Pääbo (2004), who suggested that those clusters were artefacts generated by heterogeneous sampling and that they would vanish if many more populations were analysed. Our results support their view. Indeed the relation between geographic distance from East Africa and genetic diversity is very smooth (Fig. 2.2)

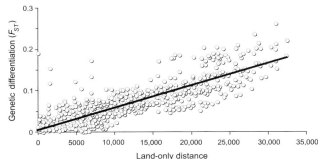

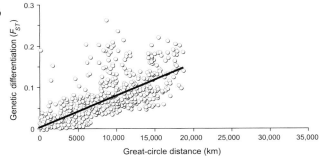

Figure 2.3. *Relationship between pairwise F_{ST} and (a) land-only distance or (b) great-circle distance for all possible pairs of populations in the data set. The increase in F_{ST} with distance is better explained by using land-only routes ($R^2 = 0.73$, $p < 0.001$) than simple great-circle distances ($R^2 = 0.55$). The relationship is not much affected if the outliers above the line (all including the Surui) are removed ($R^2 = 0.74$, $p < 0.001$).*

and does not suggest any obvious macro-geographic pattern such as a stepwise decrease in genetic diversity corresponding for instance to a severe bottleneck following the colonization of a continent. While this result questions the existence of previously defined genetic clusters (Prugnolle *et al.* 2005a), the power of the approach in detecting genetic discontinuities is arguably weak, as only the genetic diversity within each population was considered, thus discarding all the information about allele sharing between populations.

In order to specifically tackle this issue, we can build upon our geographically explicit approach and test whether such clusters are genuine. The gain in statistical power is obtained by correlating genetic differentiation with geographic distance and previously defined clusters (or continents) over all possible pairs of populations. To obtain geographic distances between populations that are meaningful in the context of human migrations, we computed all shortest pair-wise geographic distances through landmasses. Subsequently, we estimated genetic differentiation between all pairs of population as F_{ST} values. These two matrices are highly correlated ($R^2 = 0.73; p < 0.001$; Fig. 2.3a). F_{ST} is a function of migration but also of the genetic diversity of the populations analysed, and the Surui are characterized by exceptionally low genetic diversity. The few outliers on the left-hand side in Figure 2.3a all include the Surui population in America, but these have no important effect on the correlation (without Surui, $R^2 = 0.74; p < 0.001$). While this is partly due to this population being far from Africa, it also underwent an extremely severe bottleneck in 1961, when one year after their first contact with the Western world, smallpox and flu reduced the population to 34 individuals (Laraia & Damatta 1979). The population has since then been recovering but it is likely that some genetic variation has been lost in the process.

The correlation of 73 per cent between geography and genetic differentiation is extremely strong and is, to the best of our knowledge, the highest ever recorded. Such a strong pattern of genetic isolation by distance is particularly striking as pair-wise F_{ST} estimates are characterized by high variance even when large numbers of genetic markers are assayed (Balloux & Goudet 2002). The strength of the correlation also vindicates our choice of computing geographic distances along landmasses only. Running the same analysis with great circle distances (shortest possible paths irrespective whether the route is over land or water) significantly reduces the correlation ($R^2 = 0.55$; Fig. 2.3b).

At this stage we can ask whether previously defined genetic clusters or continental origin can explain additional variance in the pattern of genetic differentiation between populations. We tested for the presence of clusters by recovering the residuals of the genetic differentiation matrix after geographic distance had been accounted for. Many different clusters could be defined and we actually explored a variety of such options. Below we limit ourselves to presenting the results obtained for two subdivisions: continental origin and the *a posteriori* classification by Rosenberg and colleagues (2002), based on the program STRUCTURE (Pritchard *et al.* 2000). Hereafter we will simply refer to the *a posteriori* clusters as genetic clusters.

While continental origin is not significantly correlated to the residuals of the F_{ST} matrix ($R^2 < 0.001; p = 0.501$), ethnic groups still explain a small but significant proportion of the variance in population differentiation even after geography has been accounted for ($R^2 = 0.015; p < 0.001$). No other clustering strategy we considered could explain more variance in population differentiation. It should be kept in mind that the proportion of variance explained by genetic clusters, while significant, is very small compared to the proportion explained by geography. Geography explains 75 per cent of the overall genetic differentiation and genetic clusters only 1.5 per cent. Furthermore the fact that genetic clusters remain significant once geographic distances have been accounted for does not vindicate their existence, but might simply stem from our geographic distances being to crude to capture the full genetic pattern. If geographic routes are computed so to avoid passing through areas with average altitude over 2000 m the correlation between genetics clusters and F_{ST} disappears (Manica, Prugnolle, Balloux unpublished).

Worldwide genetic differentiation in humans is thus mainly continuous, monotonously increasing with distance along landmasses. We did not even detect any evidence for a genetic discontinuity between Africa and the rest of the world. This result is in variance with the commonly held view that the exit of modern humans out of Africa was associated to a strong genetic bottleneck. The evidence for an out of Africa bottleneck is mainly based on mitochondrial DNA. Indeed, extensive surveys of mitochondrial sequences have shown that all haplotypes found outside Africa are derived from a single lineage (Richards & Macaulay 2003; Watson *et al.* 1997).

This raises the question how our results can be reconciled with the body of evidence based on mtDNA, which has been accumulated over the last two decades. Possible candidate hypotheses include natural selection on mtDNA mediated through climate (Mishmar *et al.* 2003), sex-specific dispersal or a possible ascertainment bias in the microsatellite loci. While it is generally assumed that dispersal tends to be female-biased in pre-industrial human societies (Seielstad *et al.* 1998), it is possible this trend does not hold for movement over open water. A scenario based on a small number of initial migrants moving out of Africa, with subsequent male-biased gene flow could explain the discrepancy between mtDNA and autosomes. Finally Ray and colleagues (2005) have recently suggested these microsatellite loci might be affected by an ascertainment bias leading to an under-estimation of the genetic diversity of African populations, as they were initially selected on the basis of their diversity in Europeans. While we are currently not in the position to test for such a bias, we also wish to stress that mitochondrial DNA is a single non-recombining locus. The gene tree of mitochondrial DNA does not necessarily match the true history of the populations studied as the genealogy of any particular molecule is just a random draw from an extremely variable distribution of genealogies, with many possible given the actual history of the populations (Ballard & Whitlock 2004; Nichols 2001). The results presented in this chapter are based on a large number of genetic markers (377 autosomal microsatellites). It is through averaging over a large number of loci that we are able to detect smooth patterns.

Inferences on early human settlement history

So far we have demonstrated that when geography is accounted for, it is possible to characterize extremely strong associations between physical distances and genetic quantities. The simplistic diffusion model taking Addis Ababa as putative origin of modern humans allows us to capture 85 per cent of the variance in genetic diversity of the 51 populations from the Rosenberg data set (Fig. 2.2). The straightforward conclusion is that human settlement history can be accurately described with very simple models. This offers an exciting opportunity to develop explicit analytic models for gaining insight into the dynamics of human settlement history.

Below we outline the rationale for one such model and briefly present some very preliminary results. We are interested in estimating the carrying capacity and migration rate for early human populations. Let us consider a one-dimensional stepping-stone model composed of 300 demes with carrying capacity K. The distance along landmasses from East Africa to South America is 30,000 km so that each deme represents a cell of 100 × 100 km. Initially only a single deme at one extreme of the stepping stone is occupied. This founding population is already at carrying capacity and genetic equilibrium (identity by descent $1/2K$). The migration rate between neighbouring subpopulations is set to $m/2$. A deme only starts sending migrants to adjacent subpopulations after it has reached carrying capacity. Mating is random within demes, and the demographic dynamics within subpopulations follows a logistic equation with growth rate r and non-overlapping generations. In this model, four parameters (*carrying capacity, migration rate, growth rate* and *generation time*), are sufficient to describe the dynamics of the model. From the same model, we can obtain genetic identities by descent and coalescence times (Austerlitz *et al.* 1997). As we are interested in modelling genetic loci with high mutation rate (microsatellites), we cannot safely ignore mutation. We thus add an additional parameter u, the mean mutation rate appropriate for the 377 microsatellites.

Assuming a generation time of 25 years, the initial expansion of modern humans might have happened around 4000 generations ago, and most of the world was occupied by 500 generations ago. These times were used to calibrate growth r and migration rate m. While these parameters are fixed in the model, small departures from these values do not qualitatively affect our results. Growth rate r mainly affects

the pace at which the colonization wave advances. The environment is assumed to be homogeneous with r identical in every deme. This assumption can be justified at a global scale since the advance of hunter-gatherers is believed to have been relatively homogeneous (Ammerman & Cavalli-Sforza 1971; Bocquet-Appel & Demars 2000). Finally, we further assume a mutation rate $u = 10^{-4}$, a value appropriate for microsatellites (e.g. Xu *et al.* 2000).

Now we can estimate the values for subpopulation carrying capacity and migration rate per generation with simulations exploring the entire parameter range for those two parameters. The fit of individual simulations with the regression given in Figure 2.2 was assessed by calculating the square distance Δ_{SD} over the 300 demes as:

$$\Delta_{SD} = \frac{1}{300} \sqrt{\sum_{d=1}^{300} (simulation - regression)^2}.$$

Figure 2.4 displays the distance Δ_{SD} as a function of carrying capacity per deme K and the product of migration and carrying capacity (mK). There is a marked single optimum obtained for $K = 120$, $mK = 70$. The estimated value for carrying capacity corresponds to one effective individual per 0.012 km². The ratio between effective and census size is generally estimated to be between four and ten for human populations, depending on the level of polygyny. Our model thus estimates a carrying capacity around 0.04 to 0.1 per square km. This estimate falls within the

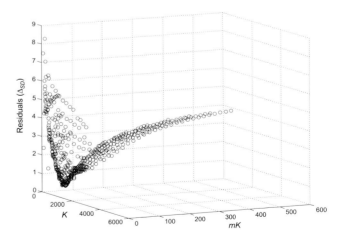

Figure 2.4. *Residuals Δ_{SD} between simulation results and actual data for varying values of carrying capacity (K) and the product of migration rate by generation and carrying capacity (mK). Small residuals indicate a better fit between the model and the actual data. The best fit is obtained under a carrying capacity (K = 120).*

0.01–0.35 densities km^{-2} estimated for ancient and modern hunter-gatherer societies (Binford 2001; Bocquet-Appel & Demars 2000; Steele *et al.* 1998)

Conclusion

The clear link between genetics and geography vindicates the use of simple models to describe the major patterns of colonization by humans. This result seems to contrast with our perception of how complex human migrations should be, at least according to the archaeological literature. So, are genetics and archaeology at odds? We believe that this is not the case, and that the discrepancies are simply a matter of scale. The genetic patterns we discussed in this chapter are on a very large scale, in the order of tens of thousand of kilometres. On the other hand, many of the migrations that archaeologists have worked hard to define are in terms of hundreds of kilometres. If we consider the populations in Figure 2.2, moving any of them by a few hundred kilometres would not affect our relationships.

Having an explicit model of the colonization of the globe by humans is not only interesting from an anthropological point of view, but it also allows us to investigate evolutionary ideas. The simple diffusion model can be considered a null model to estimate patterns of neutral diversity in humans, against which actual patterns of gene frequencies can compared. We have used this approach to study the genes governing the immune response in humans (HLA complex). This allowed us to show that even though the diversity of HLA at a global scale is influenced by human settlement history, deviations from the expected patterns are linked to the diversity of pathogens to which each population is exposed (Prugnolle *et al.* 2005b).

Global patterns of genetic diversity in current human populations offer exciting possibilities to reconstruct past colonization events, tracking down migrations that happened tens of thousand of years ago. With the recent technical developments in molecular biology, large data sets are becoming available, the research often being driven by medical interests. These same data sets could also be used for reconstructing human settlement history. The challenge is now for population geneticist to come up with new theoretical approaches that account for geography to extract distant signals from the past.

References

Ammerman, A.J. & L.L. Cavalli-Sforza, 1971. Measuring the rate of spread of early farming in Europe. *Man* 6, 674–88.

Austerlitz, F., B. Jung-Muller, B. Godelle & P.H. Gouyon, 1997. Evolution of coalescence times, genetic diversity and structure during colonisation. *Theoretical Population Biology* 51, 148–64.

Ballard, J.W.O. & M.C. Whitlock, 2004. The incomplete natural history of mitochondria. *Molecular Ecology* 13, 729–44.

Balloux, F. & J. Goudet, 2002. Statistical properties of population differentiation estimators under stepwise mutation in a finite island model. *Molecular Ecology* 11, 771–83.

Binford, L., 2001. *Constructing Frames of Reference: an Analytical Method for Archaeological Theory Building Using Hunter-gatherer and Environmental Data Sets.* Berkeley (CA): University of California Press.

Bocquet-Appel, J.P. & P.Y. Demars, 2000. Neanderthal contraction and modern human colonisation of Europe. *Antiquity* 74, 544–52.

Bowler, J.M., H. Johnston, J.M. Olley, *et al.*, 2003. New ages for human occupation and climatic change at Lake Mungo, Australia. *Nature* 421, 837–40.

Cann, R.L., M. Stoneking & A.C. Wilson, 1987. Mitochondrial DNA and human evolution. *Nature* 325, 31–6.

Cavalli-Sforza, L.L., P. Menozzi & A. Piazza, 1994. *The History and Geography of Human Genes.* Princeton (NJ): Princeton University Press.

Finlayson, C., 2005. Biogeography and evolution of the genus *Homo. Trends in Ecology and Evolution* 20, 457–63.

Forster, P. & S. Matsumura, 2005. Evolution — Did early humans go north or south? *Science* 308, 965–6.

Harpending, H.C. & A.R. Rogers, 2000. Genetic perspectives on human origins and differentiation. *Annual Review in Genomics and Human Genetics* 1, 361–85.

Hoffecker, J.F. & S.A. Elias, 2003. Environment and archaeology in Beringia. *Evolutionary Anthropology* 12, 34–49.

Jorde, L. & S. Wooding, 2004. Genetic variation, classification and 'race'. *Nature Genetics* 36, S28–S33.

Laraia, R.B. & R. Damatta, 1979. *Índios e Castanheiros: a Empresa Extrativa e os Indios no Médio Tocantins.* 2nd edition. Rio de Janeiro: Paz e Terra.

Macaulay, V., C. Hill, A. Achilli, *et al.*, 2005. Single, rapid coastal settlement of Asia revealed by analysis of complete mitochondrial genomes. *Science* 308, 1034–6.

McDermott, F., R. Grun, C.B. Stringer & C.J. Hawkesworth, 1993. Mass-spectrometric u-series dates for Israeli Neanderthal early-modern hominid sites. *Nature* 363, 252–5.

McDougall, I., F.H. Brown & J.G. Fleagle, 2005. Stratigraphic placement and age of modern humans from Kibish, Ethiopia. *Nature* 433, 733–6.

Mishmar, D., E. Ruiz-Pesini, P. Golik, *et al.*, 2003. Natural selection shaped regional mtDNA variation in humans. *Proceedings of the National Academy of Sciences of the USA* 100, 171–6.

Nei, M., 1987. *Molecular Evolutionary Genetics.* New York (NY): Columbia University Press.

Nichols, R., 2001. Gene trees and species trees are not the same. *Trends in Ecology and Evolution* 16, 358–64.

Pritchard, J.K., M. Stephens & P. Donnelly, 2000. Inference of population structure using multilocus genotype data. *Genetics* 155, 945–59.

Prugnolle, F., A. Manica & F. Balloux, 2005a. Geography predicts neutral genetic diversity of human populations. *Current Biology* 15, 159–60.

Prugnolle, F., A. Manica, M. Charpentier, J. Guégan, V. Guernier & F. Balloux, 2005b. Pathogen-driven selection and worldwide HLA class I diversity. *Current Biology* 15, 1022–7.

Ray, N., M. Currat, P. Berthier & L. Excoffier, 2005. Recovering the geographic origin of early modern humans by realistic and spatially explicit simulations. *Genome Research* 15, 1161–7.

Richards, M. & V. Macaulay, 2003. Genetic data and colonization of Europe: genealogies and founders, in *Archaeogenetics: DNA and the Population Prehistory of Europe*, eds. C. Renfrew & K. Boyle. (McDonald Institute Monographs.) Cambridge: McDonald Institute for Archaeological Research, 139–41.

Risch, N., E. Burchard, E. Ziv & H. Tang, 2002. Categorization of humans in biomedical research: genes, race and disease. *Genome Biology* 3, comment 2007.

Rosenberg, N.A., J.K. Pritchard, J.L Weber, *et al.*, 2002. Genetic structure of human populations. *Science* 298, 2381–5.

Seielstad, M.T., M. Minch & L.L. Cavalli-Sforza, 1998. Genetic evidence for higher female migration rate in humans. *Nature Genetics* 20, 278–80.

Serre, D. & S. Pääbo, 2004. Evidence for gradients of human genetic diversity within and among continents. *Genome Research* 14, 1679–85.

Steele, J., J.M. Adams & T. Sluckin, 1998. Modeling Paleoindian dispersals. *World Archaeology* 30, 286–305.

Stringer, C.B. & P. Andrews, 1988. Genetic and fossil evidence for the origin of modern humans. *Science* 239, 1263–8.

Tishkoff, S. & K.K. Kidd, 2004. Implications of biogeography of human populations for 'race' and medicine. *Nature Genetics* 36, S21–S7.

Watson, E., P. Forster, M. Richards & H.-J. Bandelt, 1997. Mitochondrial footprints of human expansions in Africa. *American Journal of Human Genetics* 61, 691–704.

White, T.D., B. Asfaw, D. DeGusta, *et al.*, 2003. Pleistocene *Homo sapiens* from Middle Awash, Ethiopia. *Nature* 423, 742–7.

Xu, X., M. Peng & Z. Fang, 2000. The direction of microsatellite mutations is dependent upon allele length. *Nature Genetics* 24, 396–9.

Zhivotovsky, L., N.A. Rosenberg & M.W. Feldman, 2003. Features of evolution and expansion of modern humans, inferred from genome-wide microsatellite markers. *American Journal of Human Genetics* 72, 1171–86.

Chapter 3

Following Populations or Molecules?
Two Contrasting Approaches and Descriptive Outcomes of
Island Colonization Arising from a Similar Knowledge-base

Stephen Oppenheimer

Two contrasting approaches to the study of human colonization arise from applying very different mathematical methods to a similar theoretical knowledge-base. One of these approaches uses established methods of classical population genetics and resembles phenetic comparison, as used in physical anthropology. It compares distance between populations on the basis of allele frequency, or conversely their similarity, and infers population genetic history. This phenetic style of comparison is exemplified by Cavalli-Sforza et al.'s 532-page magnum opus The History and Geography of Human Genes *(1994). The other approach often labelled as 'phylogeography' (e.g. Richards et al. 2000) is also interested in genetic history, but concentrates on inferences from the geographic history of particular genetic loci, rather than that of whole populations and is exemplified by a more recent two and a half page report in* Science *(Macaulay et al. 2005).*

The intention in this paper is to provide several examples to highlight some of the features of the phylogeographic approach and, in an island colonization example, contrast the outcomes of these two methods or approaches when applied to similar data. Possibly as a result of unequal splits, extreme founder effects and drift, the divergence of such outcomes are greatest when looking at island spread. In this situation, the traditional summary-statistical, phenetic approach used by some population geneticists and physical anthropologists has produced results for the Pacific, that cannot even be usefully compared with each other let alone with those obtained using a phylogeographic approach.

Phylogeography studies the prehistoric movement of individual DNA loci while population genetics studies populations. Two misunderstandings are to assume that either approach is necessarily correct or tries to depict the same thing. The phylogeographic approach has coincidental advantages over population-based phenetic studies in that, since it avoids working in terms of populations, it avoids certain assumptions about population history and

the logical (usually unintended) trap of comparing populations as if they were biological units.

Each human population contains multiple versions (or polymorphisms) of the product or DNA template of any particular locus (or whole blocks of non-recombining DNA containing many genes — as with mtDNA or the non-recombining part of the Y chromosome), each with its own phylogeny, history and different origin. The phylogeographic approach looks at the geographic distribution of the branches in individual locus phylogenies, while the summary statistical approach studies the prehistory of populations holding different mixes of those loci by comparing their relative frequencies in population samples mathematically. The term 'comparing frequencies' is of course a gross over-simplification.

Dating methods tend to be different in the two approaches, and this is particularly important when the past history of effective population size can affect the date estimation. Methods used in phylogeography to date branching points on the phylogeny of a locus (e.g. mtDNA), such as the calculation of rho (e.g. Forster *et al.* 1996) are, crudely-speaking, based on counting mutations, branches and haplotype numbers on the reconstructed tree. The validity of this method is unaffected by prior unknown variations in effective population size, but there are assumptions which affect the size of the standard error of the estimate. For instance it helps if the daughter branches from the node of interest should have a star-like distribution around the node.

What conditions make it possible to trace the movement of segments of our genome around the world?

Lack of recombination in mitochondrial DNA (mtDNA) and the major part of the Y chromosome (NRY) allows an uncorrupted cumulative record of point mutations over an extended sequence. Hence a large, detailed and unambiguous tree can be reconstructed for each stretch of non-recombining DNA studied. Because of recombination, the number of polymorphisms and degree of resolution of unambiguous phylogenetic information seen in these so-called uniparental (i.e. single parental transmission of information) loci is far greater than for most autosomal loci. That is except potentially in so-called non-recombining *autosomal frozen blocks*. Such frozen blocks are long stretches of autosomal gene sequence, found for instance in the Major Histocompatibility Complex, which show little or no recombination between different individuals and thus in effect act as single loci. As a result, while possibly thousands of haplotypes (including STRs, i.e. repetitive DNA stretches in the Y chromosome) have now been described for uniparental loci, autosomal loci used for instance by Cavalli-Sforza and colleagues (1994) have allele polymorphisms numbering typically in low single figures per locus. The exception is the case of HLA-A and HLA-B types in the Major Histocompatibility Complex, which possesses large fixed blocks of DNA and have more than ten haplotypes. The low diversity in autosomal loci reduces their resolving power to determine migration or geographic rooting of phylogenies.

The fact that autosomal alleles by their diploid nature have a much larger effective population size than uniparental markers means that drift is likely to be greater in the latter. It also means that deep-rooting possibly ancient polymorphisms in the former are more likely to be carried over and preserved in founding populations.

Mutations in the DNA segment of interest are carried on down the generations and can be used as branching points to construct a virtual spreading molecular tree on the globe, which is structurally inde-

pendent of other loci. A mitochondrial genetic tree put on the wall does not just read like a family tree and divide into regional 'races' (even if the term had validity in human populations). Regional populations as in India, Europe and China are not the same as single branches of gene trees. The 'tree' is, in reality, more like several strands of creeping ivy spreading and branching over the Earth. Multiple genetic lineages migrate in parallel, and can be studied independently.

Marked regional geographic specificity of uniparental sub-branches is self-evident (e.g. Oppenheimer 2003a, 365–75) and implies that, in the Late Pleistocene, when most people got to where they were going in the world, they stayed put in their new homes in relative isolation without demonstrating the inter-regional mixing assumed by some multiregional models of human spread and interaction. This regional conservatism is a crucial element which allows the appearance of 'new growth' on the 'ivy tree' to be plotted geographically. One region will share strands of different genetic branches with neighbouring regions; but each region has its own unique new growth, which can be observed in separate lineages.

The Out-of-Africa model as a clear example of the phylogeographic approach

A recent report in *Science* (Macaulay *et al.* 2005) argues for a single southern exit from Africa giving rise to all non-African populations. While the argument includes discussion of estimated dates, the core evidence for a single exit is topological. This report is based on the findings for only one small stretch of non-recombining DNA (mtDNA). The conclusion of a single successful population movement is logically inferred from the observation that all haplotypes on this locus outside Africa belong to a single African haplogroup. Macaulay and colleagues (2005) point out that mtDNA haplotypes from regional populations outside Africa are all derived from the three major Eurasian mtDNA founder haplogroups, M, N, and N's derivative R, and closely related and near-immediate descendants of one African haplotype L3 dated to around 83,000 years ago. It should be made clear that while this is evidence for a single geographic bottleneck it is qualitative evidence and does not necessarily provide sufficient detail to estimate the effective size of the female population at the time of the event with any degree of precision. Possibly, similar analysis of autosomal frozen block phylogenies, with their larger effective population size, may help.

Whether one looks among the so-called relict populations of Australia, New Guinea, Malaysian Orang Asli, Andamanese or in mainstream popu-

haplogroup' (Consensus haplogroup 'C2': see The Y Chromosome Consortium 2002, fig. 1). and is defined further by bi-allelic marker M38 found effectively only east of the Wallace Line. HgC is notably rare in the New Guinea Highlands, and absent from Taiwan and the Philippines. An ancestral form has been found only in India, Borneo, and Wallacea. The M38 derived form is the only type found in the rest of the Pacific and could be the male analogue of the Polynesian Motif. Age estimates for the gene cluster holding the M38 mutation are about 11,500 years for the western Pacific, with a subsequent signal of expansion dated at around 5000 years ago. When the age analysis is restricted only to Polynesian groups, a strong expansion signal appears, which can be dated to about 2200 years ago, thus indicating multiple pulsed expansions at different times (Kayser *et al.* 2000). Again lowland Melanesia or Wallacea are possible locations for the implied periods of early Holocene delay and further mutation of this Asian intrusive gene line before dispersal to the Pacific.

Conclusion

The phylogeographic and population statistical approaches to studying past human migrations differ fundamentally in what they are comparing. The former compares population distances based on allele frequency, while the latter traces individual allele movements using the geographic distribution in relation to phylogenetic structure which is greatest in specific non-recombining loci. This is reflected in different outcomes when studying the same data. The phylogeographic approach was used implicitly in the mtDNA evidence for the original Out-of-Africa scenario and was used again in a discussion of the number of successful exits from Africa. In an island colonization example, the Pacific, the phylogeographic method can be shown to give broadly reproducible inferences when compared between different loci. Genetic distance mapping does not appear to produce consistent results in island dispersals possibly resulting from different sources and multiple founder effects. This does not reduce the importance of population genetics where there is the opportunity to control for these effects. Both approaches have an important role.

References

Bellwood, P., 1997. *Prehistory of the Indo-Malaysian Archipelago.* Honolulu (HI): University of Hawaii Press.

Cann, R.L., M Stoneking & A.C. Wilson, 1987. Mitochondrial DNA and human evolution. *Nature* 325, 31–6.

Cavalli-Sforza, L.L., P. Menozzi & A. Piazza, 1994. *The History and Geography of Human Genes.* Princeton (NJ): Princeton University Press.

Denham, T., 2004. The roots of agriculture and arboriculture in New Guinea: looking beyond Austronesian expansion, Neolithic packages and indigenous origins. *World Archaeology* 36, 610–20.

Diamond, J., 1988. Express train to Polynesia. *Nature* 336, 307–8.

Diamond, J. & P. Bellwood, 2003. Farmers and their languages: the first expansions. *Science* 300, 597–603.

Eswaran, V., 2002. A diffusion wave out of Africa: the Mechanism of the modern human revolution. *Current Anthropology* 43, 749–74.

Forster, P., R. Harding, A. Torroni & H.-J. Bandelt, 1996. Origin and evolution of Native American mtDNA variation: a reappraisal. *American Journal of Human Genetics* 59, 935–45.

Forster, P., A. Torroni, C. Renfrew & R. Rohl, 2003. Asian and Papuan mtDNA evolution, in *Examining the Farming/Language Dispersal Hypothesis*, eds. P. Bellwood & C. Renfrew. (McDonald Institute Monographs.) Cambridge: McDonald Institute for Archaeological Research, 89–98.

Gaudieri, S., C. Leelayuwat, G.K. Tay, D.C. Townend & R.L. Dawkins, 1997. The Major Histocompatibility Complex (MHC) contains conserved polymorphic genomic sequences that are shuffled by recombination to form ethnic-specific haplotypes. *Journal of Molecular Evolution* 45, 17–23.

Hill, A.V.S., 1992. Molecular epidemiology of the thalassaemias (including haemoglobin E). *Baillière's Clinical Haematology* 5, 209–38.

Hill, A.V.S. & S.W. Serjeantson (eds), 1989. *The Colonisation of the Pacific: a Genetic Trail.* Oxford: Clarendon Press.

Kayser, M., S. Brauer, G. Weiss, *et al.*, 2000. Melanesian origin of Polynesian Y chromosomes. *Current Biology* 10, 1237–46.

Larson, G., K. Dobney, U. Albarella, *et al.*, 2005. Worldwide phylogeography of wild boar reveals multiple centers of pig domestication. *Science* 307, 1618–21.

Lum, J.K. & R.L. Cann, 2000. MtDNA lineage analyses: origins and migrations of Micronesians and Polynesians. *American Journal of Physical Anthropology* 113, 151–68.

Macaulay, V., C. Hill, A. Achilli, *et al.*, 2005. Single, rapid coastal settlement of Asia revealed by analysis of complete mitochondrial genomes. *Science* 308, 1034–6.

Melton, T., S. Clifford, J. Martinson, M. Batzer & M. Stoneking, 1998. Genetic evidence for the Proto-Austronesian homeland in Asia: mtDNA and nuclear DNA variation in Taiwanese aboriginal tribes. *American Journal of Human Genetics* 63, 1807–23.

Oppenheimer, S.J., 2003a. *Out of Eden: the Peopling of the World.* London: Constable.

Oppenheimer, S., 2003b. Austronesian spread into Southeast Asia and Oceania: where from and when, in *Pacific Archaeology: Assessments and Prospects*, ed. C. Sand. (Les Cahiers de l'Archéologie en Nouvelle Calédonie 15.) Nouméa: Museé de Nouvelle Calédonie, 54–70.

Oppenheimer, S., 2004. The 'Express Train from Taiwan to Polynesia': on the congruence of proxy lines of evidence. *World Archaeology* 36, 591–600.

Oppenheimer, S.J. & M. Richards, 2001. Polynesian origins: slow boat to Melanesia? *Nature* 410, 166–7.

Oppenheimer, S.J. & M. Richards, 2003. Polynesians: devolved Taiwanese rice farmers or Wallacean maritime traders with fishing, foraging and horticultural skills, in *Examining the Farming/Language Dispersal Hypothesis*, eds. P. Bellwood & C. Renfrew. (McDonald Institute Monographs.) Cambridge: McDonald Institute for Archaeological Research, 287–97.

Paz, V., 2003. Island Southeast Asia: spread or friction zone?, in *Examining the Farming/Language Dispersal Hypothesis*, eds. P. Bellwood & C. Renfrew. (McDonald Institute Monographs.) Cambridge: McDonald Institute for Archaeological Research, 275–86.

Richards, M., V. Macaulay, E. Hickey, *et al.*, 2000. Tracing European founder lineages in the Near Eastern mitochondrial gene pool. *American Journal of Human Genetics* 67, 1251–76.

Szabó, K. & S. O'Connor, 2004. Migration and complexity in Holocene Island Southeast Asia. *World Archaeology* 36, 621–8.

Wainscoat, J.S., A.V.S. Hill, A.L. Boyce, *et al.*, 1986. Evolutionary relationships of human populations from an analysis of nuclear DNA polymophisms. *Nature* 319, 491–3.

The Y Chromosome Consortium, 2002. A nomenclature system for the tree of human Y-chromosomal binary haplogroups. *Genome Research* 12, 339–48.

Part II

What Simulations Tell Us About Complex European (Pre-)histories

population of only two HG lineages, on average per deme during the whole cohabitation period between Mesolithic and Neolithic populations (lasting between 140 and 200 years per cell).

The genetic consequences of this introgression phenomenon during the two main European expansions could be the following ones:

- If admixture occurs between Neanderthals (HN) and early modern humans (HS), then HN lineages are still expected to be present in the current European gene pool. The sequencing of Neanderthal mtDNA (Krings *et al.* 1997; 1999; Ovchinnikov *et al.* 2000; Schmitz *et al.* 2002; Serre *et al.* 2004) has revealed a specific type of sequence unambiguously distinct from any modern human type. Given the fact that no sequence of Neanderthal type is currently observed among 12,000 European mtDNA (Peter Forster pers. comm.; see also Handt *et al.* 1998; Richards *et al.* 1996), we can expect the genetic input of Neanderthals into modern humans to be very low, if not absent. However, previous analytical methods have not allowed one to exclude an initial Neanderthal contribution smaller than 25 per cent to the current European genetic pool (Nordborg 1998; Serre *et al.* 2004), as all initial HN lineages would have potentially disappeared by drift since the admixture event (Hagelberg 2003; Relethford 2001). These previous estimations were made using very simple demographic models where population sizes were constant or exponential within a unique deme and admixture was instantaneous. We used a much more realistic model that took population subdivisions into account as well as progressive admixture and competition between HS and HN, and we obtained a maximum estimate of the HN contribution to the European gene pool equal to 0.1 per cent (Currat & Excoffier 2004). This value is 250 times smaller than the previous estimates obtained with less realistic models (Nordborg 1998; Serre *et al.* 2004). Our calculations imply that Neanderthals and early modern humans probably did not interbreed. Whether this absence of genetic exchange was due to inter-sterility, selection against hybrids, or an absence of ecological competition remains to be demonstrated, but a cultural separation or absence of contacts due to low densities seems to

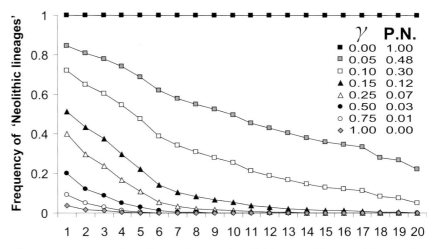

Figure 4.4. *Proportion of Near Eastern 'Neolithic genes' (see text) in a series of samples distributed regularly along the axis between Lebanon and Ireland (see arrow on Fig. 4.3D). These proportions are given for various admixture indices γ ranging from 0 to one. The average proportion of these 'Neolithic genes' over all samples on the transect is also reported as P.N.*

be excluded since technological exchanges between Neanderthals and Cro-Magnons are documented (e.g. Hublin *et al.* 1996).

- Concerning the Neolithic transition, it has been postulated that a gradient of allele frequency observed from southeast to northwest Europe was the result of the dispersion of the lineages of the first farmers from the Near East (the 'Neolithic lineages') into Europe (Barbujani & Pilastro 1993; Chikhi *et al.* 1998; Menozzi *et al.* 1978; Rosser *et al.* 2000; Sokal *et al.* 1991). We estimated that in order to get a gradient of 'Neolithic lineages' over the whole Europe, the γ index between HG and NF has to be smaller than 10 per cent. Such small γ values correspond to less than 2 HG lineages incorporated in the communities of dispersing farmers at each location (cell). The γ index must even be smaller than 5 per cent in order to get a proportion of 'Neolithic lineages' larger than 50 per cent over the whole Europe, as estimated for certain markers (Barbujani & Dupanloup 2002; Chikhi 2002; Dupanloup *et al.* 2004). This means that only an extremely low admixture between HG and NF is compatible with an European gene pool constituted of a majority of lineages brought by early farmers during the Neolithic (less than one HG lineage incorporated into the Neolithic population on average per deme: see Fig. 4.4).

Two processes can jointly explain a rapid introgression of genes from the invaded population into the genome of the invasive population. First, at each step of its expansion, the invasive population incorporates a given proportion of genes of the invaded population. The proportion of genes of the initial population in the wave front therefore decreases generation after generation, such that the larger the number of migration steps involved during the invasive processes, the stronger the dilution phenomenon. Second, the invaded lineages are incorporated into the invasive population during the cohabitation period, when the density of invaders is still low (see Fig. 4.2). It means that invaded lineages are included into the subsequent local population growth and are then amplified by the phase of logistic growth.

Molecular diversity

As the Neanderthal contribution to the current European gene pool was estimated to be almost zero (Currat & Excoffier 2004), we did not take Neanderthal lineages into account when studying the Neolithic transition. We looked at the following molecular signatures characteristic of range expansions: unimodal mismatch distribution (distribution of the number of differences between all pairs of genes within a sample) and observation of Allele Frequency Clines (AFC) along a southeast to northwest transect. Note that these typical signatures can also result from other phenomenon (e.g selection or bottlenecks), which do not directly concern the present paper. We present here the results obtained for two extreme models of the Neolithic transition. The Diffusion-Replacement model (DR) consists in a complete replacement of HG by NF without any genetic exchanges ($\gamma = 0$). Under the opposite model of Cultural Diffusion (CD), HG are adopting Neolithic technologies from invading Neolithic populations and reproduction is done randomly between the two populations ($\gamma = 1$). Note that this last model is not, strictly speaking, a purely cultural diffusion as it also implies population movements. The reality is certainly somewhere between these two models (Arias 1999; Gronenborg 1999; Mazurié de Keroualin 2003), but we focus here on their genetic consequences in order to study what pattern of diversity are expected under these two contrasting hypotheses, to which real data can be compared. Note that the classical 'Demic Diffusion' model proposed by Ammerman & Cavalli-Sforza (1984) accounts for a very limited local HG incorporation, and is thus close to our DR model.

Genealogical trees

First of all, it is necessary here to describe the genealogical trees obtained under both scenarios (Fig. 4.5A). Under DR, most of the coalescent events occur during the Neolithic expansion and lead to short terminal branches with only few long internal branches. Con-

trastingly, under the CD model coalescent events occur more regularly through time and there is an almost equal proportion of short and long branches. In both cases, the final coalescent events occur at the time of the Palaeolithic expansion.

Mismatch distributions

The difference in the shape of the trees is reflected in the mismatch distributions inferred from DNA sequences of 300 bp length (corresponding approximately to typical HV1 mtDNA sequences). DR mismatches are often bimodal with a first mode centred on 0 differences whereas almost all CD mismatch distributions are unimodal and smooth (Fig. 4.5B). The mismatch distributions simulated using 22 SNPs (corresponding to Y-chromosome data published by Semino et al. 2000) reveal approximately the same patterns but with a much larger variance (Fig. 4.5C). Note that these 22 SNPs were simulated without any ascertainment bias (see below).

Allele frequency clines

One of the typical molecular signatures of a demographic expansion is the occurrence of AFCs along the axis of the expansion, due to successive founder effects (Austerlitz et al. 2000; Barbujani et al. 1995). The observation of AFCs between the Near East and the northern part of Europe has been considered as a support for a Demic Diffusion of Neolithic farmers from the Near East and consequently for a large replacement of previous European HG populations (Ammerman & Cavalli-Sforza 1984). However, we show here that AFCs could also have been created during the expansion of early modern humans in Europe as proposed by some authors (Barbujani & Bertorelle 2001; Richards et al. 1996). Indeed, Neolithic populations followed the same routes than the early modern Europeans did about 30,000 years earlier (Mellars 2004). Under both extreme models (RD and CD) as well as under any intermediate case ($0 < \gamma < 1$), the proportion of randomly simulated mutations showing a cline from the Near East to the northern part of Europe is always smaller than 5 per cent (Table 4.1, column 3). The presence of clines is thus not a support for a large replacement of pre-existing HG people, as it is almost independent of the intensity of HG assimilation reflected by the index γ.

Ascertainment bias

One important aspect of current genetic data is the way molecular markers are selected. Except for mitochondrial DNA, there are only few loci where complete DNA sequences are available for a representative set of populations. Most of the large data sets consist

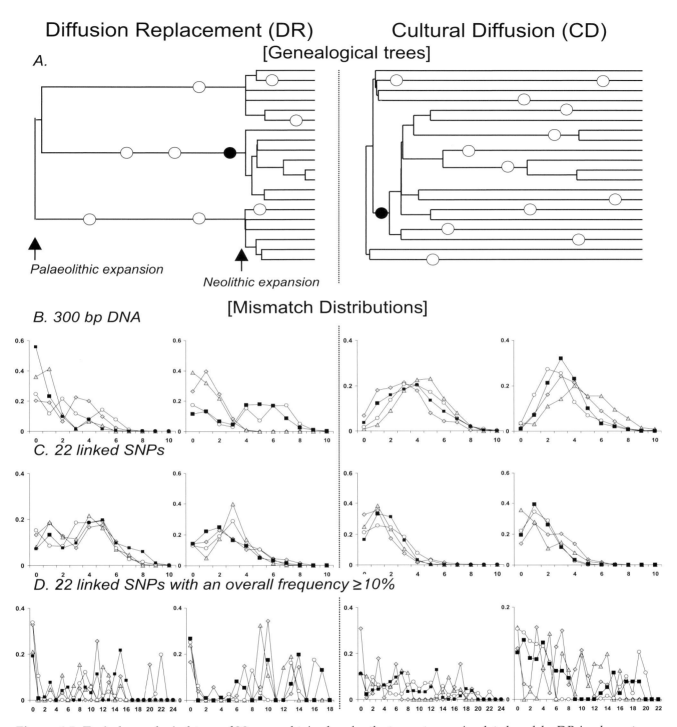

Figure 4.5. *Typical genealogical trees of 20 genes obtained under the two extreme simulated models. DR implements a complete replacement of Mesolithic hunter-gatherers by Neolithic farmers coming from the Near East and CD simulates free genetic exchanges between the two populations. For each model, we show eight random mismatch distributions replicates (x axis = number of differences, y axis = frequency). Simulations were performed with a large current Nm (= 800), where m is the migration rate and N the density, as estimated for post-Neolithic European populations (Excoffier 2004). White circles on panel A represent random mutations and black circle frequent mutations (see text).*

Table 4.1. *Proportion of simulations (over 10,000) that show a significant AFC at the 5 per cent significance level for various amount of gene flow between HG and NF demes (no gene flow: γ = 0, maximum: γ = 1). R² = average determination coefficient for the significant AFCs. Proportions are shown for random mutations but also for mutations for which the minor allele has a frequency of at least 5 per cent or 10 per cent (see text).*

Palaeolithic contribution		Allele Frequency Clines					
		All mutations		Bias (f. ≥ 5%)		Bias (f. ≥ 10%)	
γ	No. genes	Prop.	R^2	Prop.	R^2	Prop.	R^2
0.00	0	0.03	0.50	0.57	0.60	0.56	0.62
0.05	1	0.03	0.47	0.48	0.54	0.45	0.58
0.10	2	0.03	0.45	0.50	0.56	0.51	0.63
0.15	3	0.04	0.42	0.51	0.58	0.78	0.70
0.25	5	0.03	0.42	0.66	0.59	0.86	0.71
0.50	10	0.02	0.43	0.71	0.58	0.82	0.68
0.75	15	0.02	0.40	0.70	0.58	0.82	0.67
1.00	20	0.02	0.40	0.68	0.59	0.80	0.63

of SNPs, STRs or RFLPs. All these markers (as well as classical markers, like blood groups) do not necessarily represent a random set of polymorphisms on the genome. These polymorphisms are thus not very representative of random mutations on the genome, because the most frequent polymorphisms (the mutations with the highest frequencies in the population) have a larger probability to be observed and thus to be selected in human variability studies. Rare mutations are thus certainly under-represented in SNP, RFLP and classical marker data sets (Nielsen 2000), which is one kind of ascertainment bias. Corrections for ascertainment bias have been developed for some analyses such as estimation of allele frequency distributions (Nielsen *et al.* 2004), but it is still not clear how this bias can affect other studies. Thus, we have investigated the influence of ascertainment bias in our results by carrying out the same analysis as above, but keeping only mutations for which the minor allele (the less frequent) is at least 5 or 10 per cent on average along our European transect.

Mismatch distribution
Mismatch distributions computed from biased SNPs with a global frequency greater than 10 per cent are ragged and multimodal, independently of the simulated demographic scenario (Fig. 4.5D). Ascertainment bias is thus erasing the signature of an expansion in the mismatch distributions. It seems therefore difficult to infer the role played by demography in shaping the ragged and multimodal mismatch distribution inferred from European Y chromosome SNP diversity (Pereira *et al.* 2001) until the influence of ascertainment bias can be efficiently taken into account.

Allele frequency clines
We examined the effect of ascertainment bias on AFCs over Europe. The fraction of SNPs showing AFCs increases extremely (> 47 per cent, see Table 4.1) when considering SNPs with minor allele frequency larger than 5 per cent over the studied transect. This proportion is again independent of the Palaeolithic/Mesolithic contribution represented by γ (Table 4.1). It shows that the frequency of AFCs increases by an order of magnitude in cases of ascertainment bias. This results can explain why AFCs have been so commonly detected in Europe using SNPs (Rosser *et al.* 2000) and classical markers (Menozzi *et al.* 1978; Sokal *et al.* 1991), but hardly with DNA sequences (Richards *et al.* 1996; 1998; 2002). AFCs may result from demographic expansions, but the probability of observing these clines is clearly related to the age of the SNPs. Indeed, the age of a given mutation is related to its frequency (Kimura & Ohta 1973; Slatkin & Rannala 2000 and see also Fig. 4.5A). If the mutation is old enough to have been present at the time of the demographic expansion, it could have been spread by the expansion wave (Edmonds *et al.* 2004) and then been clinally distributed along the axis of the expansion (Klopfstein *et al.* 2006). One thus expects to see a correlation between the proportion of old mutations in a sample and the probability of observing AFCs.

Concluding remarks

We have presented a new simulation framework to study the effect of more realistic scenarios of range expansion on genetic variability. This approach has allowed us to exclude with much greater confidence than previous attempts, that Neanderthals ever significantly contributed to the modern human gene pool. We also showed that the amount of local Palaeolithic/Mesolithic contribution after the European Neolithic transition could potentially be estimated, since the shape of the coalescent tree depends on this contribution (Fig. 4.5). The more Near Eastern lineages that have been brought into Europe during the Neolithic diffusion, the larger the proportion of bimodal mismatch distributions that can be expected. On the contrary, mismatch distributions should be unimodal and smooth if the local Palaeolithic/Mesolithic contribution was important. We have also shown that the observation of AFCs cannot be considered as support for demic diffusion, as AFCs can be created either by a Palaeolithic expansion of early modern humans or by a Neolithic expansion of farmers. The only way to determine if European AFCs were created during the Neolithic or during the Palaeolithic would be to date them. This seems difficult without a very precise

Chapter 5

A Combined Markov Chain Monte Carlo and Simulation-based Approach for Inferring the Colonization History of the British Isles

William Amos, Howsun Jow & Nigel Burroughs

More than with just about any other species, the genetic analysis of human populations is complicated by extensive mixing, brought about by migration, trade and invasions. Such mixing increases similarity by eroding differences that accrued during previous periods of isolation. Simple approaches at measuring mixing are confounded by two unresolved ambiguities. First, the populations are usually assumed to be in equilibrium, with divergence due to drift being balanced by a small but constant and continuing exchange of individuals between populations. Thus, there is no allowance for mixing to change over time. Second, if mixing does change over time, current methods do not distinguish between mixing followed by isolation and the converse, isolation followed by mixing. We have explored this problem by developing a Markov chain Monte Carlo approach for analysing data from linked (Y-chromosome) microsatellites and applying this to an analysis of a model system, the demographic history of Britain and Ireland. In our method, we define a mixing statistic based on the extent to which nodes in the underlying phyologenetic tree link individuals from the same as opposed to different populations. This statistic can be estimated for every coalescent event in the tree, along with the age of each event measured in terms of the number of mutations before the present. Averaged over all trees accepted by the Markov chain algorithm, the net result is a profile that reflects how the historical rates of mixing between any pair of populations has varied over time. To calibrate the output, we conducted extensive simulations of plausible scenarios. Our results indicate that the method captures many expected aspects of how continental European populations have contributed to the modern British and Irish populations. Surprisingly, the method seems more consistent when applied to real as opposed to simulated data, suggesting that factors such as population expansion or a meta-population structure may act to stabilize the underlying signal.

Unravelling the history of human populations presents one of the greatest challenges to population geneticists (Cavalli-Sforza *et al.* 1994). Thus, while there is general agreement that modern humans evolved in Africa and then migrated out to colonize the rest of the world some time around 100,000 years ago (Jorde *et al.* 2000; Prugnolle *et al.* 2005; Quintana-Murci *et al.* 1999), beyond this details remain surprisingly sketchy.

Did we replace Neanderthals and all other hominids or was there significant introgression (Caramelli *et al.* 2003)? What were the migration routes (Quintana-Murci *et al.* 1999) and how many people used them? There is quite a lot of evidence that a population bottleneck took place (Harpending & Rogers 2000; Pritchard *et al.* 1999; Prugnolle *et al.* 2005), but to what extent and were there multiple events?

Many of the key questions about human demographic history appear tractable using genetic analysis, particularly following the recent massive increase in the rate at which genetic data have been collected. Ten years ago studies using more than twenty markers were unusual, yet today the largest study examined more than one million polymorphisms! (Hinds *et al.* 2005). With such remarkable power it might be expected that almost any question one might wish to pose could be answered. However, a pioneering study based on a powerful Bayesian approach implemented in the program STRUCTURE (Pritchard *et al.* 2000) and applied to data from almost 400 markers typed in 50 diverse populations nonetheless failed to find convincing population groups at a finer scale than continent level divisions (Rosenberg *et al.* 2002).

Given the level of linguistic, morphological and cultural differentiation between the populations studied by Rosenberg and colleagues (2002) it is tempting to conclude that large genetic differences should exist, and the fact that they are so hard to detect indicates that much of the signal has been lost due to widespread mixing and population movement. A more positive view is that the Rosenberg *et al.* study was based on autosomal loci, where recombination and random assortment act rapidly to scramble genetic clues about where an immigrant's descendents came from. In contrast, linked, non-recombining markers such as those on the Y chromosome should retain a 'memory' of their origin indefinitely and hence may provide a powerful tool to explore how much mixing has occurred and when.

Linked markers are unusually informative because they can be used to construct relatively unambiguous gene trees based on individuals. The underlying structure of these trees then reflects the demographic history of the populations from which they derive (Bahlo & Griffiths 2000; Kuhner *et al.* 1998; Nee *et al.* 1995). For example, people from a long-term small population will reveal thin, shallow trees with little diversity, while those from large populations yield large bushy trees with high diversity. Similarly, people from two isolated populations will generate a joint tree that divides neatly into two distinct sub-trees, while the presence of migration will be betrayed by a tendency for the two sub-trees to be linked by branches that start in one but end in the other. Tree shape can also reflect changes over time, with, for example, declining populations having very different branching patterns compared with expanding populations (Drummond *et al.* 2005). Moreover, if the mutation rate of the markers being used is known or can be estimated, it then becomes possible to add a timescale to the tree's history and infer actual population sizes from the level of diversity observed.

To extract the information contained in tree shape requires powerful statistical approaches capable simultaneously of estimating a range of parameter values that together determine the most likely tree shape given the data being considered. Since mutation rates and the exact structure of the underlying gene tree are poorly known, the method of choice is often the Bayesian approach called Markov chain Monte Carlo (MCMC) (Beaumont 1999; Drummond *et al.* 2005; Gilks *et al.* 1996; Wilson & Balding 1998), in which parameter values are sampled from uninformative prior distributions and those combinations that yield trees that better fit the data are stored. After a very large number of iterations, the distribution of stored values is used to estimate the most likely value for each parameter, along with associated confidence intervals.

MCMC approaches have already been used to analyse linked markers in the form of mitochondrial DNA sequence data. For example, Drummond *et al.* (2005) have developed a method to estimate how population size varies over time and applied it to find evidence of a previously unrecognized bottleneck in the history of Beringian bison. Such results are extremely encouraging, particularly in view of the relatively low variability of mitochondrial sequences compared with data emerging from human studies where panels of Y-chromosome microsatellites can distinguish between almost every individual tested. Indeed, MCMC approaches that exploit the high diversity and relatively simple mutation patterns of Y-chromosome microsatellites (Cooper *et al.* 1999; Wilson & Balding 1998). For example, in an early study, Cooper and colleagues examined one African and one European population and successfully estimated population size, time to most recent common ancestor and aspects of the underlying mutation process (Cooper *et al.* 1999). Furthermore, there was also evidence of a strong signal relating to population expansion that could potentially be exploited through methods analogous to those used by Drummond *et al.* (2005).

In this paper we explore the potential of a MCMC-based approach to uncover signals of mixing in human populations, using the British Isles as a model system.

Methods and results

We have now extended our basic algorithm (Cooper *et al.* 1999) to consider mixing between pairs of populations. As previously, we make the simplifying assumption of constant population size and estimate the parameters μN (mutation rate × population size), μT (mutation rate × time to most recent common ancestor) and ω (the mutation bias in favour of contraction or expansion). In addition, we now jointly consider pairs of populations in which all individuals are first labelled with either ones or zeros according to the population they were sampled from. As previously, the algorithm constructs a series of trees and stores a small subset according to how likely they are given the model, the parameter values and the input data.

To model mixing, at every node in a tree we record the tendency for like as opposed to dissimilar numbers to pair, calculated as $s = (m1 + m2)/2$, where $m1$ and $m2$ are the values at the immediate daughter nodes. Since trees are constructed from the present backwards in time, the first coalescent events mainly join 1 to 1, 0 to 0 and 1 to 0, giving values of $s = 1$, 0 and 0.5 respectively, while deeper in the tree fractional values are formed. Ideally, mixing should be measured on a scale that varies between 0 for like-like nodes and 1 for opposite type nodes. We therefore calculate a derivative 'mixing statistic' $= 2 (|s - 0.5|)$ that varies between 0 when two dissimilar nodes and 1 for two '1's or two '0's. Averaged across all nodes in all accepted trees, this mixing statistic provides a measure of the extent that the joint tree contains pure branches, where most individuals derive from the same population, as opposed to branches that are more mixed.

The mixing statistic has no absolute meaning, in the sense that the algorithm cannot directly distinguish between similarity due to lack of divergence and similarity due to poor genetic resolution (too few genetic markers). To address this problem, we introduce a control. In every tree accepted by the MCMC algorithm the mixing statistic is recalculated at every node after first scrambling the ones and zeros so as to remove all information about population origin. The difference in average mixing statistic between the observed and the scrambled data then provides a convenient measure of the degree of mixing relative to a null hypothesis that both sets of samples were drawn from the same homogeneous population (Jow *et al.* submitted). In practice, it is convenient to combine the observed and scrambled values by expressing the observed value as a proportion of the maximum possible deviation from random $= (mix - rmix)/(1 - rmix)$, where mix is the observed mixing statistic and $rmix$ is the equivalent value calculated from the randomized data set. In this way, a value close to zero indicates populations that behave indistinguishably from a single, homogeneous population, while increasingly non-zero values indicate divergence.

Although useful in its own right, the mixing statistic approach can be taken further. As explained, during tree construction the algorithm records the mixing statistic at every node. As part of the likelihood calculations, every node is also assessed for age,

expressed as the expected number of mutation events since the node formed. Consequently, by plotting node age against the associated mixing statistic a profile is generated that in principle reflects how branch-swapping between the two populations varies over time. Such mixing profiles have the potential to shed light on the key question of whether any given level of mixing between two populations occurred early, late or was homogeneously distributed through time.

To discover whether our method produces plausible results when applied to real data, we first analysed published data from a study exploring the Viking influence on the Britain (Capelli *et al.* 2003). These data comprise the 'Blood of the Vikings' sample set, a minimum of 44 males collected from each of 25 market towns chosen to be more or less evenly spaced across Britain and Ireland, as well as control populations from the Viking homelands of North Germany/Denmark (NGD, $n = 190$) and Norway ($n = 201$), augmented by six other control populations from around Europe: Basque (García *et al.* 2004), Spanish ($n = 147$, YHRD: www.ystr.org), French (Paris, $n = 212$, YHRD), Italians from Tuscany (Ricci *et al.* 2001), Frisians (Weale *et al.* 2002) and Croatians (Barać *et al.* 2003). The Croatians are included as an outgroup that has had little or no interaction with Britain, while the Frisians comprise people from a region in northern Netherlands, neighbouring NGD and who are thought to have had a strong genetic input into eastern and central England (Weale *et al.* 2002).

Examples from the range of mixing profiles we observe are illustrated in Figure 5.1. In each profile the vertical axis represents the level of mixing (0 = completely mixed, 1 = complete divergence) while the horizontal axis represents time running backwards from the present, left to right. Thus NGD–York show little evidence of divergence, the mixing statistic remaining close to zero; Croatia–York is typical of two populations that have been diverging continuously over the time course we examine; France–Oban and Basque–Morpeth reveal more complicated histories that include dips near the present suggesting a period of increased mixing, originating either as two already quite separate populations (France–Oban) or as a single population that split around 1 unit back in time (Basque–Morpeth). Over all profiles it is noticeable that similar comparisons yield similar profiles. Thus, the Frisian and NGD samples come from neighbouring continental areas and reveal very similar profiles across much of Britain (Fig. 5.2), while British populations in similar locations (e.g. west Wales, south England, north Scottish Isles) also reveal similar profiles with each of the eight European comparisons (data not shown). A second observation is that the profiles generally agree

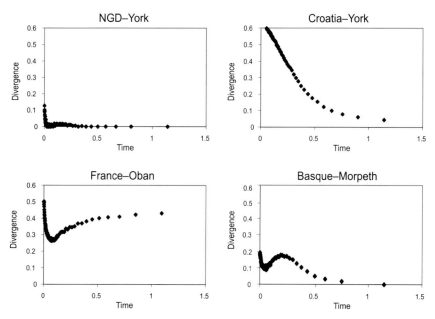

Figure 5.1. *Mixing profiles illustrating the range of patterns seen. Time is measured in mutational events ago (0 = the present) and divergence is measured by the mixing statistic (0 = indistinguishable from a single homogeneous population, maximum possible value = 1). NGD = North German/Danish.*

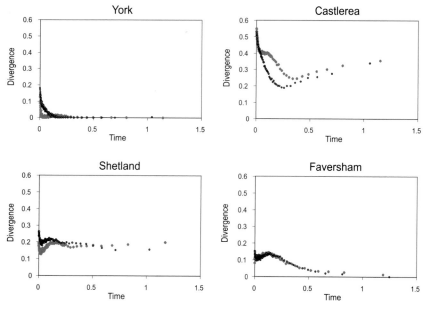

Figure 5.2. *Mixing profiles showing the similarity of profile shape generated by comparisons involving NGD (grey symbols) and the Frisian (black circles), samples collected from the same geographic area. Four British populations are shown, chosen to show a range of profile shapes and both the most divergent (Castlerea) and most congruent (Faversham) cases.*

NGD and Frisians; Croatian profiles all reveal a pattern indicating continuing divergence; Norwegians show a strong affinity with Orkney and Shetland where Norse place names abound; and while 'English' towns reveal shared ancestry with NGD and Frisians, people from the historically Celtic-speaking areas of Ireland, Scotland and Wales have profiles that indicate divergent ancestry.

Although these profiles indicate qualitatively the way in which populations have interacted, there are several factors that preclude drawing quantitative conclusions. Most importantly, the rate of divergence between two populations will depend on the effective size of the populations concerned, and this is both unknown and will inevitably vary over time. In addition, the mixing profiles are constrained by the fact that, instead of fitting a mixing parameter for every node in the tree, we fit a single homogeneous mixing rate and then examine how the events are distributed over time. Under this model, it is unlikely that mixing events will be strongly clumped and hence the size of sudden large changes in migration rate will tend to be under-estimated.

In view of these limitations, we explored the likely meaning of the observed mixing profiles by using a simulation approach. First, we used Monte Carlo simulation to create a wide range of plausible scenarios covering the sorts of population histories we might expect, using six markers each with a realistic mutation rate of 0.001 per generation (a compromise between recently reported rates of 6.9×10^{-4} (Zhivitovsky *et al.* 2004) and 3.17×10^{-3} (Kayser *et al.* 2000)) and evolving through a strict stepwise process (Di Rienzo *et al.* 1994; Moran 1975). Next, each simulated data set was analysed using our MCMC algorithm to generate a corresponding set of mixing profiles with known histories. Finally, each of the empirically observed profiles was compared with every simulated profile to find the one that yielded the closest possible fit, based on minimizing the sum

quite well with expectations: the east coast in general and the Viking city of York in particular show strong mixing with the two nearest continental populations

Table 5.1. *Summary table of parameter values for each of the eight non-British populations, averaged across all 25 British population comparisons. Mix1, mix2 and mix3 refer to rates of mixing during the early, 'invasion' and recent phases respectively. Period1 and period2 refer to the lengths of the early and recent phases respectively. Population codes are: NGD = North German/Danish, NOR = Norway, FRC = France, BAS = Basque, CRO = Croatia, FRI = Frisian, TUS = Tuscany, SPN = Spanish.*

	mix1	mix2	mix3	period1	period2
NGD	0.32%	15.2%	2.4%	820	59.0
NOR	0.48%	6.8%	1.0%	820	52.0
FRC	0.44%	13.6%	0.5%	820	53.0
BAS	0.33%	21.7%	1.7%	729	53.1
CRO	0.54%	16.7%	0.0%	896	89.6
FRI	0.64%	17.6%	2.4%	820	49.0
TUS	0.60%	14.8%	0.2%	760	60.0
SPN	0.64%	15.2%	2.1%	720	56.0

of the squared deviations between the points along the profile. Since the density of points is greatest near the present, the current unweighted approach tends to pay less attention to more ancient part of the profile and this is a bias that we are currently working to reduce.

To simulate pairs of European populations we considered four demographic phases. In the first, a homogeneous single population of 2000 is allowed to evolve to mutation drift equilibrium to create an ancestral population. In the next phase we allow divergence to occur by splitting the population randomly into two and then allowing independent evolution for either 500 or 1000 generations with no or minimal (1%) migration between them. This period is meant to represent differentiation following the last ice age. We then allow for a possible 'invasion/migration event', simulated by a period of five generations where mixing varies between 0% (no mixing) and 50% (complete mixing). Finally there is a period of stability where low levels of mixing (0%, 1%, 2% or 5%) continue for 25, 50 or 100 generations, corresponding to the 'invasion' occurring approximately 500, 1000 or 2000 years ago. For each set of conditions, two replicate data sets are generated, hereafter referred to as 'duplicate runs'.

The results of the simulation calibration are summarized in Table 5.1. For each of the eight control European (non British) populations we present the average for each of the simulation parameters, calculated across all 25 comparisons with British populations. Overall, the biggest variation in parameter values among the eight European populations occurs in the more recent time period, where the level of mixing varies from 0.0% (Croatia) up to 2.4% (NGD and Frisians). The 'invasion' period shows less variation, though perhaps surprisingly Norwegians show the lowest mixing! The earliest period is remarkably constant both in length (approximately 800 genera-

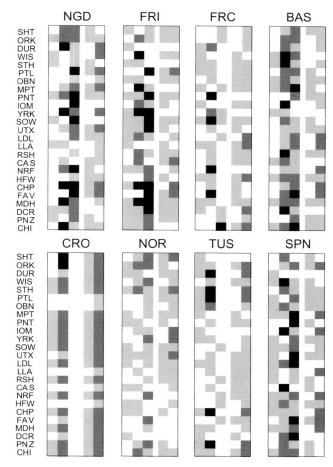

Figure 5.3. *Summary of calibrated mixing profiles. In each panel, all 25 British and Irish populations are compared against one of the eight European populations. Data are coded according to the estimated parameter value, light = small, dark = large. From left to right the columns represent mixing period one (white = 0, grey = 1%), invasion mixing (white to black = 0, 10%, 20% and 50%), settlement mixing (white to black = 0, 1%, 2% and 5%), a spacer column then length of isolation period (white = 500, grey = 1000 generations) and length of the settlement period (white to dark grey = 25, 50 or 100 generations).*

tions) and level of mixing (around 0.5%). Determining whether this constancy genuinely reflects shared demographic history or instead arises due to poor resolution deeper in the tree giving rise to more or less random parameter estimates will require further work.

To see more detail, we also constructed summary graphics for the full data set, where higher levels of mixing and longer time phases are both represented by darker blocks (Fig. 5.3). Again, although individual blocks should not be taken at face value, a meaningful overall signal is indicated by the similarities and

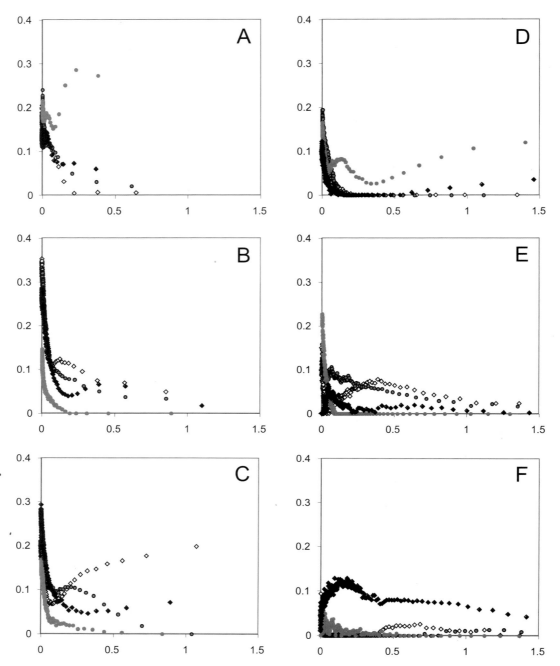

Figure 5.4. *Test of consistency of mixing profiles. Each panel shows four mixing profiles generated from two independent sub-samples drawn from each of two independent simulations with the same input parameters. Sub-samples from the same run are both either light or dark. Initial population size increases from 500 in panel A through 1000, 2000, 4000 and 8000 to 16,000 in panel F.*

differences in patterning among the European populations. For example, Croatia stands out for its consistency across all populations, particularly when it is realized that the light horizontal bands (low mixing, short time periods) all correspond to the populations from historically Celtic-speaking regions. There is

also noticeable similarity between the patterns for NGD and Friesland, for the Basques and Spain and for France and Tuscany. Interestingly, Norway has no high mixing values.

In addition to conducting simulations to calibrate the results from empirical data, we also explored the extent to which our MCMC approach extracts a consistent signal. For this we chose one set of experimental conditions (500 generation separation with no mixing, 5 generations of mixing at 50% then 25 generations of partial isolation with mixing at 2%) and re-ran simulations for a range of different population sizes (500, 1000, 2000, 4000, 8000, 16,000). For each population size we examined how profile consistency was influenced both by sampling error and by the stochasticity of the simulation itself. Sampling error was tested by drawing two independent samples of 100 individuals from each of the two sub-populations, while the stochasticity of the simulation process was tested by comparing two replicate runs with the same input parameters.

Figure 5.4 shows the results from these consistency-test simulations. The panels are labelled A ($N = 500$) though to F ($N = 16,000$). In each graph there are four traces: two light profiles generated from two independent subsets drawn from the first replicate run, and two dark profiles generated from two subsets drawn from a second replicate run. Comparisons between dark and light thus reflect the effect of stochasticity while dark-dark and light-light comparisons indicate the effect of sampling. *A priori* we would expect to find that deeper divergence values will be smaller in larger populations, light-light and dark-dark comparisons will show greater similarity than comparable light-dark comparisons and that, overall, smaller populations should reduce similarity between profiles. In practice, any trends are at best weak, though with the eye of faith they do appear to go in the expected directions.

Interestingly, the consistency of the repeat simulations summarized in Figure 5.4 appears less than that seen between real populations, as exemplified by comparisons involving NGD and Friesland in Figure 5.2. To test whether this is a real effect, we compared the maximum separation between pairs of profiles in real and simulated data. For real data we used profile pairs comprising those of NGD and Friesland compared with each of the 25 British populations. For simulated data we used the full set of calibration profiles, treating the two replicate runs of each set of parameter values as the profile pair to be compared. We found that real data (average maximum difference = 0.092±0.006) were indeed significantly more consistent that replicate simulations based on the same input parameter values (average maximum difference = 0.147±0.006).

As a further test of profile consistency between similar populations we compared the best fit parameter estimates generated by the two most similar European populations, NGD and Frisians, and a third

Table 5.2. *Correlations among parameter estimates for three European populations compared against a panel of 25 populations sampled from around Britain and Ireland. Abbreviations are as in the legend to Table 5.1.*

Early mixing			Invasion mixing			Recent mixing		
	NGD	NOR		NGD	NOR		NGD	NOR
FRI	0.16	0.05	FRI	0.37	−0.17	FRI	0.62	−0.03
NGD		0.20	NGD		0.16	NGD		0.16

Early time						Recent time		
	NGD	NOR					NGD	NOR
FRI	0.21	−0.45				FRI	−0.21	−0.21
NGD		0.01				NGD		0.33

group, the Norwegians. In each pairwise comparison we calculated correlation coefficients for each of the five parameters (Table 5.2). As expected, the level of concordance in comparisons involving Norway was generally poor. In contrast, recent mixing was highly correlated ($r = 0.62$) between NGD and FRI, indicating that these two populations tend to yield similar estimates when compared with the same British populations, in line with their geographic proximity.

Discussion

We present the results from a new form of analysis based on Markov chain Monte Carlo in which Y-chromosome polymorphisms are used to reconstruct profiles of how mixing varies over time between any given pair of populations. We have applied this analysis to both simulated data and to a large published data set concerning populations sampled across Great Britain and Ireland, and also from key populations in continental Europe. The empirical data reveal two classes of British sample: those with and those without a strong Celtic-speaking history, the latter revealing stronger recent coancestry with continental Europe. Real data appear to contain a more consistent signal compared with simulated data.

Previous studies interested in population mixing have faced the problem that any given level of genetic similarity can be arrived at via a number of different histories. In particular mixing may be constant over time or take place in a burst at some unknown time. We have therefore exploited the way that non-recombining markers can be used to construct a population tree to infer when and how often branches are swapped between pairs populations, testing the method on data from the British Isles. The resulting mixing profiles vary greatly among comparisons and in a way that is consistent with *a priori* expectations. Thus, neighbouring towns generally yield similar profiles, and the Croatians give profiles suggesting little or no recent mixing while Britain's nearest continental neighbours show high levels of mixing, particularly with eastern English towns.

The consistency of profiles between neighbouring towns is to some extent surprising, given the rather lower levels of consistency shown by profiles either from simulated data with the same input parameters or even from different samples drawn from the same simulated data set. There are several possible explanations for this discrepancy. Most obviously, current populations are large and have experienced periods of more or less exponential expansion. Both these properties are likely to buffer against the stochasticity of genetic drift. Additional buffering may come from mixing with other unsampled populations, a process that acts to increase the effective size of the local population. A further possibility is that the sampling of the real populations focused on individuals whose grandparents tended to live in the same town, and this might impose greater structure on the data than would be achieved by random sampling. To discover the exact reason will require further work, including the development of models that incorporate both mixing and changes in population size over time.

At present our approach does not directly estimate migration rates but instead records the average purity of each node in the population tree. In this sense the mixing profiles are only relative depictions, both in the sense of comparisons between profiles and in the extent to which the level of mixing changes a long a profile. The profiles are also relative in an absolute sense, since trials with larger numbers of markers reveal reduced mixing, highlighting the fact that there are two sources of similarity between populations, the degree of mixing and the degree to which limited marker variability creates some degree of homoplasy. None the less, it is possible to gain some insight into what the profiles mean through extensive simulations covering a range of likely scenarios. In our study we assumed that there were four phases: a single homogeneous populations splits into two, diverges through isolation, experiences an invasion and then spends a modern period when mixing can occur through trade and low level settlement. Although necessarily some way from total realism, these simulations did cover a wide range of levels of mixing and possible timescales.

How realistic are the profiles? Given the degree of variation between the outputs of simulations with the same input parameters, it seems clear that the parameter estimates cannot be taken at face value. Indeed, with sample sizes as low as 44 there is clearly a limit to the amount of information even a perfect joint population tree can hold. Having said this, there is some room for optimism. While the parameter

estimates for the early phase of the simulations may be little better than random, the more recent phase does seem informative, differing greatly between the different European populations. For example, while Croatians never once yield profiles that indicate mixing in the recent phase, while for Basques only two British populations fail to indicate mixing. Furthermore, there is excellent correlation between the recent phase parameter estimates generated by Frisian and NGD profiles, two independent samples from neighbouring continental regions. Such close agreement indicates that the observed variation we observe across Britain in the best-fit parameter values for how much mixing occurred and for how long is by no means random.

Previous studies looking at the Y-chromosome history of Britain found similarities between Basques and people from historically Celtic-speaking regions (Capelli *et al.* 2003; Wilson *et al.* 2001), between Norway and Shetland/Orkney (Capelli *et al.* 2003) and between Friesland and towns in central and eastern England (Weale *et al.* 2002). Our results appear broadly consistent with these trends, with both Basques and Spanish showing lots of mixing, Norway showing greatest affinity with Shetland and Orkney and Friesland mixing most with towns in central and eastern England. In addition, our data suggest other trends, with Friesland and Spain both showing much greater early mixing compared with NGD and the Basques respectively. Croatia, France and Tuscany all reveal some level of early mixing/common ancestry but little or no recent mixing, with Croatia in particular mixing little but more with 'English' than with 'Celtic' towns. These patterns suggest a number of interesting hypotheses that can be tested in future studies.

In conclusion, this initial exploration of a method for generating mixing profiles over time is encouraging in that it appears capable of distinguishing between recent and past mixing, and yields similar profiles in similar comparisons. Calibrating the method through simulation has been rather less successful, the main problem being that real populations appear to contain a more stable signal than is currently apparent in simple constant size, two population simulations. It is possible that the simulation of larger and/or expanding populations will improve inter-run consistency and allow improved calibration, thereby providing a route by which currently qualitative results could be interpreted more quantitatively.

Acknowledgements

This work was conducted under funding from the Leverhulme Trust. Catherine Hills provided invaluable insight

References

Bahlo, M. & R.C. Griffiths, 2000. Inferences from gene trees in a subdivided population. *Theoretical Population Biology* 57, 79–95.

Barać, L., M. Pericić, I.M. Klarić, *et al.*, 2003. Y chromosome STRs in Croatians. *Forensic Science International* 138, 127–33.

Beaumont, M.A., 1999. Detecting population expansion and decline using microsatellites. *Genetics* 153, 2013–29.

Capelli, C., N. Redhead, J.K. Abernethy, *et al.*, 2003. A Y chromosome census of the British Isles. *Current Biology* 13, 979–84.

Caramelli, D., C. Lalueza-Fox, C. Vernesi, *et al.*, 2003. Evidence for a genetic disconinuity between Neandertals and 24,000-year-old anatomically modern humans. *Proceedings of the National Academy of Sciences of the USA* 100, 6593–7.

Cavalli-Sforza, L.L., A. Piazza & P. Menozzi, 1994. *History and Geography of Human Genes*. Princeton (NJ): Princeton University Press.

Cooper, G., N.J. Burroughs, D.A. Rand, D.C. Rubinsztein & W. Amos, 1999. Markov Chain Monte Carlo analysis of human Y-chromosome microsatellites provides evidence of biased mutation. *Proceedings of the National Academy of Sciences of the USA* 96, 11,916–21.

Di Rienzo, A., A.C. Peterson, J.C. Garza, A.M. Valdes & M. Slatkin, 1994. Mutational processes of simple sequence repeat loci in human populations. *Proceedings of the National Academy of Sciences of the USA* 91, 3166–70.

Drummond, A.J., A. Rambaut, B. Shapiro & O.G. Pybus, 2005. Bayesian coalescent inference of past population dynmaics from molecular sequences. *Molecular Biology and Evolution* 22, 1185–92.

García, O., P. Martín, L. Gusmão, *et al.*, 2004. A Basque Country autochthonous population study of 11 Y-chromosome STR loci. *Forensic Science International* 145, 65–8.

Gilks, W.R., S. Richardson & D.J. Spiegelhalter (eds.), 1996. *Markov Chain Monte Carlo in Practice*. London: Chapman and Hall.

Harpending, H. & A. Rogers, 2000. Genetic perspectives on human origins and differentiation. *Annual Review of Genomics Human Genetics* 1, 361–85.

Hinds, D.A., L.L. Stuve, G.B. Nilsen, *et al.*, 2005. Whole-genome patterns of common DNA variation in three human populations. *Science* 307, 1072–9.

Jorde, L.B., W.S. Watkins, M.J. Bamshad, *et al.*, 2000 The distribution of human genetic diversity: a comparison of mitochondrial, autosomal and Y-chromosome data. *American Journal of Human Genetics* 66, 979–88.

Kayser, M., L. Roewer, M. Hedman, *et al.*, 2000. Characteristics and frequency of germline mutations at microsatellite loci from the human Y chromosome, as revealed by direct observation in father/son pairs. *American Journal of Human Genetics* 66, 1580–88.

Kuhner, M.K., J. Yamato & J. Felsenstein, 1998. Maximum likelihood estimation of population growth rates based on the coalescent. *Genetics* 149, 429–34.

Moran, P.A.P., 1975. Wandering distributions and the electrophoretic profile. *Theoretical Population Biology* 8, 318–39.

Nee, S., E.C. Holmes, A. Rambaut & P.H. Harvey, 1995. Inferring population histories from molecular phylogenies. *Philosophical Transactions of the Royal Society London B* 349, 25–31.

Pritchard, J.K., M.T. Seielstad, A. Perez-Lezaun & M.W. Feldman, 1999. Population growth of human Y chromosomes: a study of Y chromosome microsatellites. *Molecular Biology and Evolution* 16, 1791–8.

Pritchard, J.K., M. Stephens & P. Donnelly, 2000. Inference of population structure using multilocus genotype data. *Genetics* 155, 945–59.

Prugnolle, F., A. Manica & F. Balloux, 2005 Geography predicts neutral genetic diversity of human populations. *Current Biology* 15, R159–R160.

Quintana-Murci, L., O. Semino, H.-J. Bandelt, G. Passarino, K. McElreavy & A.S. Santachiara-Benerecetti, 1999. Genetic evidence of an early exit of *Homo sapiens* from Africa through eastern Africa. *Nature Genetics* 23, 437–41.

Ricci, U., I. Sani & M.L. Giovannucci Uzielle, 2001. Y-chromosome STR haplotype in Toscany (central Italy). *Forensic Science International* 120, 210–12.

Rosenberg, N.A., J.K. Pritchard, J.L. Weber, *et al.*, 2002. Genetic structure of human populations. *Science* 298, 2381–5.

Weale, M.E., D.A. Weiss, R.F. Jager, N. Bradman & M.G. Thomas, 2002. Y chromosome evidence of Anglo-Saxon mass migration. *Molecular Biology and Evolution* 19, 1008–21.

Wilson, I.J. & D.J. Balding, 1998. Genealogical inference from microsatellite data. *Genetics* 150, 499–510.

Wilson, J.F., D.A. Weiss, M. Richards, M.G. Thomas, N. Bradman & D.B. Goldstein, 2001. Genetic evidence for different male and female roles during cultural transitions in the British Isles. *Proceedings of the National Academy of Sciences of the USA* 98, 5078–83.

Zhivitovsky, L.A., P. Underhill, C. Cinnioglu, *et al.*, 2004. The effective mutation rate at Y chromosome short tandem repeats, with application to human population-divergence times. *American Journal of Human Genetics* 74, 50–61.

into theories about early British history. We thank two anonymous reviewers for their constructive comments.

Chapter 6

Social Constraints on Interethnic Marriage/Unions, Differential Reproductive Success and the Spread of 'Continental' Y Chromosomes in Early Anglo-Saxon England

Mark G. Thomas, Heinrich Härke, Gary German & Michael P.H. Stumpf

The extent and role of migration from northwest Continental Europe during the Anglo-Saxon transition in England has been intensely debated over the last 30 years. Archaeological and historical evidence is inconclusive but current estimates of the contribution made by migrants to the English population are typically less than 10%. In contrast, recent studies based on Y-chromosome variation posit a considerably higher contribution to the modern English gene pool (50–100%). Historical evidence suggests that following the Anglo-Saxon transition, people of indigenous ethnicity were at an economic and legal disadvantage compared to those seen as having an Anglo-Saxon ethnicity. It is likely that such a disadvantage would lead to differential reproductive success. We examine the effect of differential reproductive success coupled with limited intermarriage between distinct ethnic groups on the spread of genetic variants and language. Computer simulations indicate that a social structure limiting intermarriage between indigenous Britons and an initially small Anglo-Saxon immigrant population provides a plausible explanation of the high degree of Continental male-line ancestry in England. The existence of such a social structure will have consequences for our understanding of linguistic change in Britain. Here, we present a case for the spread of Old English as being the result of a language shift within a 'caste society', not as the consequence of language and population replacement, a view which coincides with recent linguistic and sociolinguistic research concerning a possible Brittonic substratum.

The traditional model of the Anglo-Saxon immigration into fifth-century Britain was based on the scanty written sources (Gildas, Bede, Anglo-Saxon Chronicle) and envisaged mass 'invasion' from the Continent and large-scale replacement of the natives (Stenton 1947). This model, with minor variations, remained largely undisputed until the later 1980s (Jackson 1953; Myres 1985; Chadwick 1963). At that time, many historians and archaeologists began to favour the elite replacement model: the immigration of a small elite which achieved military, political and social ascendancy (Hodges 1989; Higham 1992). Within a decade or so,

this had become the majority opinion among Anglo-Saxonist scholars (Hills 2003), with a critical discussion of the new model only emerging in the late 1990s (Härke 1998; 2002). While studies of stable isotopes in Anglo-Saxon skeletal material (Budd *et al.* 2004; Montgomery *et al.* 2005) promise for the future a better idea of the proportion of first-generation immigrants, molecular genetics has already succeeded in making a major contribution to this debate in recent years.

Weale *et al.* (2002) found a striking similarity in the distribution of Y-chromosome haplotypes in central England and Friesland but a dissimilarity between central England and north Wales. Using a population-genetic model that was specifically tailored to the question of the scale of Anglo-Saxon migration, one that incorporated both continuous gene flow between England and Northwest Continental Europe and mass migration, they concluded that the observed similarity in the distribution of Y chromosomes is best explained by a substantial migration of Anglo-Saxon men into central England (contributing 50–100% to the gene pool at that time) but not into North Wales. Capelli and colleagues (2003) examined the distribution of Y chromosomes throughout the British Isles as well as in southern Denmark, northern Germany and Norway. Using an likelihood-based admixture approach (Chikhi *et al.* 2001) they found a more heterogeneous pattern of Continental input into the English gene pool. However, using southern Danish and northern German populations as the descendants of putative Anglo-Saxon source populations their median estimates for Continental introgression into England ranged between 24.4% and 72.5% (mean 54.1%).

Explaining such a high proportion of Continental genetic input with immigration alone would require migration on a massive scale (approx. 500,000+), well above documented population movements of the Early Middle Ages (see for example Heather (1991)). An alternative explanation would be provided by a combination of a smaller-scale immigration but with a degree of post-migration reproductive isolation and social and economic conditions that give the immigrants a higher reproductive success (Woolf 2004; 2007). Such conditions would be met in a situation in which the immigrants would throughout have a higher social status than the native population and would avoid intermarriage or keep it at a low level, at least for several generations (Hughes 1986; Mulder 1987; Mace 1996).

Reproductive isolation and differential social status along ethnic lines is a not infrequent, temporary consequence of conquest and settlement, the best-known modern case being the Apartheid system in South Africa. In the post-Roman period, intermarriage between dominant immigrants and subject natives was banned in Visigothic France and Spain in the late fifth and early sixth century (King 1972). The Normans in eleventh- and twelfth-century England operated a conquest society in which the native English and Welsh had a lower legal status than Normans (Garnett 1985), and intermarriage, where it happened, was predominantly unidirectional, i.e. Norman men marrying English women. In Anglo-Saxon England, elements of ethnic difference in social and economic status in a conquest society can also be perceived in a Wessex law code of the seventh century which distinguishes clearly between Saxons and 'Welsh' (Britons) and gives the former a significantly higher legal status, some two centuries after the initial immigration (Whitelock 1979). Archaeological and skeletal data (Härke 1990; 1992), as well as textual evidence (Woolf 2004), have been used to suggest a situation of limited intermarriage between immigrant Anglo-Saxons and native Britons until the seventh century when this distinction began to break down.

Under a model of cross-generation mating isolation coupled with differential reproductive success it is expected that the chromosomes of the advantaged ethnic group would increase in overall frequency. However, intermarriage between ethnic groups would serve to homogenize the genetic makeup of those groups. Once homogeneity is attained, the reproductive advantage of an ethnic group would not systematically affect the overall frequency of any chromosome type. Here we describe the results of computer simulations performed to examine the rate of increase in overall frequency of chromosomes that are found initially only among the advantaged group, in the period leading up to homogenization. These simulations were first reported elsewhere (Thomas *et al.* 2006) and have provided a plausible explanation for differences in the estimates of the scale of Anglo-Saxon migration into fifth-century Britain.

Methods and results

The model employed is schematically illustrated in Figure 6.1. It should be noted that while Figure 6.1 describes a deterministic process, the actual model also contains stochastic elements to represent random genetic drift. Details of the model are available in Thomas *et al.* (2006).

Initially, the effects of different combinations of selective advantage and intermarriage rate ($U = D$) on the proportion of 'incoming' Y chromosomes in the total population after 15 generations were explored. Values for the proportion of individuals available to marry out of their ethnic group ranged from 0–10% per generation in steps of 0.1%. Values of selective advantage ranged from 1 to 2 per generation in steps of 0.01. Figure 6.2 shows the results assuming the population was made up of (a) 5%, (b) 10% and (c) 20% immigrants immediately following migration.

Next, the rate of increase in the proportion of 'incoming' Y chromosomes under different values of selective advantage and intermarriage ($U = D$) were explored, starting with 10% immigrants immediately following migration. Figure 6.3 shows this increase assuming selective advantage values of (a) 1.2, (b) 1.5 and (c) 1.8. For each value of selective advantage,

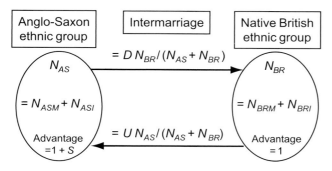

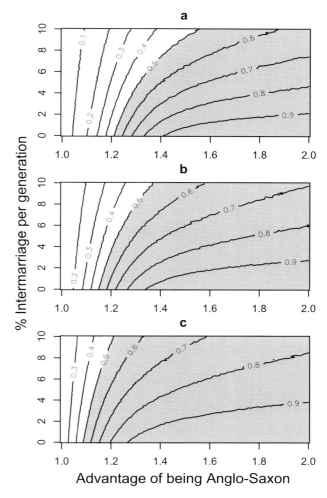

Figure 6.1. *Schematic representation of the simulation model used. N_{AS} and N_{BR} represent the numbers of Anglo-Saxons and Native British men in any generation, respectively. N_{ASM} and N_{BRM} represent Anglo-Saxons and Native British men, respectively, who carry Y chromosomes that originate in northwest Continental Europe and were carried to England with the Anglo-Saxon migration. N_{ASI} and N_{BRI} represent Anglo-Saxons and Native British men, respectively, who carry Y chromosomes that were of indigenous British origin at the outset of the Anglo-Saxon migration. D and U represent the proportion of Anglo-Saxons and Native British men that are available in each generation to change ethnic group. It should be noted that the actual number of individuals that change ethnic group is scaled by the proportion of the total population that belong to the receiving ethnic group. In each generation, N_{ASM} and N_{ASI} increase in number by a factor of $1 + S$ (the selective advantage of being Anglo-Saxon).*

Figure 6.2. *The simulated proportion of 'Anglo-Saxon' Y chromosomes in the total population, after 15 generations, under different combinations of selective advantage and intermarriage rate (U = D), assuming the population was made up of (a) 5%, (b) 10% and (c) 20% immigrants immediately following migration. Shaded area of graph indicates parameter combinations that lead to greater than 50% 'Anglo-Saxon' Y chromosomes (Weale et al. 2002; Capelli et al. 2003).*

values of intermarriage of 0.02, 0.04, 0.06, 0.08 and 0.1 were used.

Given a conservative estimate of 50% for the proportion of Y chromosomes in central England that originate among Anglo-Saxon migrants (Weale *et al.* 2002; Capelli *et al.* 2003), the effects of different combinations of selective advantage and intermarriage ($U = D$) on the number of generations that would be required to reach 50% 'incoming' Y chromosomes, assuming the population was made up of (a) 5%, (b) 10% and (c) 20% immigrants immediately following migration, were explored (Fig. 6.4).

Finally, the change through time in the proportion of individuals belonging to the 'Anglo-Saxon' ethnic group, assuming a selective advantage of (a) 1.2, (b) 1.5, and (c) 1.8 to being Anglo-Saxon, were examined (Fig. 6.5). This rate is unaffected by the intermarriage rate given that $U = D$, but is strongly affected by the selection parameter.

Discussion

The most striking results of the simulations is the wide and plausible range of combinations of selective advantage to being Anglo-Saxon and intermarriage rate that would allow the proportion of 'immigrant' Y chromosomes to rise from 20% or less immediately following migration to greater than 50% in 15 generations. Following previous genetic studies (Weale *et al.* 2002; Capelli *et al.* 2003), 50% is a conservative estimate of the proportion of Y chromosomes in the present-day English gene pool that originate among Anglo-Saxon

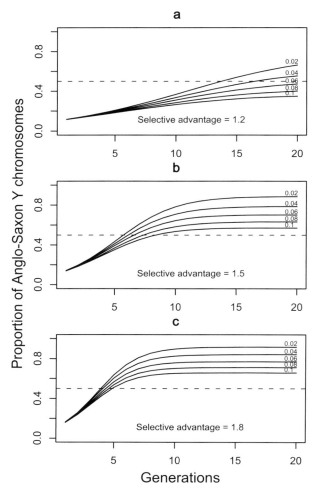

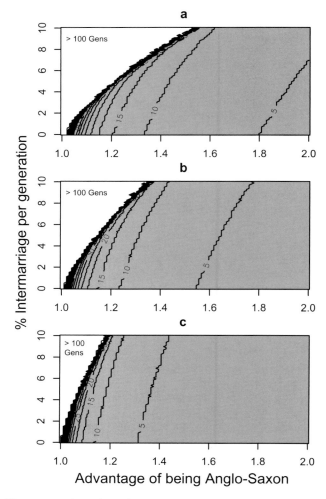

Figure 6.3. *Increase in the proportion of 'Anglo-Saxon' Y chromosomes through time under different combinations of selective advantage and intermarriage (U = D), starting with 10% immigrants immediately following migration. Selective advantage values of (a) 1.2, (b) 1.5 and (c) 1.8 were modelled. For each value of selective advantage, values of intermarriage of 0.02, 0.04, 0.06, 0.08 and 0.1 were used, as indicated above lines.*

Figure 6.4. *Number of generations required to reach 50% 'Anglo-Saxon' Y chromosomes (Weale et al. 2002; Capelli et al. 2003), under different combinations of selective advantage and intermarriage rate (U = D), assuming the population was made up of (a) 5%, (b) 10% and (c) 20% immigrants immediately following migration. Shaded area of graph indicates parameter combinations that lead to greater than 50% 'Anglo-Saxon' Y chromosomes in less than 100 generations.*

migrants in the fifth century. Fifteen generations marks the upper limit for the duration of an Anglo-Saxon/British ethnic division in social status since, by assuming an intergenerational time of between 25 and 30 years, this is the approximate time span between the initial immigration in the middle of the fifth century and the Laws of Alfred the Great (issued around AD 890) which do not contain any indications of legal status differences between Britons and Anglo-Saxons (Whitelock 1979). We note that although others have reported a male-specific intergeneration time of around 35 years (Tremblay & Vezina 2000), this estimate is based on genealogical

records from a rapidly growing population between the seventeenth and the twentieth centuries. It is likely that in Anglo-Saxon England, life expectancy, and as a consequence, intergeneration time would have been shorter. However, 15 generations cannot be considered as a conservative estimate of the duration of such a social structure. For this reason, the rate of increase in the proportion of 'immigrant' Y chromosomes over time under a range of parameter values was also examined (Fig. 6.3). As can be seen, the proportion of 'immigrant' Y chromosomes typically rises rapidly at first then levels off to its ceiling value. It is notable that the time

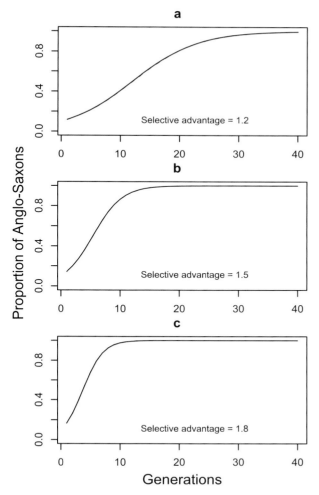

Figure 6.5. *Change through time in the proportion of individuals belonging to the 'Anglo-Saxon' ethnic group assuming a selective advantage of (a) 1.2, (b) 1.5, and (c) 1.8 to being Anglo-Saxon.*

taken to reach a near-ceiling value is largely determined by the relative reproductive advantage of being of Anglo-Saxon ethnicity and is less influenced by the intermarriage rate. Most importantly, the proportion of 'immigrant' Y chromosomes can rise from 10% to in excess of 50% in considerably less than 15 generation under a range of plausible parameter values. This is best illustrated in Figure 6.4, where the effects of different parameter values on the number of generations required to reach 50% 'incoming' Y chromosomes in the whole population is explored. Comparing Figure 6.4a, b and c (representing 5%, 10% and 20% Anglo-Saxon migration respectively), it is evident that the initial size of the migration has a highly influential effect.

The model presented (Thomas *et al.* 2006) is necessarily simple but serves to illustrate some of the effects of differential reproductive success among

groups, with a degree of reproductive isolation, on patterns of genetic variation (Woolf 2004). Figures 6.2 to 6.5 only present the results of simulations assuming symmetric intermarriage rates ($U = D$). However, asymmetric intermarriage rates whereby we multiplied U by 0.5 and D by 1.5, or vice versa, were tested and very similar results to the previous simulations obtained (Thomas *et al.* 2006).

Restricted ethnic intermarriage and a reproductive advantage to being Anglo-Saxon are likely outcomes of the Anglo-Saxon immigration into post-Roman Britain for a number of reasons. These reasons are detailed in Thomas *et al.* (2006). Here, we briefly summarize those reasons. Firstly, Anglo-Saxon immigration led to an encounter of two groups with different, mutually incomprehensible languages. The minority immigrants would have faced losing their identity and their political and military control had they assimilated into the much larger indigenous population. Reproductive isolation would have provided a strategy for a dominant ethnic minority to avoid this (Thurnwald 1931). Direct evidence for Anglo-Saxon reproductive isolation rests on a textual source and some skeletal evidence. The late seventh-century laws of Ine distinguish clearly between Saxons and 'Welsh' (native Britons) (Whitelock 1979). The 'late' date for this ethnic distinction, and its formalization in law, suggest some mechanism that perpetuated it from its likely inception in the fifth and early sixth centuries. Since the laws of Ine imply no physical segregation, reproductive isolation seems to be the most obvious mechanism. Skeletal evidence suggests a stature differential between men thought to be Anglo-Saxon and those thought to be mainly native British (Härke 1990; 1992). These differences persisted from the later fifth until the end of the sixth century, but most importantly, began to break down in the seventh century. The absence of a change in environmental factors in the seventh century (Fuller *et al.* 2006) is consistent with the breakdown of that differential being the consequence of increasing intermarriage. Evidence for legally restricted ethnic intermarriage can be seen in Visigothic southern France and Spain (King 1972) and Norman England (Garnett 1985). Even in modern times, in the absence of formal laws, low ethnic intermarriage rates (*c.* 6.6% and 4%) have been noted in modern Mauritius (Nave 2000) and southern Pembrokeshire (Woolley 1986), respectively. It is likely that pre-modern rates were even lower.

The late seventh-century laws of King Ine of Wessex, which differentiate between natives and Saxons, also indicate wealth differentials between those groups through wergild, the blood money payable to the family of the victim of a killing (Whitelock 1979).

Similar wergild differences between immigrants and natives are found in the early seventh-century laws of King Ethelbert of Kent (Whitelock 1979), and elsewhere in early medieval Europe such as in the Frankish kingdom (Ward-Perkins 2005). There is a considerable literature on a positive correlation between wealth and reproductive success, based both on empirical evidence (Hull & Hull 1977; Hughes 1986; Mace 1996; Mulder 1987; Boone 1986) and evolutionary theory (Fisher 1958; Mace 1998; Beauchamp 1994).

We have only considered the effects of differences in ethnic reproductive advantage and inter-ethnic marriage rate on patterns of Y-chromosome variation. If there were no sex-bias in the intermarriage rate, then we would expect these effects to be equal for the different genetic systems (mitochondrial DNA, Y chromosome, X chromosome, autosomes). However, part of the motivation for the study of Thomas and colleagues (2006) was to seek an explanation for the discrepancy between archaeological estimates of the size of the Anglo-Saxon migration (Hills 2003; Härke 1998; 2002) and estimates based on Y-chromosome data (Weale et al. 2002; Capelli et al. 2003). Three further factors could increase the rate of replacement of indigenous Y chromosomes. The first is that when intermarriage does occur, the offspring may be more likely to assume the ethnic identity of the father, thus reducing the effective intermarriage rate, as it would affect patterns of Y-chromosome diversity. The second is that forced extra-marital matings are more likely to occur between Anglo-Saxon men and native British women than the reverse since, as the law codes of Ine indicate, the degree of punishment was determined by the social status of the victim. The third is based on the theory that relatively 'good-condition' males tend to out-reproduce females of a similar condition, whereas relatively 'poor-condition' females tend to out-reproduce their male counterparts (Trivers & Willard 1973). From this, a strategy of sex-biased parental investment, whereby relatively wealthy parents favour wealth transfer to their sons, should emerge (Hartung 1976). Such a phenomenon is supported by genealogical data (Boone 1986) and should lead to an asymmetric increase in the population frequency of Y chromosomes carried by wealthy men, when compared to the other genetic systems.

Implications for language change in the Anglo-Saxon transition

Recent linguistic and sociolinguistic research examining a possible Brittonic (British Celtic) substratum in early basilectal varieties of Old English is consistent with an Anglo-Saxon transition following the proc-

esses described above. While few have ever ventured to make the case (cf. Keller 1925; Preusler 1956), the pioneering work of Tristram (1995; 1997; 1999; 2002; 2007) has encouraged a growing number of scholars (Filppula et al. 2002; German 1996; 2000a,b; 2003; Poppe 2006; White 2002; 2006; Venneman 2000; 2001; Klemola 2000) to investigate certain morphosyntactic traits shared by the Brittonic languages and English. Nevertheless, it should be noted that most linguists are still wary of this idea, partly due to the fact that few have ever challenged the traditional belief that the Britons were exterminated and/or expelled from Britain — so how could Brittonic have influenced the development of English? — but also because there is little direct Old English text-based evidence which unambiguously demonstrates its existence (Mossé 1958). The paucity of Brittonic vocabulary in English has long been used as an argument in favour of the 'clean sweep' theory (Freeman 1867; Stubbs 1926). The logic, of course, is circular.

Here are a few elements of the discussions. Given that nominal inflexions were lost in Brittonic by around the fifth to the sixth centuries (Jackson 1953; Simms-Williams 1990), it has been proposed that a similar erosion of nominal inflexions in late Old English may have been sparked by the inability of British learners to master their use. Later Scandinavian influence has also been suggested as the cause (Milroy 1996), but the typological similarity of Old Norse and Old English makes this less likely (Tristram 2002; Thomason & Kaufman 1988). Another particularly striking similarity is the existence in Old English of two paradigms of S-forms and B-forms of the verb BE with the B-forms conveying habitual or future aspect, a feature unknown in the other Germanic languages but common in Celtic. Other Brittonic-like features in English include DO-periphrasis (often expressing habitual aspect in non-standard varieties); a progressive construction (BE + preverbal particle + verbal noun); an 'it-cleft' construction (invariable copula + subject + relative pronoun + verb); preposition stranding, phrasal verbs; similar functions of the third person possessive adjective in Brittonic and English; 'small clauses' and so on. It is significant that, diachronically, each of these characteristics first appears in the Brittonic languages and only later in English. Significantly, they are either unattested or uncommon in the western Germanic languages.

The comparative wealth of morphosyntactic examples and the dearth of Brittonic vocabulary can be explained by the fact that words are the most salient features of language. When a language shift occurs under the sociolinguistic conditions of the model outlined above, the long-term trend is for successive generations to purge the vocabulary of the stigmatized source language from the freshly acquired target language in an effort to blend into the higher-status group (Thomason & Kaufman 1988). This process is clearly at work in the language shifts currently under way in the Celtic-speaking areas of Wales, Scotland, Ireland and western Brittany (German 2003). While the speech of the older generations is often filled with Celtic loanwords, the language of the younger generations is often characterized by a notable lack of them. Interestingly, the ability to identify and eliminate words belonging to the lower-status language requires that the younger generation should have at least a passive knowledge of the source language. This is why a language shift does not normally occur in fewer than three generations, and usually takes far longer. Meanwhile, symbolically neutral features of language, such as morphology, syntax as well as phonological characteristics which cannot be mastered, have a tendency to go unnoticed by the learners.

In their study of the sociolinguistic situation in Kupwar, India, Gumperz & Wilson (1971) offer a tantalizing analogy with our model. The community is composed of three separate castes that have been living side by side for the past 600 years. Yet, for social reasons, each has succeeded in maintaining its own linguistic, ethnic and religious identity. What is particularly noteworthy is that while the lexicon of each language has remained strictly separate, for the reasons outlined above, their morphology and syntax gradually merged into a common grammatical system which virtually allows speakers to translate word for word from one language to the other. While it seems clear that the social conditions between Britons and Anglo-Saxons were not as socially complex nor as long-lasting, the Kupwar example does provide a cogent explanation for the lack of Brittonic vocabulary in English, on the one hand, and the morphosyntactic parallels, on the other.

The linguistic picture that emerges is consistent with the model present above and suggests that considerable numbers of the British peasantry cohabited with the Anglo-Saxons and acquired basilectal forms of Brittonic-influenced Old English. Davies (1993) has posited that these Britons were better treated under Anglo-Saxon rule than by their own Romano-British elites. If so, this would have presumably encouraged the shift towards Old English. Considering the primordial role of women in the transmission of language, if one takes into account the high probability of extra-marital matings between Anglo-Saxon men and British women referred to above, the social incentive for the latter to learn Old English is even greater and makes the hypothesis for the development of basilectal Anglo-Brittonic varieties of Old English a distinct possibility.

The outcome of this diglossic situation was that stigmatized Anglo-Brittonic speech habits were certainly shunned by the higher-status Anglo-Saxons. It is probably for this reason that relatively few Celticisms ever entered the Old English *Schriftsprache*, particularly in Wessex where the earliest laws suggest that Britons were numerous. The diglossia which characterized the linguistic relationship between the two communities probably persisted as long as the Brittonic (and Anglo-Brittonic) speech communities survived in England, and that is probably later than many have considered. Jackson (1953; 1963) points out, for example, that Brittonic was still spoken in Exeter during the reign of Athelstan (tenth century) and at least until the eleventh century in Cumbria and Strathclyde. It almost certainly continued to be spoken for even longer among the peasantry in scattered areas of western England along the Welsh border. The use by modern Lincolnshire, Cambridgeshire and Cumbrian farmers of Brittonic numerals for counting sheep, as well as the survival of Brittonic laws (bearing their Celtic names) into the twelfth and thirteenth centuries in northern and western England, appear to reinforce this possibility (Rees 1963). This would have left ample time for Brittonic characteristics to penetrate the lower-status varieties of 'vulgar' Old English (cf. Burchfield 1985). The linguistic implications are profound: Old English spread as the result of a language shift, not as a consequence of language and population replacement.

The fact that a number of these Celtic-looking morphosyntactic features arise in writing only during the Middle English period (DO periphrasis, it-clefting) can be explained by the collapse of the Anglo-Saxon social order after 1066 which ushered in another period of diglossia during which the English language was in its turn downgraded to the status of a peasant language (German 2000b). The sociolinguistic consequence of this situation was the liberation of hitherto stigmatized Brittonic constructions, combined with more recent Scandinavian and French adstratal influences (especially lexical), which flooded into the newly developing written language. Thus, the rapid transition from Old English to Middle English may be more apparent than real.

Conclusions

The motivation for the study of Thomas *et al.* (2006) was to reconcile the discrepancy between, on the one hand, archaeological and historical ideas about the scale of the Anglo-Saxon immigration (Hills 2003), and on the other, estimates of the genetic contribution of the Anglo-Saxon immigrants to the modern English gene pool (Weale *et al.* 2002; Capelli *et al.* 2003). We have shown that this discrepancy can be resolved by the assumption of an apartheid-like social structure within a range of plausible values for inter-ethnic marriage and socially-driven reproductive advantage following immigration (Woolf 2004). In this paper we have sought to summarize the arguments presented in Thomas *et al.* (2006) and develop them further by adding a linguistic perspective. The apartheid-like model is a testable hypothesis of social structure in Anglo-Saxon England and we speculate that modern techniques, such as, for example, stable isotope analysis, may provide a means to test this. Perhaps the most striking aspect our model is that, by using parameter values derived from historical and modern cases, the genetic contribution of an immigrant population can rise from less than 10% to more than 50% in as little as five generations, and certainly less than fifteen generations. This model, we propose, also provides a hitherto unconsidered mechanism for the spread of Old English in England: one that suggests that Old English spread as the result of a prolonged language shift rather than a simple language replacement. Similar processes are likely to have shaped patterns of genetic variation and perhaps linguistic change in other 'conquest societies' of the period, including post-Roman western Continental Europe, Viking Britain and Norman England. The social structures described here may have been of wider significance in processes of language replacement and the interactions of hunter-gatherers and early farmers. This is of particular relevance in cases where genetic and linguistic data indicate a demographic expansion of farmers, such as the Bantu (Beleza *et al.* 2005; Salas *et al.* 2002; Thomas *et al.* 2000; Passarino *et al.* 1998; Luis *et al.* 2004; Cruciani *et al.* 2002; Scozzari *et al.* 1999) and the Austronesian expansions (Lum *et al.* 2002; Hagelberg *et al.* 1999; Melton *et al.* 1998; Hurles *et al.* 2002).

Acknowledgements

We thank A. Woolf, S. Shennan, R. Mace, L. Fortunato, H. Harpending, M.E. Weale, C. Hills, P. Forster, S. Matsumura and C. Renfrew for valuable discussion.

References

Beauchamp, G., 1994. The functional-analysis of human-fertility decisions. *Ethology and Sociobiology* 15(1), 31–53.

Beleza, S., L. Gusmao, A. Amorim, A. Carracedo & A. Salas, 2005. The genetic legacy of western Bantu migrations. *Human Genetics* 117(4), 366–75.

Boone, J.L., 1986. Parental investment and elite family structure in preindustrial states: a case study of late medieval–early modern Portuguese genealogies. *American Anthropologist* 88(4), 859–78.

Budd, P., A. Millard, C. Chenery, S. Lucy & C. Roberts, 2004. Investigating population movement by stable isotope analysis: a report from Britain. *Antiquity* 78(298), 127–40.

Burchfield, R.W., 1985. *The English Language.* Oxford: Oxford University Press.

Capelli, C., N. Redhead, J.K. Abernethy, *et al.*, 2003. A Y chromosome census of the British Isles. *Current Biology* 13(11), 979–84.

Chadwick, N., 1963. *Angles and Britons.* Cardiff: Cardiff University Press.

Chikhi, L., M.W. Bruford & M.A. Beaumont, 2001. Estimation of admixture proportions: a likelihood-based approach using Markov chain Monte Carlo. *Genetics* 158(3), 1347–62.

Cruciani, F., P. Santolamazza, P. Shen, *et al.*, 2002. A back migration from Asia to sub-Saharan Africa is supported by high-resolution analysis of human Y-chromosome haplotypes. *American Journal of Human Genetics* 70(5), 1197–214.

Davies, J., 1993. *A History of Wales.* London: Penguin Books.

Filppula, M., J. Klemola & H. Pitkänen, 2002. *The Celtic Roots of English.* Joensuu: Joensuu University Press.

Fisher, R.A., 1958. *The Genetical Theory of Natural Selection.* New York (NY): Dover.

Freeman, E.A., 1867. *The History of the Norman Conquest of England: Its Causes and Results.* Oxford: Clarendon Press.

Fuller, B.T., T.I. Molleson, D.A. Harris, L.T. Gilmour & R.E. Hedges, 2006. Isotopic evidence for breastfeeding and possible adult dietary differences from Late/Sub-Roman Britain. *American Journal of Physical Anthropology* 129(1), 45–54.

Garnett, G., 1985. Franci et Angli: the legal distinctions between peoples after the conquest. *Anglo-Norman Studies* 8, 109–37.

German, G.D., 1996. *Etude sociolinguistique de l'anglais du Pays de Galles.* Calais: Université du Littoral.

German, G.D., 2000a. Britons, Anglo-Saxons and scholars: 19th century attitudes towards the survival of Britons in Anglo-Saxon England, in *The Celtic Englishes*, vol. II, ed. H. Tristram. Heidelberg: Carl Winter, 347–74.

German, G.D., 2000b. The genesis of analytic structure in English: the case for a Brittonic substratum, in *Travaux de Diachronie*, vol. 2, ed. J.-P. Régis. Tours: Publications de l'Université de François Rabelais, 125–41.

German, G.D., 2003. The French of western Brittany in light of the Celtic-Englishes, in *The Celtic Englishes*, vol. III, ed. H. Tristram. Heidelberg: Carl Winter, 390–412.

Gumperz, J.J. & R.Wilson, 1971. Convergence and Creolization: a case from the Indo-Aryan/Dravidian border of India, in *Pidginization and Creolization of Languages*, ed. D. Hymes. Cambridge: Cambridge University Press, 151–67.

Hagelberg, E., M. Kayser, M. Nagy, *et al.*, 1999. Molecular genetic evidence for the human settlement of the

Pacific: analysis of mitochondrial DNA, Y chromosome and HLA markers. *Philosophical Transactions of the Royal Society of London B Biological Sciences* 354(1379), 141–52.

Härke, H., 1990. 'Warrior Graves'? The background of the Anglo-Saxon weapon burial rite. *Past & Present* 126, 22–43.

Härke, H., 1992. *Angelsächsische Waffengräber des 5. bis 7. Jahrhunderts*. Cologne & Bonn: Rheinland-Verlag & Habelt.

Härke, H., 1998. Archaeologists and migrations: a problem of attitude? *Current Anthropology* 39(1), 19–45.

Härke, H., 2002. Kings and warriors: population and landscape from post-Roman to Norman Britain, in *The Peopling of Britain: the Shaping of a Human Landscape*, eds. P. Slack & R. Ward. (The Linacre Lectures 1999.) Oxford: Oxford University Press, 145–75.

Hartung, J., 1976. Natural-selection and inheritance of wealth. *Current Anthropology* 17(4), 607–22.

Heather, P.J., 1991. *Goths and Romans 332–489*. Oxford: Clarendon Press.

Higham, N.J., 1992. *Rome, Britain and the Anglo-Saxons*. London: Seaby.

Hills, C., 2003. *Origins of the English*. London: Duckworth.

Hodges, R., 1989. *The Anglo-Saxon Achievement: Archaeology & the Beginnings of English Society*. Ithaca (NY): Cornell University Press.

Hughes, A.L., 1986. Reproductive success and occupational class in eighteenth-century Lancashire, England. *Social Biology* 33(1–2), 109–15.

Hull, T.H. & V.J. Hull, 1977. The relation of economic class and fertility: an analysis of some Indonesian data. *Population Studies* 31(1), 43–57.

Hurles, M.E., J. Nicholson, E. Bosch, C. Renfrew, B.C. Sykes & M.A. Jobling, 2002. Y chromosomal evidence for the origins of oceanic-speaking peoples. *Genetics* 160(1), 289–303.

Jackson, K., 1953. *Language and History in Early Britain: a Chronological Survey of the Brittonic Languages, 1st to 10th Century AD*. Edinburgh: Edinburgh University Press.

Jackson, K., 1963. Angles, Britons in Northumbria and Cumbria, in *Angles and Britons*, ed. N. Chadwick. Cardiff: University of Wales Press, 60–84.

Keller, W., 1925. Keltisches im englischen Verbum. Anglica. *Untersuchungen zur englischen Philologie* 1, 55–66.

King, P.D., 1972. *Law and Society in the Visigothic Kingdom*. Cambridge: Cambridge University Press.

Klemola, J., 2000. The origins of the northern subject rule: a case of early contact?, in *Celtic Englishes*, vol. II, ed. H. Tristram. Heidelberg: Carl Winter, 329–46.

Luis, J.R., D.J. Rowold, M. Regueiro, *et al.*, 2004. The Levant versus the Horn of Africa: evidence for bidirectional corridors of human migrations. *American Journal of Human Genetics* 74(3), 532–44.

Lum, J.K., L.B. Jorde & W. Schiefenhovel, 2002. Affinities among Melanesians, Micronesians, and Polynesians: a neutral biparental genetic perspective. *Human Biology* 74(3), 413–30.

Mace, R., 1996. Biased parental investment and reproductive success in Gabbra pastoralists. *Behavioral Ecology and Sociobiology* 38(2), 75–81.

Mace, R., 1998. The coevolution of human fertility and wealth inheritance strategies. *Philosophical Transactions of the Royal Society of London B Biological Sciences* 353(1367), 389–97.

Melton, T., S. Clifford, J. Martinson, M. Batzer & M. Stoneking, 1998. Genetic evidence for the proto-Austronesian homeland in Asia: mtDNA and nuclear DNA variation in Taiwanese aboriginal tribes. *American Journal of Human Genetics* 63(6), 1807–23.

Milroy, J., 1996. Linguistic ideology and the Anglo-Saxon lineage of English, in *Speech Past and Present: Studies in English Dialectology in Memory of Ossi Ihalainen*, eds. J. Klemola, M. Kytö & M. Rissanen. Frankfurt am Main: Peter Lang, 169–86.

Montgomery, J., J.A. Evans, D. Powlesland & C.A. Roberts, 2005. Continuity or colonization in Anglo-Saxon England? Isotope evidence for mobility, subsistence practice, and status at West Heslerton. *American Journal of Physical Anthropology* 126(2), 123–38.

Mossé, F., 1958. *Esquisse d'une histoire de la langue anglaise*. Lyons: Imprimerie artistique en couleur.

Mulder, M.B., 1987. Resources and reproductive success in women with an example from the Kipsigis of Kenya. *Journal of Zoology* 213(3), 489–505.

Myres, J.N.L., 1985. *The English Settlements*. Oxford: Clarendon.

Nave, A., 2000. Marriage and the maintenance of ethnic group boundaries: the case of Mauritius. *Ethnic and Racial Studies* 23(2), 329–52.

Passarino, G., O. Semino, L. Quintana-Murci, L. Excoffier, M. Hammer & A.S. Santachiara-Benerecetti, 1998. Different genetic components in the Ethiopian population, identified by mtDNA and Y-chromosome polymorphisms. *American Journal of Human Genetics* 62(2), 420–34.

Poppe, E., 2006. Celtic influence on the relative clause, in *The Celtic Englishes*, vol. IV, ed. H. Tristram. Potsdam: Potsdam University Press, 191–211.

Preusler, W., 1956. Keltischer Einfluss im Englischen. *Revue des langues vivantes* 22, 322–50.

Rees, W., 1963. Survivals of ancient Celtic custom in medieval England, in *Angles and Britons*, ed. N. Chadwick. Cardiff: Cardiff University Press, 148–68.

Salas, A., M. Richards, T. De la Fe, *et al.*, 2002. The making of the African mtDNA landscape. *American Journal of Human Genetics* 71(5), 1082–111.

Scozzari, R., F. Cruciani, P. Santolamazza, *et al.*, 1999. Combined use of biallelic and microsatellite Y-chromosome polymorphisms to infer affinities among African populations. *American Journal of Human Genetics* 65(3), 829–46.

Simms-Williams, P., 1990. Dating the transition to Neo-Brittonic: phonology and history, 400–600, in *Britain 400–600: Language and History*, ed. A.B.A.A. Wollmann. Heidelberg: Carl Winter, 217–62.

Stenton, F.M., 1947. *Anglo-Saxon England*. Oxford: Clarendon Press.

Stubbs, W., 1926. *The Constitutional History of England*. Oxford: Clarendon Press.

Thomas, M.G., T. Parfitt, D.A. Weiss, *et al.*, 2000. Y chromosomes traveling south: the cohen modal haplotype and the origins of the Lemba — the 'Black Jews of Southern Africa'. *American Journal of Human Genetics* 66(2), 674–86.

Thomas, M.G., M.P. Stumpf & H. Härke, 2006. Evidence for an apartheid-like social structure in early Anglo-Saxon England. *Proceedings of the Royal Society of London B Biological Sciences* 273(1601), 2651–7.

Thomason, S.G. & T. Kaufman, 1988. *Language Contact, Creolization and Genetic Linguistics.* Berkeley & Los Angeles (CA): University of California Press.

Thurnwald, R., 1931. *Die menschliche Gesellschaft in ihren ethno-soziologischen Grundlagen.* Berlin: W. de Gruyter.

Tremblay, M. & H. Vezina, 2000. New estimates of intergenerational time intervals for the calculation of age and origins of mutations. *American Journal of Human Genetics* 66(2), 651–8.

Tristram, H., 1995. Aspect in contact. *Anglia* 113.3, 269–94.

Tristram, H., 1997. DO-periphrasis in contact, in *Language in Time and Space*, ed. H.K.W. Ramisch. Stuttgart: Franz Steiner, 401–17.

Tristram, H., 1999. *How Celtic is Standard English?* St Petersburg: Nauka.

Tristram, H., 2002. Attrition of inflections in English and in Welsh, in *The Celtic Roots of English*, eds. M. Filppula, J. Klemola & H. Pitkänen. Joensuu: Joensuu University Press, 111–49.

Tristram, H., 2007. Why don't Englishmen speak Welsh?, in *The Britons in Anglo-Saxon England*, ed. N.J. Higham. Rochester (NY): Boydell & Brewer 2007, 192–214.

Trivers, R.L. & D.E. Willard, 1973. Natural selection of parental ability to vary the sex ratio of offspring. *Science* 179(68), 90–92.

Venneman, T., 2000. English as a 'Celtic' language, in *Celtic-Englishes*, vol. II, ed. H. Tristram. Heidelberg: Carl Winter, 399–406.

Venneman, T., 2001. Atlantis Semitica: structural contact features in Celtic and English, in *Historical Linguistics*, ed. L. Brinton. Amsterdam & Philadelphia (PA): John Benjamins Publishing Company, 351–69.

Ward-Perkins, B., 2005. *The Fall of Rome and the End of Civilization.* Oxford: Oxford University Press.

Weale, M.E., D.A. Weiss, R.F. Jager, N. Bradman & M.G. Thomas, 2002. Y chromosome evidence for Anglo-Saxon mass migration. *Molecular Biology and Evolution* 19(7), 1008–21.

White, D., 2002. Explaining the innovations of Middle English: what, where, and why, in *The Celtic Roots of English*, eds. M. Filppula, J. Klemola & H. Pitkänen. Joensuu: Joensuu University Press, 153–74.

White, D., 2006. On the areal patterns of Brittonicity, in *The Celtic Englishes*, vol. IV, ed. H. Tristram. Potsdam: Potsdam University Press, 306–35.

Whitelock, D., 1979. *English Historical Documents*, c. *500–1042.* London: Eyre Methuen.

Woolf, A., 2004. Apartheid and Genocide: Legal Theory and Economic Reality. Presentation given at a conference 'Britons in Anglo-Saxon England', Manchester, UK, 14–16 April 2004.

Woolf, A., 2007. Apartheid and economics in Anglo-Saxon England, in *The Britons in Anglo-Saxon England*, ed. N.J. Higham. Rochester (NY): Boydell & Brewer, 115–29.

Woolley, V., 1986. Demographic studies in Pembrokeshire., in *Genetic and Population Studies in Wales*, eds. P.S. Harper & E. Sunderland. Cardiff: University of Wales Press, 236–50.

Part III

Human Dispersal from Asia

Chapter 7

The Genetic Prehistory of Madagascar's Female Asian Lineages

Peter Forster, Shuichi Matsumura, Matthieu Vizuete-Forster, Petya Belinda Blumbach & Robert Dewar

Archaeological sites demonstrate that humans settled permanently in Madagascar as recently as c. 1500 years ago, even though mainland Africa has been inhabited by modern humans for over 100,000 years. Another paradox is that linguists have traced the Malagasy language to an Indonesian origin, more than 5000 km across the Indian Ocean, despite the fact that Madagascar lies less than 500 km off the African coast. A recent genetic publication from our laboratory demonstrated that roughly half the female and male lineages in the Malagasy are from Southeast Asia, while the other lineages are from Africa, with a small minority from Europe or the Near East. Here, we investigate the female Asian component of the Malagasy lineages more closely and confirm their Southeast Asian origin using additional samples from around the Indian Ocean. Furthermore, we apply coalescent simulations to provide an estimate of the number of Asians arriving in Madagascar. The simulations suggest a most likely effective female founder population size of about 30 Asian women, which probably corresponds to a total census founder population of 60–200 Asian men and women of all ages arriving in Madagascar some 1500 years ago.

Geneticists and palaeontologists mostly agree that *Homo sapiens* evolved first in continental Africa around 150,000 years ago (Clark *et al.* 2003; McDougall *et al.* 2005) before migrating out to Europe and Asia 60–80,000 years ago (Forster 2004). The settlement of far-flung islands by trans-oceanic navigation is one of the most absorbing features of human evolutionary history. The island of Madagascar, the largest in the Indian Ocean, lies some 250 miles (400 km) from Africa and 4000 miles (6400 km) from Indonesia. Its population today is a genetic witness to prehistoric navigational achievement.

The archaeological evidence for the earliest human presence in Madagascar comes from Andavakoera near Diego Suarez and is dated to AD 420 (AD 250–590, 2 SDs) (Dewar & Wright 1993). There is some indirect evidence for earlier human presence, but it is ambiguous. The oldest such potential evidence to our knowledge is a cutmarked subfossil lemur bone from a palaeontological site, Taolambiby, in the southwest.

One date was obtained, calibrated as 530 BC to 300 BC (Godfrey & Jungers 2003). The cutmarking looks plausible, but there is a potential problem of old carbon from the limestone landscape compromising the date, and there are no associated artefacts or archaeological sites in the vicinity. Nearly contemporaneous potential evidence comes from *Cannabis/Humulus* pollen which occurs in a pollen column from the central highlands at an interpolated date of *c.* 2200 BP (Burney 1987). There is some suspicion however that cannabis may have reached Africa 3000 years ago, and in any case, there is no archaeological evidence for human occupation in the highlands until *c.* AD 1200. Finally, a cutmarked pygmy hippo bone from Ambolisatra has been dated and calibrated to between 60 BC and AD 130 (2 SDs), but it is from a coastal swamp without indications of settlement, in a heavily karstic region. Moreover, a similar bone from the same collection from a nearby site gave two widely divergent dates of 2020 BP and 3495 BP (MacPhee & Burney 1991). Transient visits to

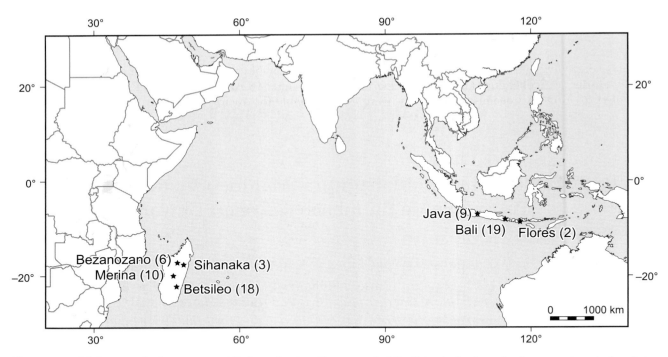

Figure 7.1. *Malagasy ethnic groups and Indonesian locations sampled for this study. Sample sizes are given in brackets. The Malagasy samples were published by Hurles* et al. *(2005). The Indonesian sequences were newly generated in our laboratory in order to improve the coverage across potential sea exits which early voyagers from Borneo may have taken to reach Madagascar. The Indonesian sequences were added to the worldwide data base of over 35,000 published mtDNA sequences.*

Madagascar that did not result in enduring settlement cannot be ruled out, and may have left some traces. For the purposes of this paper we hence assume a continuous presence for humans in Madagascar from about AD 500 onwards.

From about AD 1500, Madagascar was visited first by the Portuguese and then by other European seafarers. These European visitors soon noticed that the native inhabitants of Madagascar, the Malagasy, were phenotypically intermediate between Africans and Asians. In the middle of the twentieth century, linguists recognized that their language was Southeast Asian, and in particular, was most similar to the Maanyan language of the Barito valley in southern Borneo (reviewed by Dewar 2006).

Motivated by this well-known paradox of an Asian language on an African island, in our recent paper (Hurles *et al.* 2005) we had genotyped and compared Y-chromosomal lineages among 362 males from Madagascar and from Southeast Asia and the Pacific. We had also typed mitochondrial DNA (mtDNA) in the Malagasy and analysed it in a global data base of 19,371 mtDNA samples. We found approximately equal African and Southeast Asian contributions to both paternal and maternal Malagasy lineages. The

most likely origin of the Asian-derived paternal lineages within the Malagasy was in Southeast Asia. This agreed strikingly with the linguistic evidence that the languages spoken around the Barito River in southern Borneo are the closest extant relatives of Malagasy languages.

Now, we seek to elaborate on two aspects of the female (mtDNA) lineages within the Malagasy. First, we wish to confirm our previous conclusion that the Asian mtDNA lineages within the Malagasy are indeed of a Southeast Asian origin rather than anywhere else in Asia. Previously, the geographic coverage around the Indian Ocean in the worldwide data base of nearly 20,000 individuals was rather poor, and we have since added new data for Indonesia (Fig. 7.1), Thailand, Sri Lanka, India, Pakistan and Iran. Secondly, generous support from the Sloan Foundation now allows us to carry out computer simulations to tackle the challenging task of reconstructing prehistoric population sizes. We are therefore in a position to ask the question of how many Asian individuals might have arrived across the Indian Ocean 1500 years ago as founders of the present Asian component in the Malagasy population.

Materials and methods

Malagasy mtDNA data

Malagasy data were taken from our previous publication by Hurles and colleagues (2005). The paper had presented 37 mtDNA lineages of which 14 were of African genetic origin, and these 14 are disregarded in the present study. The sample labels for the four published Malagasy groups (Betsileo, Bezanozano, Merina and Sihanaka) are F, A, T and AO, respectively (Matthew Hurles pers. comm.). The approximate geographical locations of the four tribes are shown in Figure 7.1.

DNA sequencing

Saliva samples were obtained from 30 healthy Balinese (some of whom had maternal origins in neighbouring Java and Flores: see Fig. 7.1) with informed consent and sequenced for diagnostic nucleotide positions (nps) of the mtDNA control region (minimally nps 16025–16569 and nps 00001–00241 in the numbering of Anderson *et al.* 1981). Primers, protocols and methods were as published previously (Haack & Vizuete-Forster 2000; L. Forster *et al.* 2002). The sequence data are included in Hill *et al.* (2007).

Centre-of-Gravity (CoG) data base search

For this analysis we use a worldwide mtDNA data base which holds both information on the mtDNA profile of an individual and on the geographical location of the birthplace either of the individual or of his or her maternal mother or grandmother. The search program is based on the work published by Röhl *et al.* (2001) and finds the closest genetic matches for the entered sequence, and displays these matches on a map; the program also calculates a centre of gravity (CoG), which is a theoretical average location for the matches found in the data base, along with its standard deviation (or more precisely, the standard deviation of the matches from the CoG). The CoG calculation is based on the local frequency for each match, whereby the local frequency is determined from the grid square surrounding each match. It follows that the local frequency determination will vary according to the chosen size of the local grid square; we have therefore varied the grid size from 1 degree by 1 degree to 8 degrees by 8 degrees (thus a difference by a factor of 64) to empirically assess the effect of choosing different grid sizes. Further details are described in Forster *et al.* (2002). The CoG interpolates, from the available geographic sample coverage, the potential location with the highest frequency of a given allele. Here, this geographic location is assumed to represent the most likely origin of a given allele of unknown provenance,

especially for recent time depths where geographic allele patterns have not had sufficient time to change substantially. For example, the Malagasy mtDNA types can be considered as recent arrivals of unknown provenance. Any single CoG may not be particularly reliable for tracing the alleles' point of departure (or origins) prior to the arrival in Madagascar, especially if the standard deviation of the CoG is large. Therefore, it is desirable to calculate an exhaustive list of CoGs for a population sample (such as for the Malagasy in this case) to more reliably delineate areas of origins (such as mainland Africa and Southeast Asia in the Malagasy example). The individual CoGs for each Malagasy mtDNA type are then combined to form a single CoG which indicates the possible origin of the Asian Malagasy lineages. When calculating this combined overall centre of gravity, we weight each individual centre of gravity according to the mutational distance between a Malagasy mtDNA type and its most similar match, according to the standard deviation of the CoG of each match, and according to the frequency of each type within Madagascar. This weighting scheme caused the eighth Malagasy Asian mtDNA type to drop out of the CoG analysis (see Fig. 7.2). Details on the weighting scheme are given in the Supplementary Information of Hurles *et al.* (2005).

Coalescent simulations

Coalescent simulations were carried out using software programmed by SM. The basic assumptions of the simulations are: 55 generations of exponential growth (1485 years if we assume 27 years for female generation time) and a current population size of 3,000,000 females (calculated from a total census of 14,800,000 Malagasy of which half are female and 23/(23+14) are of Asian matrilineal descent. This Asian subset is then multiplied by 0.7 to convert census females to effective females (Matsumura & Forster this volume). For each founding size 100,000 iterations were performed.

Results

Malagasy homeland

In our previous paper (Hurles *et al.* 2005) the CoG analysis had suggested a Southeast Asian origin for Asian Malagasy mtDNA. For the present study, we felt that in order to confirm or reappraise this result, we needed to include more population data from around the Indian Ocean that had not previously been available, and we accordingly added new data for Indonesia, Thailand, Sri Lanka, India, Pakistan and Iran. Most of these Indian Ocean data were taken from the literature, but the Indonesian mtDNA data was freshly sequenced from 30 individuals with maternal birthplaces in Bali, Java and the immediately surrounding islands. Including the Bali data also has the secondary aim of covering one of the potential, albeit less likely, sea exits available for the long journey from Borneo to Madagascar. We recalculated the CoG for the Asian Malagasy using this extended data base, and confirmed the previous result.

In detail, as shown in Figure 7.2, the CoG indicating the Asian Malagasy homeland shifted by only 750 kilometres to a point northwest of Borneo compared to Hurles *et al.* (2005), despite the large additional amount of new data to the west (covering Thailand to Iran). The standard deviation (1700 km) of the CoG was also similar to that of Hurles *et al.* (2005). The CoG and its standard error also remained relatively stable when we changed the frequency grid size from 1 by 1 degree through 4 by 4 degrees to 8 by 8 degrees, i.e. a grid size increase by a factor of approximately 64. Taken together, these empirical results indicate that the Southeast Asian origin of the Malagasy Asian lineages is a stable result even despite adding many non-Southeast Asian lineages to the data base and despite drastically resetting the grid size for the calculation.

On the other hand, the addition of the new Indonesian and other Asian lineages has not resulted in improved genetic matches to the Malagasy mtDNA types: of the 23 Malagasy lineages, only seven matched precisely with other sequences in the worldwide data

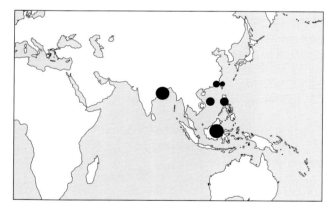

Figure 7.2. *Centres of Gravity for seven Asian mtDNA types in the Malagasy. The individual Centres of Gravity are displayed as black circles, with the circle area being proportional to their weighting (see Materials and Methods). The white circle labelled 'C' represents the overall Centre of Gravity of the individual CoGs. The locations of the CoGs are very similar to the earlier analysis in Hurles* et al. *(2005), despite the formerly poorer sample coverage around the Indian Ocean. The concordance between these studies demonstrates the robustness of the CoG analysis.*

base, while the other 16 Malagasy resulted in only approximate matches (i.e. difference of one or two mutations in the HV1 sequence stretch considered) in the worldwide data base. This clearly indicates that a denser sampling of Southeast Asia is still required to pinpoint genetically the Malagasy homeland.

Mysterious Malagasy: Arabian-Indonesian match
The centre of gravity for nearly every Malagasy mtDNA type can be unambiguously assigned either to Africa or to East Asia. There is one intriguing exception. Malagasy T25 (from the highland Merina tribe) has exact mtDNA matches in Yemen (in the Hadramawt of Thomas *et al.* 2002) and in Borneo (in the Banjarmasin sample of Hurles *et al.* 2005). The mtDNA motif is quite distinctive (16086C-16148T-16223T-16259T-16278T-16319A) and no sequence similar to within three mutations is found anywhere else in the worldwide data base.

It is at present not clear how this mtDNA lineage shared between Yemen, Borneo and highland Madagascar is best explained. Perhaps these three lineages are rare remnants of the early out-of-Africa migration which spread from East Africa and then possibly along the Indian Ocean (Forster *et al.* 2001; Oppenheimer 2003). However, further genotyping demonstrated that this mtDNA sequence is an M type and therefore most probably of non-African origin (only the sub-branch M1 is found in Africa, and even that is nearly restricted to Afro-Asiatic-speaking areas: see Forster 2004). This may leave two explanations: either a Southeast Asian migrant group containing women paused in Arabia, leaving female offspring there, before continuing to Madagascar; or Arabian women with this particular mtDNA type independently migrated from Arabia to Madagascar and from Arabia to Indonesia. Intuitively, neither of these two explanations appears very likely, and further expansion of the worldwide data base is needed to solve this interesting problem.

Malagasy founder population size
In the following, we shall assume that we can accept the linguistic evidence that Borneo is the source area for the Asian genetic component in the Malagasy population. What is quite clear is that Malagasy mtDNA diversity is reduced compared to mtDNA diversity in Borneo today. The mtDNA diversity (i.e. the probability of selecting two different mtDNA HV1 types at random) is 99% (SE 2%) in Borneo, but only 84% (SE 5%) among Malagasy Asian mtDNA. Much of this decreased diversity is due to the high proportion in Madagascar of a major mtDNA type (motif 16223T-16263C-16311C) which is found in 8

out of 24 Asian Malagasy mtDNA sequences, and in three out of the four sampled Malagasy tribes, but not elsewhere in the worldwide data base so far. This clearly indicates a strongly bottlenecked founder event, which we have tried to quantify by simulation as follows.

In **Simulation 1** we assume a uniform composition in the source population. The assumptions are that the source population contains 80 mtDNA types at a frequency of 1.25% each. The descendant population contains 23 sampled individuals sharing 8 types with a distribution of (1,2,3,3,1,8,3,2). If the mtDNA type composition of a population is as described above (80 types), random sampling from it produces a similar pattern to Borneo (Poisson distribution, result not shown). Hence, it is not necessarily assumed that the source population was Borneo, but any population showing a high diversity as in Borneo.

In **Simulation 2** we considered one major type only. The assumptions are that the descendant population contains 23 sampled individuals, the major type having a frequency of 8, and the others 15. The source population contains the major type at 5%, and the others 95%. The graph in Figure 7.4 shows the likelihood that a particular type is not sampled at all (in 63 samples) in relation to its proportion in the population. It is highly unlikely (with a probability of less than 0.05) that its proportion in the source population is 5% or more. So, we chose 5% for conservatively estimating the bottleneck (i.e. the founding population size could be overestimated by using this value) and the resulting simulation is shown in Figure 7.5.

Conclusions from the simulations
The simulations indicate that the maximum likelihood effective value of founding females in Madagascar peaks quite sharply at 30 females if we attempt to model all the Asian

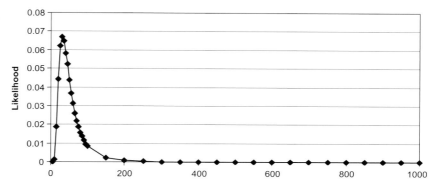

Figure 7.3. *Simulation 1. The maximum likelihood (ML) value is an effective female population size of 30, with a 95% confidence interval (CI) of about [10–250]. It is understood that this number represents an effective female population size, i.e. a model population with a number of idealized characteristics, including a Poisson-distributed number of offspring per female, a uniform generation time, and synchronized reproduction in each generation.*

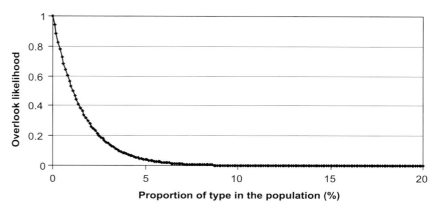

Figure 7.4. *Likelihood function that a particular type is overlooked in a small sample of 63 individuals. For example, if a type has a frequency of 1% in the real population, then the probability of overlooking it in a sample of 63 is about 50%.*

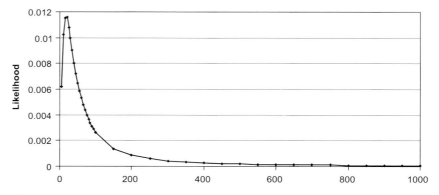

Figure 7.5. *Simulation 2. The ML value is an effective female population size of 20, with a 95% CI of about [5–650]. Note that this simulation allows an effective female founder size of 5, but in fact we observe at least 8 distinct mtDNA types in Madagascar, so if we disregard the possibility of mutation, at least 8 women must have founded the female Malagasy lineages.*

mtDNA lineages in the Malagasy sample, or 20 females if we simulate only the striking major Asian mtDNA type in Madagascar (about one third of all Asian Malagasy types). An effective value of 30 females may correspond to 30–100 census females using empirical conversion factors (Frankham 1995), and if we assume a one-to-one sex ratio in the founding Malagasy populations, then perhaps 60–200 individuals may have arrived in Madagascar 1500 years ago.

The peak around this maximum likelihood value is quite sharp, but as always there is a range of uncertainty. In the Malagasy case, the absolute minimum value is 8 female founders (i.e. the number of distinct mtDNA lineages we see in Madagascar today), and the upper 95% confidence limit is an effective female founder population size of 650, which may correspond to 500–2000 actual female founders.

Discussion

Population sizes and shipping capacity

According to our simulations, between 8 and 2000 women may have crossed from Asia into Madagascar, with a maximum likelihood value of about 60–200 women and men (this is our census size estimate rather than the effective size estimate). Could the prehistoric technology to ship this number of people and the stores necessary to keep them alive, plausibly have been available?

There was a diversity of ships and boats in the Indian Ocean in the first millennium AD, ranging from small to quite large, and of varying degrees of sea-worthiness. Maritime activity was vibrant by the middle of the first century AD, when the Periplus Maris Erythraei was written by an Egyptian Greek merchant (Casson 1989) who described the trade and ports from Tanzania to south India and beyond. Merchant ships in the Mediterranean were large, in some cases reaching 1000 tons burden, though perhaps more commonly 100 to 500 tons (Casson 1971, 171–2), and Greek shipping in the Indian Ocean was likely in the same types of ships. The voyage from the Red Sea to south India was a dangerous one, and was only attempted by relatively large ships (Casson 1989, 284). The author of the Periplus commented on the 'very big kolandiophônta that sail across to Chrysê [Malaya or Sumatra] and the Gangês region' from southern India. Casson (1989, 230) is in accord with Christie (1957) and Needham (1971, 459–60) that kolandiophônta is a corrupted Greek form of a Chinese phrase meaning 'large ocean-going ships of Southeast Asia'. While the size of the ships that established Indonesians on the coast of Madagascar cannot be known, it is very unlikely they were small,

and there is no reason to suppose that they could not have transported scores of settlers.

In 1985, a group of German, English and Australians set out to prove this could be done. They built a double outrigger canoe (the 'Sarimanok') similar to what would have been used by the early Malays. The group took 50 days to travel non-stop from Bali in the 20-m-long pirogue built entirely of wood without the use of a single nail. They arrived in July at Nosy Be island in Madagascar without the benefit of navigation instruments or modern equipment (cited from the website www.malaysia.net).

Future work on other possible scenarios

We have assumed a scenario of a single Asian migration directly arriving in Madagascar without first stopping in Africa and admixing with Bantu women. There are alternative scenarios which we have not explicitly considered, for example the Asian migrants may have stopped in Africa and admixed with the Bantu before continuing to Madagascar. Such an admixture event would tend to increase the founder population size estimated here. Another possibility we have not considered is multiple arrivals of migrants from Asia to Madagascar. There is some linguistic evidence of multiple periods of borrowing from Southeast Asian languages into Malagasy (reviewed in Dewar 2006). One or more subsequent Asian migrations to Madagascar would be expected to contribute additional distinct mtDNA types to Madagascar, say for example 3 new types. If we subtract these hypothetical 3 newcomer types from the present total of 8 Malagasy mtDNA types, then we would be left with only 5 types deriving from the first migration. In other words, in the Malagasy context, subsequent migration from Asia would necessitate decreasing the estimated Asian female founder population size of the first migration.

Another priority needs to be an increase of the Malagasy sample size, which is currently only 37 individuals from four locations. In this context, Erika Hagelberg has kindly shown us additional unpublished Malagasy data from the same four groups, and a preliminary simulation analysis reveals the enlarged sample hardly changes our most likely founder population size of 30 females, but does have a significant and beneficial effect in narrowing the confidence interval. On the African side, increasing coverage of mainland Africa will also allow estimates of African participation in the prehistoric settlement of Madagascar. Within Madagascar, there are reported to be differences between groups, for example coastal versus inland, which may impact the general applicability of our conclusions and should motivate better sampling coverage in future projects on Madagascar.

Data sets

997 males sampled from 27 populations from China, Mongolia, Korea and Japan, a subset of those described previously (Zerjal *et al.* 2003; Xue *et al.* 2005), were included in this analysis (Fig. 8.1). The mean sample size was 37 per population, and the range was 27–65. Males were typed at 45 Y binary marker sites and 16 Y-STRs using routine methods; most experimental details were reported by Zerjal *et al.* or Xue *et al.* and further information can be obtained from the authors on request. In some analyses, we compared the findings from East Asia with those from an independent published data set consisting of 532 males from Anatolia typed with 89 binary Y markers and 10 Y-STRs (Cinnioglu *et al.* 2004).

For BATWING runs, we reduced the sizes of the data sets in a number of ways. Twenty-eight binary markers were chosen from each data set, retaining those that captured most of the phylogenetic information by omitting first, those that detected no variation; second, those that were redundant because another marker was phylogenetically equivalent; and third, those that distinguished only one or a small number of phylogenetically-unimportant chromosomes. We also reduced the number of STRs, for two reasons. One STR, *DYS19*, was duplicated in some East Asian individuals, and so it was not clear how information from this locus could be incorporated correctly; it was therefore excluded from all work on the East Asian data set reported here. In addition, mutation rates have been measured in father/son pairs for some STRs, but not for others (Kayser *et al.* 2000; Dupuy *et al.* 2004; Kurihara *et al.* 2004; Budowle *et al.* 2005; Goés *et al.* 2005). When an inferred average mutation rate (Zhivotovsky *et al.* 2004) was used, this did not matter, but when pedigree mutation rates were used, only the subset of loci with measurements were included

because the other loci would increase the size of the data set and thus the time to run BATWING without contributing greatly to inferences on the timing of events measured. The data set used in BATWING analyses thus consisted of 28 binary markers in each case and 10, 15 or 8, 10 STRs (pedigree mutation rate, average mutation rate) from East Asia and Anatolia, respectively.

BATWING run conditions

The BATWING program includes population and mutation models. Choices must be made about which implementations of these models to use; prior values for the relevant parameters then need to be specified. In the work described here, we always used the demographic model where a population remains at a constant size N_a for a period, then at time β begins to grow exponentially at rate α (size model 2); we did not incorporate population subdivision. Priors for N_a, α and β were set as shown in Table 8.1. Binary markers were used solely to condition the trees to be consistent with the SNP phylogeny and its known root (option 2). Each STR was allowed to have an individual mutation rate. Mutation rate priors were derived either from pedigree mutation rates (Table 8.2), or from a slower estimated 'evolutionary' mutation rate averaged over all loci (Zhivotovsky *et al.* 2004). The former provide mutation rates per generation, and a generation time of 30 years, appropriate for males over this timescale (Tremblay & Vézina 2000), was used to convert them into times measured in years; the latter is expressed in years and must be divided by 25 to give a mutation rate per generation. The evolutionary rate was used in the analyses described here, unless otherwise specified.

In all runs, we took 13,000 samples of the output, and discarded the first 3,000 as 'burn-in'. Thus

Table 8.1. *BATWING priors for* N, α *and* β.

Npriors							
mean = 1000		mean = 10,000		mean = 30,000		mean = 100,000	
SD	Nprior	SD	Nprior	SD	Nprior	SD	Nprior
100	gamma (100, 0.1)	1000	gamma (100, 0.01)	3162	gamma (90, 0.003)	10,000	gamma (100, 0.001)
316	gamma (10, 0.01)	3162	gamma (10, 0.001)	10,000	gamma (9, 0.0003)	31,623	gamma (10, 0.0001)
632	gamma (2.5, 0.0025)	6325	gamma (2.5, 0.00025)	19,365	gamma (2.4, 0.00008)	63,246	gamma (2.5, 0.000025)
1000	gamma (1, 0.001)	10,000	gamma (1, 0.0001)	31,623	gamma (0.9, 0.00003)	100,000	gamma (1, 0.00001)
1414	gamma (0.5, 0.0005)	14,142	gamma (0.5, 0.00005)	42,008	gamma (0.51, 0.000017)	141,421	gamma (0.5, 0.000005)
1826	gamma (0.3, 0.0003)	18,257	gamma (0.3, 0.00003)	54,772	gamma (0.3, 0.00001)	182,574	gamma (0.3, 0.000003)

α **prior**   gamma (2, 400): mean = 0.005, SD = 0.0035
β **prior**   gamma (2, 1): mean = 2, SD = 1.41

Note: for Nprior values, see discussion in text; α prior and β prior are from Wilson *et al.* (2003).

Table 8.2. *Mutation rate measurements used and BATWING mupriors.*

Locus	Kayser *et al.* (2000) mut	mei	Dupuy *et al.* (2004) mut	mei	Budowle *et al.* (2005) mut	mei	Goés *et al.* (2005) mut	mei	Kurihara *et al.* (2004) mut	mei	Total mut	mei	BATWING muprior
DYS19	2	996	3	1766							5	2762	gamma (5, 2763)
DYS388			1	1766							1	1766	gamma (1, 1767)
DYS389I	1	425	4	1766							5	2191	gamma (5, 2192)
DYS389b	2	425	4	1766							6	2191	gamma (6, 2192)
DYS390	4	466	8	1766							12	2232	gamma (12, 2233)
DYS391	2	415	8	1766							10	2181	gamma (10, 2182)
DYS392	0	415	0	1766							0	2181	gamma (1, 2182)
DYS393	0	415	1	1766							1	2181	gamma (1, 2182)
DYS437					2	692	0	119	0	161	2	972	gamma (2, 973)
DYS438					0	692	1	119	0	161	1	972	gamma (1, 973)
DYS439					2	692	1	119	1	161	4	972	gamma (4, 973)
Total	11	3557	29	14,128							40	17,685	
Average											5	2211	

Zhivotovsky *et al.* average 'evolutionary' mutation rate, 25-year generation time: gamma (1.47, 2130)
mean = 0.00069, SD = 0.00057

Note: mut = number of mutations; mei = number of meioses.

all results are based on 10,000 samples. The number of MCMC iterations between each sample varied between runs, from 10^2 to c. 10^5, so the runs ranged from 10^6 to c. 10^9 MCMC cycles.

Initial results: a lack of convergence with a large data set

We carried out our initial analyses using the entire data set. With 10^6 MCMC cycles, N_a, the effective population size before the population began to expand, appeared to converge (i.e. reach a stable posterior value) from a range of prior distributions to a value of c. 25,000. This value was surprisingly large: N for a worldwide set of Y chromosomes is usually reported at about 5000 (e.g. Hammer 1995). We repeated the analysis with the Anatolian data set and saw similar apparent convergence to a high value, in this case c. 10,000. We therefore investigated the convergence properties of the program in more detail by increasing the number of MCMC cycles. Starting from an Nprior (i.e. a prior distribution for N_a, the population size for the constant period) with mean 10,000 and standard deviation 10,000 (also used by Weale *et al.* 2001), which converged to the Nposterior (i.e. the distribution of N_a after performing the analyses) values of c. 25,000 and c. 10,000 in the initial runs, but would also be compatible with smaller values, we changed the sampling procedure so that the number of MCMC cycles examined would range from 10^6 (10,000 samples with

Nbetsamp = 10 and treebetN = 10), to approximately 10^7, 10^8 or 10^9. The last runs took around one week on a c. 2.7 GHz machine. The results are shown in Figure 8.2a. Median Nposterior decreases as the number of cycles is increased, and in the longest runs is c. 700 (360–1600) and 1300 (470–3000) in East Asia and Anatolia, respectively. Have these values stabilized? There is no indication that they have: Nposterior continues to decrease between the 10^8 and 10^9 cycles. A run of 10^{10} cycles would take around two months, so has not been tested. We wondered whether the failure to reach a stable state might be due to the choice of an unsuitable Nprior that was too high and had a large standard deviation. We therefore repeated the runs with a lower Nprior, using a mean of 1000 and standard deviation of 1000 (Fig. 8.2b). The Nposterior values are very similar, and show a similar dependence on the length of the run.

Different parameters may converge at different rates. Another of the demographic parameters of interest to us was the time when the population started to grow. We have examined this in the runs described above (Fig. 8.2c, d). Like Nposterior, it is little affected by the different values of Nprior, but does not stabilize: it increases with run length. With the longest runs, it reaches a value of around 30,000 years with both data sets. This absolute value is directly dependent on the generation time assumed, and would be 20,000 years if a generation time of 20 years was used, but, more importantly, its failure to reach a stable value

82

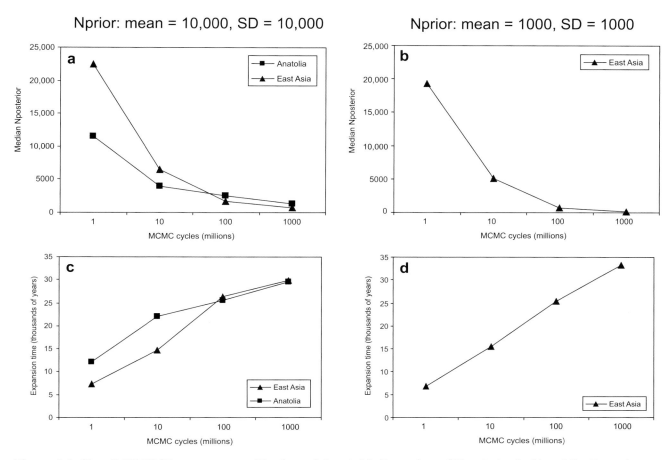

Figure 8.2. *Slow BATWING convergence with a large data set. Median values of Nposterior (a, b) and the time when population growth started (c, d) in East Asian (a, c) and Anatolian (b, d) data for different numbers of MCMC cycles.*

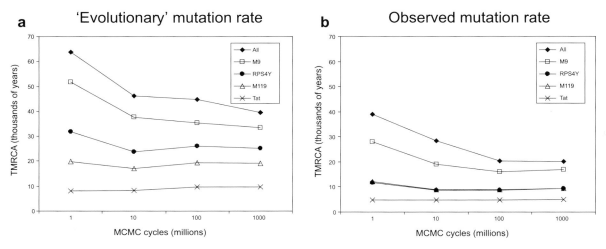

Figure 8.3. *Satisfactory convergence of TMRCAs with a large data set. TMRCAs for the complete set of Y chromosomes (All), or for individual lineages (M9, RPS4Y, M119, Tat). Mutation rate priors (Table 8.2) are based on an inferred evolutionary mutation rate (a), or pedigree mutation rates in father-son pairs (b).*

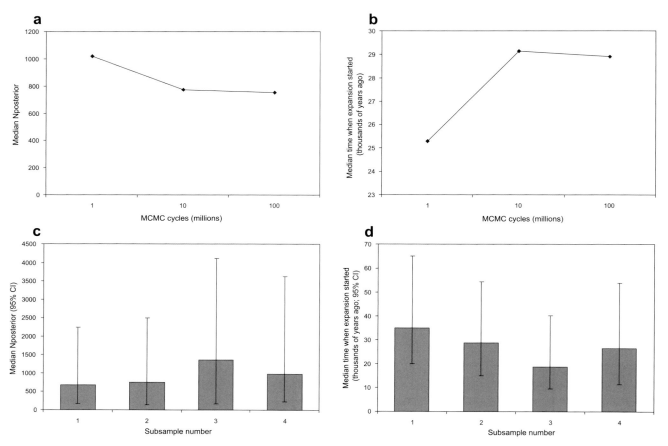

Figure 8.4. *Rapid BATWING convergence with small data sets. Median values of Nposterior (a, c) and the time when population growth started (b, d) for different numbers of MCMC cycles using a data set of 54 individuals (a, b) or independent subsamples (c, d).*

suggests that any historical interpretation must be made with caution.

The TMRCA of the complete set of Y chromosomes in a population is also of interest (Wilson *et al.* 2003; Macpherson *et al.* 2004); in addition, the derived state of each SNP defines a unique lineage with its own geographical distribution, and the TMRCA of the lineage provides an important constraint to its spread (it must have spread after this time), so is of interest as well. We have therefore examined TMRCAs for the complete data set, and of individual lineages (Fig. 8.3a, b). These, in contrast to the demographic parameters, did reach a stable value in these runs. For the more recent TMRCAs, this was achieved by 10^6 cycles, and for most of the sets of chromosomes by 10^7 cycles. As expected, the TMRCA depends substantially on whether the mutation priors are derived from observed or evolutionary rates, being considerably lower with the former. Moreover, the relationship between the two is not simple: for example, RPS4Y and M119 have quite different TMRCAs when the evolu-

tionary rate is used (Fig. 8.3a), but are very similar when the pedigree rate is used (Fig. 8.3b). A similar stability of TMRCA in runs of different length was seen in the Anatolian data set (results not shown). It therefore appears that TMRCAs are determined in a more stable fashion by the program, although they of course still depend on the mutation rate and generation times used.

Satisfactory convergence with smaller data sets

The most practical way to analyse our data further appeared to be to examine small subsets of the data. We therefore chose two or three males from each population at random to produce subsamples containing 54 or 81 individuals, and tested the convergence of BATWING. We observed similar values of Nposterior and expansion time after 10^7 or 10^8 MCMC cycles (Fig. 8.4a, b), showing that the program had converged after 10^7 cycles. These parameters differed somewhat in independent subsamples, as expected, but suggested a value of N_a for the region of around 1000, consistent with a worldwide value of c. 5000. The time at which population growth began similarly differed between subsamples, but showed median values between c. 19 and c. 35 kya. Although the 95% confidence intervals associated with these values were wide, the results all suggested that demographic expansion had started in the Palaeolithic: there was no support for a start to growth after 10 kya in the Neolithic (Fig. 8.4b).

These results showed that male demographic parameters could be determined satisfactorily from small data sets and provided average values for East Asia. Since there might be variation between populations in this large area, we next examined single populations.

Individual populations

All samples derived from single populations consisted of 65 or fewer individuals, and so produced data sets that converged satisfactorily after 10^7 MCMC cycles. We therefore determined N_a, the start of population growth and the growth rate for each population separately (Fig. 8.5). Median values of Nposterior ranged from c. 450 (200–1180) for the Hui to c. 1300 (340–3670) for one of the Uygur populations (Fig. 8.5a), similar to subsets of the whole area. Median values for the growth rate ranged from 0.11% per generation (0.01–0.62%) for the Yao from Bama to 0.46% (0.20–0.98%) for the Manchu (Fig. 8.5b). Median estimates of the time when expansion started ranged from c. 11.9 (1.1–44.6) kya for the Yao from Bama, to 34.4 (17.7–68.3) kya for the Inner Mongolians (Fig. 8.5c), a wider range than the average for the whole area.

Although both the smallest and the largest population sizes were observed in the north, the median values for the northern populations were, on average, larger than the southern populations by about 200 individuals, a result of borderline significance ($P = 0.04$ by T test). The rate of growth was slightly higher in the south (mean = 0.31% per generation) than in the north (mean = 0.26%), but the difference between the regions was not significant. In contrast, the difference in north/south expansion times was very marked. The median values did not overlap between the two groups, being <18 kya in the south and >21 kya in the north, a highly significant difference ($P = 4 \times 10^{-7}$ by T test).

There thus appear to be demographic differences between the north and south of East Asia, with the northern populations being slightly larger and beginning their expansion significantly earlier than in the south.

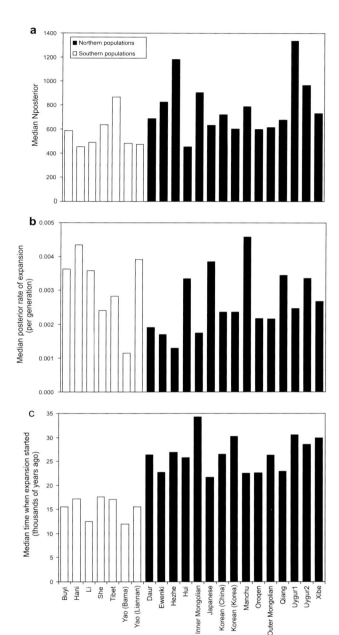

Figure 8.5. *Demographic parameters for individual populations. Median posterior values from BATWING for Nposterior (a), the population growth rate (b), and the time when population expansion started (c). Northern populations are indicated by closed bars, southern populations by open bars. Five of the 27 populations in our set belonged to the major Chinese ethnic group, the Han. The Han have been very mobile during historical times (Wen et al. 2004) and especially in recent decades, and so were excluded from these analyses.*

Discussion

BATWING is the most powerful tool currently available for analysing combinations of Y-chromosomal SNP and STR data. Because of its incorporation of a population model, it can provide information on male demographic parameters which can then lead to insights into the male prehistory of a region, in this case East Asia. We were unable to obtain reliable estimates of ancestral population size or time of expansion using our entire data set, but could do so with smaller subsamples. We will first discuss these limitations to BATWING, and then the more general implications of our findings.

BATWING's use has previously been explored in detail on data sets consisting of 115 chromosomes typed with 6 STRs and 2 binary markers, or 212 chromosomes typed with 5 STRs and 1 binary marker (Wilson *et al.* 2003), 667 males typed with 7 STRs alone (Macpherson *et al.* 2004) and 734 males typed with 6 STRs and 11 binary markers (7 variable) (Weale *et al.* 2001), and in limited ways on many other data sets. Wilson *et al.* used 1.6×10^8 MCMC cycles; Macpherson *et al.* tested 4×10^6 and 2×10^8 cycles with four different prior sets (and 8×10^8 with one set); Weale *et al.* used 3.1×10^8 cycles. Macpherson *et al.* found a decrease of approximately two- to threefold in Nposterior between their shorter and longer runs, but concluded that the program had reached convergence after 2×10^8 cycles because the TMRCA had stabilized. A comparison of Figures 8.2 and 8.3 shows that TMRCA convergence can be a poor guide to whether or not Nposterior or expansion time have converged. It seems that the very slow convergence of some parameters in large data sets is a general but little-appreciated property of BATWING, and needs to be taken into account when such analyses are carried out.

It is notable that the sum of the Nposterior values for the individual populations (Fig. 8.5a) is far greater than Nposterior for the region considered as a whole (Fig. 8.4a, c). This reflects the fact that N represents the effective population size over a long time span and that the populations carry related rather than independent sets of Y chromosomes. If, for example, a population splits into two halves, Nposterior for each half would be similar to that in the original population.

In addition to these rather technical points, our work leads to two conclusions of more general significance. The first is that the genetically-detectable demographic expansion began in the Palaeolithic period. This conclusion carries a number of caveats. First, the time estimates depend on the mutation rate used. Use of the observed father-son mutation rate would lead

to more recent estimates. Might these be more appropriate and lie within the Neolithic or later periods, thus radically changing this conclusion? A difference between pedigree-based and evolutionary estimates of mutation rates is seen in both Y-chromosomal and mitochondrial DNA studies, and evolutionary rates are generally considered more appropriate for studies involving time depths of more than a few generations (e.g. Howell *et al.* 2003). Zhivotovsky *et al.* (2004) calibrated their evolutionary rate using timescales of about 1000 years, and this rate is unlikely to overestimate older times. Second, the demographic model used, involving a period with constant population size followed by a period of exponential expansion, is a gross oversimplification of the real demography. Does imposing such a model nevertheless capture significant features of the real demography? This question is difficult to answer, but might be addressed using data sets where the real demography is known in reasonable detail, or by using more extensive simulations. Third, and related to the second point, it is obvious from the archaeological and historical records that later expansions have occurred as well. Our conclusion does not conflict with these observations: it simply identifies the time when detectable demographic expansion *began*.

There has been some controversy among geneticists about the interpretation of the signal of expansion carried by genetic data sets (Wall & Przeworski 2000; Ptak & Przeworski 2002). Some populations show no clear evidence of expansion, but one of the most comprehensive studies, involving 377 STRs and over 1000 individuals, suggested expansion in African farmers starting *c.* 35 kya, in Eurasians *c.* 25 kya and in East Asians *c.* 18 kya (Zhivotovsky *et al.* 2003). Y-chromosomal analyses have generally shown a strong signal of expansion, beginning *c.* 18 kya (7–41 kya: Pritchard *et al.* 1999) or *c.* 22 kya (8.5–50 kya: Macpherson *et al.* 2004) in worldwide studies, with some variation between continents. In contrast, a detailed study of one country, Armenia, suggested a start of expansion in the Neolithic *c.* 4.8 kya (2.0–11.1 kya: Weale *et al.* 2001). Our finding of a Palaeolithic start to expansion in East Asia is thus consistent with most previous work.

The second general conclusion is that fine-scale regional differences in expansion time can be detected, and that, in East Asia, expansion began earlier in the north than in the south. Expansion time estimates for individual populations have wide confidence intervals, but the north–south difference is robust. Notably, expansion in the north preceded the LGM (*c.* 18–21 kya), while expansion in the south post-dated it. The northern and southern populations have different histories which may trace back to separate migrations out of Africa (Oppenheimer 2003), but distinct origins would not necessarily lead to the different starts to demographic expansion. A simple explanation is that resources may have been available to northern populations during the period *c.* 40–21 kya that were not available to southern populations, and the highly-productive steppe environment with its extensive megafauna including mammoths, could have provided these (Guthrie 1990). In contrast, southern populations would only have expanded when the climate began to ameliorate after the LGM. This hypothesis needs to be tested using archaeological data from East Asia, and comparisons with other regions of Eurasia would be of interest.

Overall, we conclude that Y-chromosomal data, together with appropriate analytical techniques, can provide novel insights into human prehistory, and suggest directions for future interdisciplinary research.

Acknowledgements

We thank all sample donors for making this work possible, Andrew Flint and Tim Cutts for setting up BATWING, and Mike Shield for maintaining the Sanger computer system. On a number of occasions, our enthusiasm for BATWING exceeded the computing capacity available to us, and we thank our colleagues for their forbearance when their vital projects slowed down as a result. We also thank Mike Weale and Ian Wilson for helpful comments on the first draft of this manuscript, and all participants at the conference 'Simulations, genetics and human prehistory — a focus on islands' for making the meeting so constructive and stimulating. This work was supported by a Joint Project from the National Natural Science Foundation in China and The Royal Society in the UK, and by the Wellcome Trust.

References

Budowle, B., M. Adamowicz, X.G. Aranda, *et al.*, 2005. Twelve short tandem repeat loci Y chromosome haplotypes: Genetic analysis on populations residing in North America. *Forensic Science International* 150, 1–15.

Cinnioglu, C., R. King, T. Kivisild, *et al.*, 2004. Excavating Y-chromosome haplotype strata in Anatolia. *Human Genetics* 114, 127–48.

Dupuy, B.M., M. Stenersen, T. Egeland & B. Olaisen, 2004. Y-chromosomal microsatellite mutation rates: differences in mutation rate between and within loci. *Human Mutation* 23, 117–24.

Goés, A.C. d. S., E. de Carvalho, I. Gomes, *et al.*, 2005. Population and mutation analysis of 17 Y-STR loci from Rio de Janeiro (Brazil). *International Journal of Legal Medicine* 119, 70–76.

Guthrie, R.D., 1990. *Frozen Fauna of the Mammoth Steppe.* Chicago (IL): University of Chicago Press.

Hammer, M.F., 1995. A recent common ancestry for human Y chromosomes. *Nature* 378, 376–8.

Howell, N., C.B. Smejkal, D.A. Mackey, P.F. Chinnery, D.M. Turnbull & C. Herrnstadt, 2003. The pedigree rate of sequence divergence in the human mitochondrial genome: there is a difference between phylogenetic and pedigree rates. *American Journal of Human Genetics* 72, 659–70.

Jin, L. & B. Su, 2000. Natives or immigrants: modern human origin in East Asia. *Nature Reviews Genetics* 1, 126–33.

Jobling, M.A. & C. Tyler-Smith, 2003. The human Y chromosome: an evolutionary marker comes of age. *Nature Reviews Genetics* 4, 598–612.

Jobling, M.A., M.E. Hurles & C. Tyler-Smith, 2004. *Human Evolutionary Genetics.* New York (NY) & Abingdon: Garland Science.

Karafet, T., L. Xu, R. Du, *et al.*, 2001. Paternal population history of East Asia: sources, patterns, and micro-evolutionary processes. *American Journal of Human Genetics* 69, 615–28.

Kayser, M., L. Roewer, M. Hedman, *et al.*, 2000. Characteristics and frequency of germline mutations at microsatellite loci from the human Y chromosome, as revealed by direct observation in father/son pairs. *American Journal of Human Genetics* 66, 1580–88.

Kurihara, R., T. Yamamoto, R. Uchihi, *et al.*, 2004. Mutations in 14 Y-STR loci among Japanese father–son haplotypes. *International Journal of Legal Medicine* 118, 125–31.

Macpherson, J.M., S. Ramachandran, L. Diamond & M.W. Feldman, 2004. Demographic estimates from Y chromosome microsatellite polymorphisms: analysis of a worldwide sample. *Human Genomics* 1, 345–54.

Oppenheimer, S., 2003. *Out of Eden: the Peopling of the World.* London: Constable and Robinson.

Pritchard, J.K., M.T. Seielstad, A. Perez-Lezaun & M.W. Feldman, 1999. Population growth of human Y chromosomes: a study of Y chromosome microsatellites. *Molecular Biology and Evolution* 16, 1791–8.

Ptak, S.E. & M. Przeworski, 2002. Evidence for population growth in humans is confounded by fine-scale population structure. *Trends in Genetics* 18, 559–63.

Shen, G., W. Wang, Q. Wang, *et al.*, 2002. U-Series dating of Liujiang hominid site in Guangxi, southern China. *Journal of Human Evolution* 43, 817–29.

Tavaré, S., D.J. Balding, R.C. Griffiths & P. Donnelly, 1997. Inferring coalescence times from DNA sequence data. *Genetics* 145, 505–18.

Tremblay, M. & H. Vézina, 2000. New estimates of intergenerational time intervals for the calculation of age and origins of mutations. *American Journal of Human Genetics* 66, 651–8.

Trinkaus, E., 2005. Early modern humans. *Annual Review of Anthropology* 34, 207–230.

Wall, J.D. & M. Przeworski, 2000. When did the human population size start increasing? *Genetics* 155, 1865–74.

Weale, M.E., L. Yepiskoposyan, R.F. Jager, *et al.*, 2001. Armenian Y chromosome haplotypes reveal strong regional structure within a single ethno-national group. *Human Genetics* 109, 659–74.

Wen, B., H. Li, D. Lu, *et al.*, 2004. Genetic evidence supports demic diffusion of Han culture. *Nature* 431, 302–5.

Wilson, I.J., M.E. Weale & D.J. Balding, 2003. Inferences from DNA data: population histories, evolutionary processes and forensic match probabilities. *Journal of the Royal Statistical Society: Series A (Statistics in Society)* 166, 155–88.

Xiao, C.J., L.L. Cavalli-Sforza, E. Minch & R.F. Du, 2000. [Geographic distribution maps of human genes in China (in Chinese)]. *Yi Chuan Xue Bao* 27, 1–6.

Xue, Y., T. Zerjal, W. Bao, *et al.*, 2005. Recent spread of a Y-chromosomal lineage in northern China and Mongolia. *American Journal of Human Genetics* 77, 1112–16.

Zerjal, T., Y. Xue, G. Bertorelle, *et al.*, 2003. The genetic legacy of the Mongols. *American Journal of Human Genetics* 72, 717–21.

Zhivotovsky, L.A., N.A. Rosenberg & M.W. Feldman, 2003. Features of evolution and expansion of modern humans, inferred from genomewide microsatellite markers. *American Journal of Human Genetics* 72, 1171–86.

Zhivotovsky, L.A., P.A. Underhill, C. Cinnioglu, *et al.*, 2004. The effective mutation rate at Y chromosome short tandem repeats, with application to human population-divergence time. *American Journal of Human Genetics* 74, 50–61.

Chapter 9

Genetic Relationships of Human Populations in and around the Japanese Archipelago

Saitou Naruya
Dedicated to the memory of the late Hanihara Kazuro

Genetic and linguistic studies on the phylogenetic relationships of populations in and around the Japanese Archipelago are presented. The genetic data suggest a weak affinity between Ainu and Okinawan, compatible with the Dual Structure hypothesis of the late Hanihara Kazuro. Linguistically, Okinawan is a Japanese dialect, and the Ainu language is distant from Japanese. However, some possibility of similarity between the Ainu and Okinawa languages is suggested through phylogenetic network analysis.

The Japanese Archipelago consists of four major islands (Hokkaido, Honshu, Shikoku, and Kyushu) and many surrounding small islands (Fig. 9.1). Owing to its vicinity to the Eurasian Continent, frequent waves of migration from the continent to the islands took place during at least the last 50,000 years. There are six major migration routes to the Japanese Archipelago (Fig. 9.1). Route 1, the most plausible pathway, is through the Korean Peninsula, and the next possible one, route 2, is via Sakhalin Island. The northernmost route 3 is via the Kamchatkan Peninsula and the Chishima (Kurile) Archipelago, while the southernmost route 4 is via Taiwan and the Ryukyu Archipelago. In Japan route 4 is known as the 'Sea Road' (Yanagita 1961). There are two other routes, but both of them need relatively long crossings of either the East China Sea (route 5) or the Sea of Japan (route 6), and probably became important only recently, perhaps within the past 3000 years. There is another possible human migration, from the Pacific Ocean, i.e. visitors from Polynesia, but the relative contribution to the genetic constitution of the people in the Japanese Archipelago is small.

It may be pertinent to divide the population of the Japanese Archipelago into three groups in terms of their cultural and historical perspectives; the Ainu, the mainland Japanese, and the Okinawans. The Ainu people, who currently live mainly in Hokkaido, also lived in Sakhalin and the Chishima Archipelago until

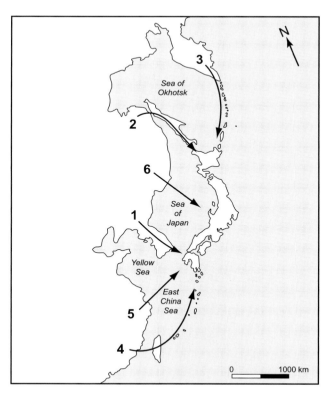

Figure 9.1. *Six possible routes of migration to the Japanese Archipelago. (Drawing: D. Kemp from Saitou 2005.)*

89

Table 9.1. *Cultural periods of the central part of the Japanese Archipelago. (From Saitou 2005.)*

Period	Time
Palaeolithic	–13,000 BP
Jomon	13,000–3000 BP
Yayoi	3000–1800 BP
Kofun-Historical	1800 BP–Present

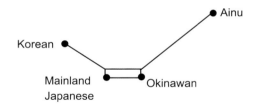

(A) Genetic Network

(B) Language Network

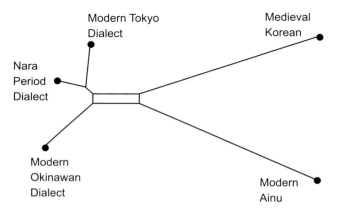

Figure 9.2. *Phylogenetic networks for (A) genetic data and for (B) language data. ((A) is based on Omoto & Saitou (1997), and (B) is from Saitou (2005).)*

recently. The Ainu population was about 23,000 in 1993 (Ainu Museum web; www.ainu-museum.or.jp/), and Hokkaido is now mostly populated by immigrants from the mainland (Honshu and the other two major islands). Mainland Japanese form the majority of current 'Japanese', and their population size was approximately 130 million in 2005. Okinawans are the majority in the Ryukyu Archipelago, but there are many migrants and their descendants from mainland Japan. Although there are now several ancient (more than 15,000 BP) human remains found from Okinawa, the real start of Okinawan prehistory was about 6000 BP (Asato & Doi 1999).

Table 9.1 shows the historical framework of the central part of the Japanese Archipelago. Archaeological details of these prehistoric periods are reviewed in Imamura (1996). Hanihara (1991) proposed a 'Dual Structure' hypothesis to explain the current geographical distribution pattern of the Japanese population. This hypothesis consists of two parts: 1) that the Upper Palaeolithic population of Japan that gave rise to the Jomon people was of southeast Asian origin; and 2) that the modern Ainu and Okinawa populations are direct descendants of the Jomon people, while mainland Japanese are mainly derived from migrants from the northeast Asian continent after the Yayoi period.

Genetic studies

Omoto & Saitou (1997) studied the genetic relationship of three human populations (Ainu, mainland Japanese, and Okinawan) in Japan and Korean using 25 classic markers. When they used the neighbour-joining method (Saitou & Nei 1987), Ainu and Okinawans became neighbours, as did mainland Japanese with Koreans. Bootstrap probabilities for clustering between these two populations were 85% and 74% for the DA distance and the Dst distance, respectively, somewhat lower than statistically significance levels. However, those bootstrap probabilities were much higher than the random expectation (33%). Omoto & Saitou (1997) therefore provided partial support for Hanihara's (1991) Dual Structure hypothesis for explaining the genetic structure of the Japanese.

Figure 9.2A shows a split decomposition network (Bandelt & Dress 1992) based on the DA distances given in Omoto & Saitou (1997). The split ((Ainu, Okinawan)–(Korean, mainland Japanese)) is longest, followed by ((Okinawan, mainland Japanese)–(Ainu, Korean)). The remaining possible split ((Ainu, mainland Japanese)–(Okinawan, Korean)) does not exist in this network. This network suggests that Ainu and Okinawan share some genetic similarity, even though Ainu is quite distantly related from the three other populations. The similarity between mainland Japanese and Okinawan, shown by the second split, suggests the existence of gene flow between these two populations. The genetic similarity between Ainu and Okinawan supports Hanihara's (1991) dual structure hypothesis on the origin of the Japanese at least partially.

A similar relationship was also observed for the Y chromosome (Hammer & Horai 1995), HLA (Bannai *et al.* 2000), and for mtDNA (Tajima *et al.* 2003).

Tajima and colleagues (2003) determined mtDNA sequences for Ainu and some other human populations surrounding Japan, and they found that haplotypes 2 and 4 found in the Ainu were also found in the Nivkhi and Kamchatkan populations, respectively. This clearly indicates a genetic influence of Northeastern Asian populations on the Ainu.

Tanaka and colleagues (2004) determined complete mitochondrial DNA sequences for 672 Japanese individuals and compared them with many other Asian sequences. They also found a clear genetic similarity between mainland Japanese and Asian continental populations such as Korean and Han Chinese.

Li and colleagues (2005) recently examined more than 100 STR loci for five Han Chinese populations and two Japanese populations (mainland and Okinawa). Two Japanese populations were tightly clustered with 100% bootstrap probabilities, but interestingly, this Japanese cluster was more similar to southern Han Chinese populations than to northern ones. This pattern is somewhat different from the phylogenetic relationship of Chinese and surrounding Asian populations using HLA data (Saitou *et al.* 1992), where both Japanese and Korean were genetically much closer to northern Han Chinese. However, when Alu insertion/deletion polymorphism was used for the same Han Chinese samples and Japanese, the northern Han were somewhat closer to the Japanese (Ishibashi and Saitou, unpublished). This discrepancy is worth examining in future studies.

Linguistic studies

The origin of the Japanese language has long been debated. Arai Hakuseki, a high-ranking Tokugawa Shogun government official in the eighteenth century, suggested that Japanese was similar to the Korean language, and since then many people have proposed an affinity of these two languages. Some linguists considered these two languages as well as the Ainu language as belonging to the Altaic language family (see Vovin & Osada 2003). The Okinawan language is considered to be a dialect of Japanese because of their close relationship, while the phylogenetic language relationship between Ainu and Japanese is not clear; some linguists such as Kindaichi Kyosuke and Chiri Mashio concluded that these two languages were not related, while others such as Murayama Shichiro and Hattori Shiro accepted a weak similarity of these two languages, though indirectly (Saitou 2005). It seems that the majority of linguists do not currently conduct numerical and statistical analyses in studying the phylogenetic relationship of languages.

Yasumoto & Honda (1978) compared lists of 100 and 200 basic words of many languages around the Japanese Archipelago, and proposed the existence of a common ancestral language for the contemporary

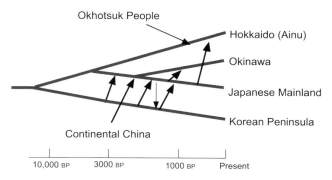

Figure 9.3. *Scenario for temporal changes of human populations in the Japanese Archipelago and the Korean Peninsula. (From Saitou 2005.)*

Japanese, Ainu, and Korean languages based on their results. Saitou (2005) constructed a phylogenetic network (Fig. 9.2B) for these three languages (three dialects for Japanese, Ainu, and medieval Korean) using data collected by Yasumoto & Honda (1978). As expected, the three Japanese dialects clearly formed one cluster, in particular, the Nara period (eighth century AD) dialect was closest to contemporary Japanese, followed by the contemporary dialect of Okinawa's Shuri area. Interestingly, there were three words that showed similarity between the Okinawan and Ainu languages.

Although the genetic and linguistic relationships of human populations in and around the Japanese Archipelago are not consistent, this difference itself may tell something about the history of human populations in this region. Figure 9.3 summarizes one plausible scenario of temporal changes of human populations in the Japanese Archipelago. I hope this can explain both genetic and linguistic patterns shown in Figure 9.2.

Acknowledgements

I would like to thank Peter Forster for showing me his phylogenetic network study on languages. This facilitated my analysis of language data in and around the Japanese Archipelago. I also thank Peter Forster, Merritt Ruhlen, and Shuichi Matsumura for their comments on an earlier version of this paper. This work was partially supported by a grant-in-aid to SN for scientific research from the Ministry of Education, Culture, Sport, Science, and Technology, Japan.

References

Asato, S. & N. Doi, 1999. *Okinawajinwa Dokokara Kitaka* [*Where did the Okinawan People Originate?*]. Naha: Border. [In Japanese.]

Bandelt, H.-J. & A.W. Dress, 1992. Split decomposition: a new and useful approach to phylogenetic analysis of distance data. *Molecular Phylogenetics and Evolution* 1, 242–52.

Bannai, M., J. Ohashi, S. Harihara, *et al.*, 2000. Analysis of HLA genes and haplotypes in Ainu (from Hokkaido, northern Japan) supports the premise that they descent from Upper Paleolithic populations of East Asia. *Tissue Antigens* 55, 128–39.

Hammer, M.F. & S. Horai, 1995. Y chromosomal DNA variation and the peopling of Japan. *American Journal of Human Genetics* 56, 951–62.

Hanihara, K., 1991. Dual structure model for the population history of the Japanese. *Japan Review* 2, 1–33.

Imamura, K., 1996. *Prehistoric Japan*. Honolulu (HI): University of Hawaii Press.

Li, S.-L., T. Yamamoto, T. Yoshimoto, *et al.*, 2005. Phylogenetic relationship of the populations within and around Japan using 105 short tandem repeat polymorphic loci. *Human Genetics* 118(6), 695–707.

Omoto, K. & N. Saitou, 1997. Genetic origins of the Japanese: a partial support for the 'dual structure hypothesis'. *American Journal of Physical Anthropology* 102(4), 437–46.

Saitou, N., 2005. DNA *Kara Mita Nihonnjin* [*Japanese Viewed from DNA*]. Tokyo: Chikuma Shobo. [In Japanese.]

Saitou, N. & M. Nei, 1987. The neighbor-joining method: a new method for reconstructing phylogenetic trees. *Molecular Biology and Evolution* 4(4), 406–25.

Saitou, N., K. Tokunaga & K. Omoto, 1992. Genetic affinities of human populations, in *Isolation, Migration, and Health: 33rd Symposium Volume of the Society for the Study of Human Biology*, eds. D.F. Roberts, N. Fujiki & K. Torizuka. NewYork (NY): Cambridge University Press, 118–29.

Tajima, A., M. Hayami, K. Tokunaga, *et al.*, 2003. Genetic origins of the Ainu inferred from combined DNA analyses of maternal and paternal lineages. *Journal of Human Genetics* 49, 187–93.

Tanaka, M., V.M. Cabrera, A.M. Gonzalez, *et al.*, 2004. Mitochondrial genome variation in eastern Asia and the peopling of Japan. *Genome Research* 14, 1832–50.

Vovin, A. & T. Osada (eds.), 2003. *Perspectives on the Origin of the Japanese Language*. (Nichibunken Japanese Studies Series 31.) Kyoto: International Research Center for Japanese Studies. [In English and Japanese.]

Yanagita, K., 1961. *Kaijo no Michi* [*Sea Road*]. Tokyo: Chikuma Shobo. [In Japanese.]

Yasumoto, B. & M. Honda, 1978. *Nihongo No Tanjo* [*Emergence of the Japanese Language*]. Tokyo: Taishukan Shoten. [In Japanese.]

Chapter 10

Reconstruction of the Prehistory of Greenland Eskimos from Genetic Data

Shuichi Matsumura & Peter Forster

According to the archaeological records, the colonization of Greenland from North Alaska occurred within the past 5000 years. The aim of this study is to infer the population dynamics, especially the founding population size, of Greenland Eskimos from genetic data. Consulting the historical family trees of Polar Eskimos of North Greenland, we firstly determined recent generation intervals and effective population size. We found that the average mother–daughter interval was 27.0 years, while the average father–son interval was 32.1 years. The ratio of the effective size to the census size was about 0.7 and 0.5 for mitochondrial DNA and Y-chromosomal DNA, respectively. Simulation of the change in the allele frequency suggested that Y-chromosomal DNA lineages may change proportions by genetic drift a little faster than mitochondrial DNA lineages in the Polar Eskimo population. To penetrate further into prehistory, we carried out coalescent simulations using published archaeological and genetic information as well as the parameter values determined above. The simulations based on a typical scenario showed a founding size of c. 200 as the most likely, with a large confidence interval of [31, 990]. Our sensitivity analyses showed that the inference of the founding population size considerably depended on model assumptions.

Introduction

The colonization of Greenland is one of the most recent demographic expansions of modern humans. Archaeological records suggest human presence in Greenland at 2500 BC. Several different cultures, e.g. Independence-I, II, or Dorset, have been recognized. A distinct culture called the Thule or neo-Eskimo culture appeared in Greenland by AD 1200. The Thule is characterized by maritime activities such as whale hunting. It is seen in a wide area of the coastal Arctic, from Siberia (around the Chukchi Peninsula), to Greenland. Many archaeologists assume a population migration in relation to the rapid spread of the Thule culture. The location and time of the origin of the neo-Eskimos is still debatable (Dames 1984; Maxwell 1985), but they appeared to emerge in North Alaska around Point Barrow c. AD 900–1000. Then the culture spread eastward very rapidly within one or two centuries (Maxwell 1985).

Mitochondrial DNA (mtDNA) data from people living in high latitudes of North America show a sign of recent demographic expansion after a population bottleneck. The four major mtDNA types, A, B, C, D are commonly found among Amerindian-speaking people from North to South America, whereas Na Dene- and Eskimo-Aleut-speakers in North America almost exclusively have the A2 type (Forster *et al.* 1996; Schurr & Sherry 2004). This suggests that these peoples experienced a recent population bottleneck whereby mtDNA diversity was lost. One possibility is that populations that formerly inhabited Beringia expanded into northern North America after the LGM, and gave rise to Eskimo-Aleuts and Na Dene Indians (Forster 2004; Schurr & Sherry 2004). Eskimos might have experienced a further bottleneck because they lack some minor types (e.g. D2) shared by Aleut- and Na Dene-speakers. A founder analysis of Siberian and Greenlandic Eskimo mtDNA suggested that they derived from a source population 2000 years ago

(Saillard *et al.* 2000). Unfortunately, it is difficult to say whether this corresponds to the Thule (neo-Eskimo) migration or a large-scale population event that pre-dated the neo-Eskimos, because of the large standard error (1400 years) of this genetic date.

An analysis of Y-chromosomal DNA exhibited an entirely new facet of the genetic history of Greenland Eskimos (Bosch *et al.* 2003). Out of 69 samples analysed, 40 (58%) Y DNA are highly likely to have a recent European origin. This contrasts with the fact that no European trace was found in 82 mtDNA samples (Saillard *et al.* 2000). There are two potential sources for European DNA types: one is Danish–Norwegian immigration since the eighteenth century, and the other is Norse settlement which disappeared when the climate deteriorated around 500–600 years ago (Pringle 1997; Lynnerup 1998).

The speed of development in methods of population genetic analysis based on likelihood is impressive, and researchers are starting to apply these methods to inference of human demographic history (Beaumont 2004). The objective of this study is to infer the demographic prehistory of Greenland Eskimos from genetic data, and to examine factors influencing such inference. We first estimated values for some important parameters in population genetics by an analysis of genealogical records from the Polar Eskimos in North Greenland. We then carried out coalescent simulations to estimate the founding population size for Greenlanders.

Analysis of the Polar Eskimo genealogy

The Polar Eskimos, who live in the Thule District of North Greenland, are the only hunter-gatherer population, to our knowledge, who can offer precise genealogical records spanning several generations, from the 1800s until 1974 (Gilberg *et al.* 1978; Edwards 1992a). These records provide us with a valuable opportunity to measure actual values of some important parameters of population genetics in human populations. We estimated the values of the two important parameters, generation time T and the ratio of the effective population size to census size (N_e/N_a) (Matsumura & Forster 2008). On the one hand, such information from the Polar Eskimos is useful for the study of genetic prehistory of Greenland Eskimos themselves. Additionally, it is valuable to learn about the variation of these key parameters among human populations. The environment, physical characteristics and culture of Eskimos is very different from those of Europeans. If any of these factors have a great impact on these parameters then we should see it in the Eskimos. If however there is little effect, we are

more justified in using the modern parameters for prehistoric peoples.

The first estimate of Polar Eskimo population size reported about 150 or less in the mid-nineteenth century (Gilberg 1976). It was around 200–300 in the late nineteenth and the early twentieth century, then increased to 400 in 1959. Genealogical information of the people was collected and published by a resident physician and his family (Gilberg *et al.* 1978). The data base includes 1614 individuals who were born between *c.* 1805 and 1974. Edwards (1992a) studied the basic structure of their genealogy from a viewpoint of population genetics. Following his definition, 225 individuals whose parents do not appear in the data base are regarded as founders.

Maternal and paternal generation intervals in the Polar Eskimos

For generation time, the analysis was restricted to those who had finished their reproduction (Females: <50 years, Males: <69 years) or died before 1974. The average mother–daughter interval in the Polar Eskimo genealogy was 27.0 years, while the average father–son interval was 32.1 years (Matsumura & Forster 2008). These are similar to those from recent studies which investigated long-term genealogical records of Europeans (Denmark/Germany: Forster 1996; Canada: Tremblay & Vézina 2000; Iceland: Helgason *et al.* 2003). All these studies suggested that the human generation time is longer than previously assumed in population genetic models. The generation time looks rather consistent regardless of cultural and environmental differences among human societies (Fenner 2005).

The effective population size in the Polar Eskimos — a gene-flow simulation

We need the ratio of effective to actual population size (N_e/N) to apply population genetic models to real populations because inputs/outputs of population genetics models are basically in the form of the effective population size. Most previous studies estimated the effective size N_e in human populations either by analysing demographic data or by analysing genetic data (Frankham 1995). The fact that we know actual family trees of Eskimos in addition to the birth records enables us to calculate N_e directly by simulating changes in the allele frequency through the genealogy (gene-flow simulation: Edwards 1992b; allele dropping simulation: Heyer 1999).

Two common alleles were assigned to the founders and the frequency of the alleles was traced over time. This simulation was repeated 100,000 times. N_e was estimated from the increase of the genetic variance in a period from 1850 to 1940 when the genealogical data were considered as reliable enough. The increase was adjusted to the one per generation time for effective sizes for mtDNA ($N_{e\,Mit}$) and Y ($N_{e\,Y}$).

The estimated $N_{e\,Mit}$ and $N_{e\,Y}$ during the period between 1850 and 1940 was 107.6 and 79.4, respectively. If we use the actual population size in 1940 (141 females and 158 males based on the genealogy), the estimates for $N_{e\,Mit}/N_f$ and $N_{e\,Y}/N_m$ were 0.76 and 0.50, respectively. The main reason of the smaller N_e/N ratio in Y than in mtDNA is a greater variance in the offspring number among males (mean number of sons: 1.26, variance: 2.66) than among females (mean number of daughters: 1.28, variance 1.98). We also can calculate N_e/N analytically from these means and variances. Using Hill's (1979) formula with an adjustment suggested by Crow & Morton (1955), we obtained $N_{e\,Mit}/N_f = 0.65$ and $N_{e\,Y}/N_m = 0.59$. Although the estimates from the gene-flow simulation would be the most realistic values if we had a perfect genealogical record, the Eskimo genealogy contains some uncertain records even in this period. It seems reasonable to conclude that the ratio of the effective size to the census size is about 0.7 ($N_{e\,Mit}/N_f$) and 0.5 ($N_{e\,Y}/N_m$) in this population.

Inferring the founding population size for Greenland Eskimos

Murray-McIntosh *et al.* (1998) estimated the Maori founding population size using mtDNA data. They used a three-step forward simulation. In the first step, a maternal founding population was created by a random sampling from the frequencies of the 11 types observed in eastern Polynesia. In the second step, this founding population grew exponentially over 30 generations to 50,000. The third step was a sampling where 54 individuals were sampled from the resulting population and compared with the observed frequency of types in the present New Zealand Maori. They concluded that the founding population size was likely to be 50–100 females.

The three steps of their simulation were integrated into one in our backward simulation. We started with samples from the modern population and simulated genealogies backwards in time. When we reached the founding population, we allocated an mtDNA type to each ancestor randomly according to the mtDNA frequencies in the source population. The simulation program written by the authors is based on a discrete-generation coalescent method, instead of continuous-time approximation methods which have been used by many authors (e.g. Hudson 1990). The former is slower than the latter, but it has several advantages (Laval & Excoffier 2004). For example, it

works better when the population size is quite small because it allows multiple coalescent and/or migration events per generation. It has the potential to incorporate complicated demographic scenarios. This is the reason why we developed original simulation programs instead of using powerful software available for inference of past population history using Markov Chain Monte Carlo sampling or Importance Sampling techniques (BATWING, genetree etc.).

We used published Greenland Eskimo DNA data which contains mtDNA data from 82 individuals (Saillard *et al.* 2000) and Y-chromosomal DNA data from 69 individuals (Bosch *et al.* 2003). Although no European lineages were found in the mtDNA sample, a considerable proportion of the Y sample (58±6%) was identified as European. We restricted our analysis to the Eskimo lineages (29 individuals) and the binary markers.

We determined the composition of the assumed (Alaskan) source population in the following way. The candidate source types are all the mtDNA types seen in the present-day Greenland Eskimos and in Siberian Eskimos and Chukchi (Starikovskaya *et al.* 1998; Karafet *et al.* 1999; Lell *et al.* 2002). Firstly, we assumed that the source population included all the mtDNA types shared between the present-day Greenland and Siberian Eskimos (including Chukchi). We further assumed that the source population also contained types shared between either of the two and other Eskimo-Aleuts or Na Dene. The proportion of each type in the source population was proportional to the average between that of the current Greenland and Siberian Eskimos.

When we simulated mtDNA genealogies, we started from the Greenland Eskimo sample ($n = 82$) and created genealogies backwards in time until the founding age (e.g. 1000 years). The gene lineages did not usually coalesce into a single lineage but into several founding lineages. The mtDNA types of the founding lineages were determined by random sampling from the source population. Then, we simulated the mutational process along the genealogy obtained. We randomly assigned mutations to each branch according to a Poisson distribution. We assumed an infinite-sites model and an average mutation rate of one per 20,180 years (Forster *et al.* 1996). After mutations were added, the sample contained the founder types and their derivative types. We recorded the proportion of simulations where the DNA composition of the simulated sample coincided with the real sample. We assumed no mutation had occurred in the Y-chromosomal binary markers during this short period and followed only the change in the frequencies through time.

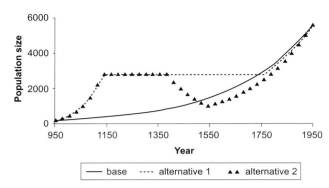

Figure 10.1. *Population dynamic scenarios for Greenland Eskimos. This example starts with a founder size of 200 females and ends with 5600: 'base' represents a simple exponential growth. In 'alternative 1', the population grows rapidly (r = 0.4) until it reaches 2800. It grows again in the last four generations (c. 100 years). In 'alternative 2', the population size declines from 2800 (1383) to 1000 (1545).*

The population size in Greenland in 1950 was about 20,000, c. 80% of which were Eskimos (Dames 1980). It is difficult to obtain reliable estimates on the population size in the past few centuries. The population size of Greenland in 1721 was estimated as 10,000 (Mooney 1928, cited in Crawford 1998) though official registry records suggest a smaller value (Dames 1984). The registry records of Western, Eastern, or Polar Eskimos do not show a clear decline since the eighteenth–nineteenth centuries (Gilberg 1976; Dames 1984), although drastic population declines were reported for many Native American populations including St Lawrence Island Eskimos (Crawford 1998). As a simple scenario, we assumed exponential growth from the founder size to 5600 females or 4000 males (i.e. 8000 actual females or males in 1950) (Fig. 10.1, base). Then, we examined the effect of rapid population growth during the initial stage of colonization and the effect of a population decline.

Result of the simulation

We started with a basic set of simulations under a simple scenario. The founder population left the source population c. 1000 years ago (37 generations for maternal lines and 31 generations for paternal lines). The population grew exponentially from the beginning, and there was no sub-structure within the population.

Figure 10.2 shows the likelihood of the founding population size for females (mtDNA) and males (Y-chromosomal binary markers). Both graphs show a single peak (mtDNA: 100, Y: 30). As the simulation

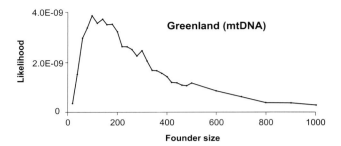

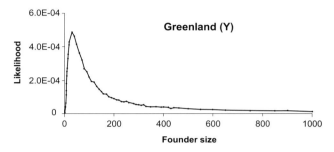

Figure 10.2. *Likelihood of the founding population size. We repeated 10,000,000 (Y) or 100,000,000,000 (mtDNA) simulations for each founder size and counted the number of simulations that yielded the pattern observed in Greenland Eskimos.*

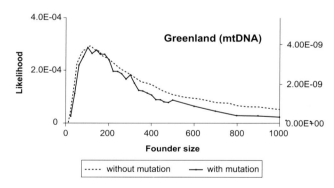

Figure 10.3. *Likelihood of the founding population size when mutation is taken into account (solid line, the right axis) or is ignored (dotted line, the left axis).*

results are shown in the form of effective numbers, these are equivalent to 140 actual females and 60 actual males if we use the values obtained from the Polar Eskimos ($N_f = N_{e\,Mit} / 0.7$ and $N_m = N_{e\,Y} / 0.5$). These results suggest that the founder size of current Greenland Eskimos may have been small. Unfortunately, the confidence intervals are large for both females and males. If we consider the effective sizes for which the log-likelihood is within two units of the maximum likelihood as approximate 95% confidence interval (Stephens 2001), we obtain [25, 735] for the female and [6, 255] for the male effective size.

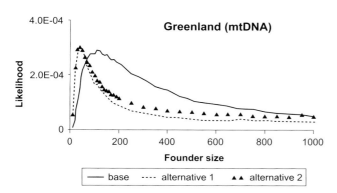

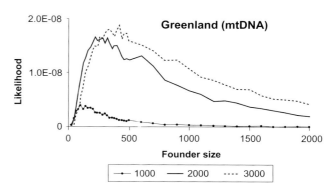

Figure 10.4. *Likelihood of the founding population size when we adopt one of the alternative population dynamics. Mutation is not considered here. Alternative 1: a rapid population growth at the beginning; alternative 2: a rapid population growth at the beginning + a population decline at a later stage. For details, see text and Figure 10.1.*

Figure 10.5. *Likelihood of the founding population size when we assume different founding ages (1000, 2000, and 3000 years before present).*

Although we considered mutation in the simulation using mtDNA, it is possible to ignore mutation like in the simulations using Y binary markers (or those of the Maori case). In other words, we just follow the change in the proportion of each 'haplogroup' and check the agreement at a haplogroup level between the simulation result and real data. In the Greenland mtDNA case, the peak of the likelihood function did not change when we disregarded mutation (Fig. 10.3), but the 95% confidence interval became even larger. In other words, we utilize less information in the data if we do not take mutation into account.

Sensitivity analyses

We investigated which assumptions or parameter values could change the simulation result drastically.

Population dynamics

The assumption of simple exponential growth after the colonization may not be valid in many occasions. We tested two alternative scenarios which appear more realistic in Greenland. Firstly, we assumed that the founding population experienced a high growth rate close to the intrinsic growth rate (we used $r = 0.4$) just after the colonization (alternative 1 in Fig. 10.1). Furthermore, we added a population decline at a later stage (alternative 2 in Fig. 10.1) due to a cold climate since 600 years ago, which is indicated by Greenland ice core data (O'Brien *et al.* 1995). In fact, archaeological records suggest that this climatic impact is likely to be a main cause of the extinction of the Norse

settlements on Greenland's west coast (Pringle 1997; Lynnerup 1998).

Figure 10.4 shows the likelihood of the founding population size inferred from the mtDNA data when we consider these two alternative demographic scenarios. The peak of the likelihood functions shifted towards smaller sizes. This suggests that the result is likely to be an overestimate if we apply a uniform exponential growth model to a population which experienced a higher growth rate at the beginning. The population decline we assumed in the alternative-2 scenario had a small effect on the likelihood across a range of large founder sizes (>100). A population decline potentially flattens the likelihood curve as it wipes out traces of the preceding period of a larger population size. It could have a larger effect if we assume more severe population declines.

Founder age

We have chosen 1000 years as the age of the founding event mainly on the basis of archaeological evidence for the emergence of the Thule culture. However, this may not be the case. A founder analysis of a mtDNA HVS-I network of Greenland and Siberian Eskimos suggested an older age (2000 years). The peaks of the likelihood function shift to a larger founding population size if we assume older founding ages (Fig. 10.5). It is noteworthy that absolute likelihood values are higher when we assume 2000 or 3000 years than when we assume 1000 years. This is expected from the fact that the founder age analysis using mtDNA HVS-I mutations yields a mean value of 2000 years (Saillard *et al.* 2000).

Identification of founder types/proportions in the source populations

Identifying founder types is usually quite a hard task for researchers. A small change in the assumptions about the composition of the source population can cause a large difference in the results. For example, if we assume that the genetic composition of the source population is almost identical to that of the subject population, simulations will not yield an obvious peak in the likelihood curve of population sizes. Researchers have to examine the genetic data of the relevant populations very carefully before determining the founder types. One way to make this procedure less arbitrary and more quantitative is to include all the relevant populations into the simulation using multiple-population models. One the other hand, such multiple-population models require more parameters and assumptions on which we do not have sufficient information. In addition, detailed multiple-population simulations may be computationally very expensive.

Conclusions

Colonization of islands is an attractive subject for those who wants to reconstruct past population histories from genetic data (Falush Chapter 12, this volume). It is often the case that islands lack meaningful spatial structure within them, and a relatively small number of discrete events are involved in their histories. Thus, inference of founding population size using DNA data and computer simulations is a promising field. However, we must be aware of their limits at the present stage. In particular, extremely large confidence intervals are one of the most discouraging points we see in the present study. One may think that the only thing we can do is to reject some extreme scenarios (e.g. colonization by a single boat). However, we do not necessarily take such a pessimistic view about the future. The large confidence intervals mainly come from the extremely low genetic diversity of the assumed source population — Alaska (this study) or Polynesia (Murray-McIntosh *et al.* 1998) — probably due to earlier severe bottlenecks. When the diversity of the source population is high (see Forster *et al.* Chapter 7, this volume), confidence intervals can be small enough to distinguish between several plausible scenarios. The confidence intervals will shrink when data from multiple genetic loci become available (e.g. Hey 2005).

Collaboration between geneticists and archaeologists will play a key role in this field. Information extractable from genetic data of present-day people is often quite limited. Without any other independent information, we can discern only basic features of the population dynamics such as a mean size of the population during a certain period of the past. Archaeological evidence enables us to make reasonable assumptions about population dynamics and founding age. Recent studies on circumpolar animals suggested that DNA extracted from ancient materials could be of great help to reconstruct the past population dynamics on a fine scale (e.g. Shapiro *et al.* 2004). The more external information we have, the better inference we can draw from population genetic simulations.

Recently, Helgason and colleagues (2006) reported new mtDNA data from Greenland Eskimos (*n* = 299) as well as Canadian Eskimos (*n* = 96) and suggested Thule groups coming from Alaska interbred with existing Dorset people. Simulations using a larger amount of data will be helpful to reconstruct the history of human migration in this region.

References

Beaumont, M., 2004. Recent developments in genetic data analysis: what can they tell us about human demographic history? *Heredity* 92, 365–79.

Bosch, E., F. Calafell, Z.H. Rosser, *et al.*, 2003. High level of male-biased Scandinavian admixture in Greenlandic Inuit shown by Y-chromosomal analysis. *Human Genetics* 112, 353–63.

Crawford, M.H., 1998. *The Origins of Native Americans: Evidence from Anthropological Genetics*. Cambridge: Cambridge University Press.

Crow, J.F. & N.E. Morton, 1955. Measurement of gene frequency drift in small populations. *Evolution* 9, 202–14.

Dames, D. (ed.), 1984. *Handbook of North American Indians*, vol. 5: *Arctic*. Washington (DC): Smithsonian Institute.

Dumond, D.E., 1984. Prehistory: summary, in *Handbook of North American Indians*, vol. 5: *Arctic*, ed. D. Dames. Washington (DC): Smithsonian Institute, 72–9.

Edwards, A.W.F., 1992a. The structure of the Polar Eskimo genealogy. *Human Heredity* 42, 242–52.

Edwards, A.W.F., 1992b. Expected number of alleles in the Polar Eskimo population (Abstract), in *Proceedings of the XVI International Biometric Conference, Hamilton, New Zealand.* (Contributed Papers.) Hamilton: University of Waikato, 106.

Fenner, J.N., 2005. Cross-cultural estimation of the human generation interval for use in genetics-based population divergence studies. *American Journal of Physical Anthropology* 128, 415–23.

Forster, P., 1996. Dispersal and Differentiation of Modern *Homo sapiens* Analyzed with Mitochondrial DNA. Unpublished PhD thesis, University of Hamburg.

Forster, P., 2004. Ice Ages and the mitochondrial DNA chronology of human dispersals: a review. *Philosophical Transactions of the Royal Society, London,* B 359, 255–64.

Forster, P., R. Harding, A. Torroni & H.-J. Bandelt, 1996. Origin and evolution of native American mtDNA variation: reappraisal. *American Journal of Human Genetics* 59, 935–45.

Frankham, R., 1995. Effective population size /adult population size ratios in wildlife: a review. *Genetic Research, Cambridge* 66, 95–107.

Gilberg, R., 1976. Polar Eskimo population, Thule district, North Greenland. *Meddelelser om Grønland* 203/3.

Gilberg, A., L. Gilberg, R. Gilberg & M. Holm, 1978. Polar Eskimo genealogy. *Meddelelser om Grønland* 203/4.

Helgason, A., B. Hrafnkelsson, J.R. Gulcher, R. Ward & K. Stefánsson, 2003. A population-wide coalescent analysis of Icelandic matrilineal and patrilineal genealogies: evidence for a faster evolutionary rate of mtDNA lineage than Y chromosomes. *American Journal of Human Genetics* 72, 1370–88.

Helgason, A., G. Pálsson, H.S. Pedersen, *et al.*, 2006. MtDNA variation in Inuit populations of Greenland and Canada: migration history and population structure. *American Journal of Physical Anthropology* 130, 123–34.

Hey, J., 2005. On the number of New World founders: a population genetic portrait of the peopling of the Americas. *PLoS Biology* 3(6), e193.

Heyer, E., 1999. One founder/one gene hypothesis in a new expanding population: Saguenay (Quebec, Canada). *Human Biology* 71, 99–109.

Hill, W.G., 1979. A note on effective population size with overlapping generations. *Genetics* 92, 317–22.

Hudson, R.R., 1990. Gene genealogies and the coalescent process, in *Oxford Surveys in Evolutionary Biology*, vol. 7, ed. D. Futuyma. Oxford: Oxford University Press, 1–44.

Karafet, T.M., S.L. Zegura, O. Posukh, *et al.*, 1999. Ancestral Asian source(s) of New World Y-chromosome founder haplotypes. *American Journal of Human Genetics* 64, 817–31.

Laval, G.L. & L. Excoffier, 2004. SIMCOAL 2.0: a program to simulate genomic diversity over large recombining regions in a subdivided population with a complex history. *Bioinformatics* 20, 2485–7.

Lell, J.T., R.I. Sukernik, Y.B. Starikovskaya, *et al.*, 2002. The dual origin and Siberian affinities of Native American Y chromosomes. *American Journal of Human Genetics* 70, 192–206.

Lynnerup, N., 1998. The Greenland Norse: a biological-anthropological study. *Meddelelser om Grønland, Man & Society* 24.

Matsumura, S. & P. Forster, 2008. Generation time and effective population size in Polar Eskimos. *Proceedings of the Royal Socety, Biological Sciences* B 275, 1501–8.

Maxwell, M.S., 1985. *Prehistory of the Eastern Arctic*. Orlando (FL): Academic Press.

Murray-McIntosh, R.P., B.J. Scrimshaw, P.J. Hatfield & D. Penny, 1998. Testing migration patterns and estimating founding population size in Polynesia by using human mtDNA sequences. *Proceedings of the National Academy of Sciences of the USA* 95, 9047–52.

O'Brien, S.R., P.A. Mayewski, L.D. Meeker, D.A. Meese, M.S. Twickler & S.I. Whitlow, 1995. Complexity of Holocene climate as reconstructed from a Greenland ice core. *Science* 270, 1962–4.

Pringle, H., 1997. Death in Norse Greenland. *Science* 275, 924–6.

Saillard, J., P. Forster, N. Lynnerup, H.-J. Bandelt & S. Nørby, 2000. MtDNA variation among Greenland Eskimos: the edge of the Beringian expansion. *American Journal of Human Genetics* 67, 718–26.

Schurr, T.G. & S.T. Sherry, 2004. Mitochondrial DNA and Y chromosome diversity and the peopling of the Americas: evolutionary and demographic evidence. *American Journal of Human Genetics* 16, 420–39.

Shapiro, B., A.J. Drummond, A. Rambaut, *et al.*, 2004. Rise and fall of the Beringian steppe bison. *Science* 306, 1561–5.

Starikovskaya, Y.B., R.I. Sukernik, T.G. Schurr, A.M. Kogelnik & D.C. Wallace, 1998. MtDNA diversity in Chukchi and Siberian Eskimos: implications for the genetic history of ancient Beringia and the peopling of the New World. *American Journal of Human Genetics* 63, 1473–91.

Stephens, M., 2001. Inference under the coalescent, in *Handbook of Statistical Genetics*, eds. D.J. Balding, M. Bishop & C. Cannings. New York (NY): John Wiley & Sons, 213–38.

Tremblay, M. & H. Vézina, 2000. New estimates of intergenerational time intervals for the calculation of age and origins of mutations. *American Journal of Human Genetics* 66, 651–8.

Part IV

Methodological Challenges in Ancestral Inference

Chapter 11

Incorporating Environmental Heterogeneity in Spatially-explicit Simulations of Human Genetic Diversity

Nicolas Ray, Mathias Currat & Laurent Excoffier

We recently developed a simulation framework (SPLATCHE) to model the past demography of human population and the resulting genetic diversity at neutral markers. Additional to range expansions and population subdivisions, we increase here the realism of our simulations by incorporating spatial and temporal heterogeneity of the environment. This heterogeneity can be translated into maps of carrying capacities (maximum density of individuals) and frictions (difficulty of moving) that will in turn influence the size of local populations and the direction and the intensity of migrations. We have considered the influence of several environmental variables: the type of vegetation directly affects the available resource and therefore the carrying capacities; streams and coastlines act as migration corridors with higher carrying capacities than the surrounding environment; a rough topography may also drastically influence migrations. We discuss in this paper each of these environmental variables and how one can estimate carrying capacities and friction values for each of them. We also present an innovative way of considering dynamic changes of vegetation through temporal vegetation heterogeneity. Finally, we examine how environmental heterogeneity might affect genetic differentiation of human populations, and discuss the limitations and perspectives of our approach.

The past demography of modern humans has certainly been complex, with a series of range expansions, contractions, and admixture events (Excoffier 2002). Deciphering the temporal and spatial patterns of these past demographic events is an exciting but very challenging task. Along with archaeological and palaeoanthropological data, contemporary genetic data at neutral markers can be used to infer past demographic events. One way to achieve this is to model genetic diversity under several demographic models and to compare simulated to observed data. This approach has been used to infer signals of past population growth, bottlenecks and relative levels of gene flows among continents (e.g. Eller 2001; Harpending *et al.* 1998; Slatkin & Hudson 1991). However, there has been a recent awareness that most of these models were not realistic enough as they were not taking into account important aspects such as population subdivisions, the progressive nature of range expansion, and the interactions between landscape features and migrating individuals. In an effort to incorporate more realism into spatially explicit modelling of past demography, we have implemented the SPLATCHE simulation framework (Currat *et al.* 2004). This modelling tool first allowed us to study the effects of spatial expansion and varying levels of gene flow on genetic diversity in a simple subdivided square world (Ray *et al.* 2003). A further step towards more realistic simulations was the incorporation of the geographical contours of the continent. At the European continental scale, we used these contours to study the interactions between early modern humans and Neanderthals (Currat & Excoffier 2004), as well as those between hunter-gatherer and farmer populations during the European Neolithic transition (Currat & Excoffier 2005). For both studies, range expansions and competition between populations were implemented (see Currat *et al.* this volume).

All the models that we have discussed so far considered a spatially uniform environment, and therefore an evenly distributed population over the surface of the simulated world. However, the spatial heterogeneity of the environment is evident in most areas of the World. This heterogeneity translates into various availabilities of resources for human populations, which may impact their demography (growth and migrations) and, as a result, their genetic differentiation. Similarly, temporal variations of the environment at continental scale have also affected these populations through a series of range contractions, range expansion, demographic bottlenecks or demographic expansions (Excoffier 2002). The temporal heterogeneity of resources is therefore an additional level of realism which warrants consideration. With the recent availability of global information layers that can be easily manipulated in Geographical Information Systems (GIS), it is now possible to merge ecological information from many sources in order to build informative maps. These environmental maps can then be linked to more realistic demographic models. A first attempt to use spatial environmental heterogeneity within our simulation framework is found in Ray *et al.* (2005), and is further detailed in Excoffier *et al.* (this volume), where various levels of spatial heterogeneity are compared using multilocus genetic data.

However, the incorporation of environmental heterogeneity is not straightforward and requires that one decides on (i) the type of environmental heterogeneity one should consider; (ii) the way variations in environmental heterogeneity should be translated into demographic parameters, and (iii) the values of these parameters and their associated uncertainties. The aim of this paper is to discuss these issues in the framework of our spatially-explicit model of past human demography implemented in SPLATCHE (Currat *et al.* 2004). We shall focus on the spatial and environmental contexts of the old World during the last 120,000 years, which corresponds approximately to the period of evolution of modern humans (Stringer 2002). We start by discussing static environmental heterogeneity, and continue by presenting an innovative way of incorporating temporal variations of resources, so-called dynamic environmental heterogeneity. Next, we examine the expected impact of these new models on the simulated genetic diversity. Finally, we discuss current data limitations and perspectives.

Simulation framework, carrying capacities and frictions

Technical descriptions of our simulation framework called SPLATCHE can be found elsewhere (Currat *et al.* 2004; and this volume), and we only discuss below specific aspects linked to the concerns of this paper. SPLATCHE is a 2D stepping-stone model where sub-populations (demes) are located on the intersection of a regular lattice. Each deme can hold independent ecological information under the form of a carrying capacity term and a friction term (see below). A typical simulation starts by simulating the demography (densities and migrations between demes) of the sub-populations forward in time. One or several origins of dispersal can be chosen, which influences the dynamic of the following range expansions. The resulting demographic information is stored into a data base, which is used to simulate genetic diversity by a backward coalescent process. An entire simulation can therefore be summarized as the translation of ecological information into demographic information, in turn translated into genetic information.

During the demographic simulations, the density of the demes is locally logistically regulated, with intrinsic rate of growth r, and carrying capacity K. Logistic growth is widely used in ecology (Tsoularis & Wallace 2002), but its use in human population dynamics requests some assumptions (Dewar 1984) which are that: (1) K is a function of the productive capacity (Cp) of the environment; (2) the realized (observed) population density N is at equilibrium ($N = K$); (3) there is a direct relationship between a given observed population density (N_i) and the productive capacity of the occupied surface (Cp_i). In other words, one needs to assume that there is a continuous feedback between the resource consumers and the density of these resources (vegetal or animal) that leads to a population/environment equilibrium. This equilibrium implies that hunter-gatherers consciously or unconsciously evaluate the carrying capacity of their environment and implement various mechanisms (e.g. emigrations, infanticide: see Kelly 1995) to stay below this threshold. When the level of resource varies either spatially or temporally, it therefore implies that populations will react accordingly and will adjust their densities. This relatively simple model has been criticized by Read & Leblanc (2003), who observe that human populations often stabilize well below K. The stabilized population size is further described by Read & Leblanc (2003) as a complex function of the distribution and the seasonality of resources, the social organization of groups of individuals, and the between-group competition. The model proposed by Read & Leblanc (2003) is certainly more realistic than the simple logistic model. However, its calibration at our temporal and spatial scales of interest is extremely difficult (see Ray 2003a). Moreover, the fact that N stabilized below K in some contemporary populations can be reconciled by using directly the stabilized carrying capacity in the simple logistic model. Although simple, we believe that the logistic model still remains a useful model to relate the available resources in a given type of environment to the local population dynamic.

The friction value F is another key demographic property of each deme. The friction associated to a deme represents the relative difficulty of moving through it, and friction values are used to compute directional probabilities of migration, assuming that movement preferentially occurs toward areas of relatively lower friction (see Excoffier *et al.* this volume). While empirical data can be used to derive relative carrying capacities among different types of environment, much less information is available to derive relative friction values.

Incorporation of static environmental heterogeneity

To incorporate heterogeneity in spatially explicit simulations, we first need to choose the environmental variables that can best reflect changes in densities, migration intensities and directions. One of the important factor that can affect densities is the quantity of food that can be extracted from the surrounding environment, and several authors have empirically demonstrated this link (e.g. Baumhoff 1958; 1963; Belovsky 1988; Rogers 1969; Thompson 1966). The quantity and quality of food available to HG groups are tightly linked to the types of vegetation present in their immediate environment. The efficiency of gathering/collecting behaviour (e.g. fruits, seeds, roots) indeed mainly depends on the available plant species, and so does the composition of animal species that can be hunted or foraged.

We start by discussing how vegetation can be taken into account, and continue by discussing three other types of landscape elements that may have played a major role in past human demography, namely the mountainous regions, the river network and the coastlines. The latter two linear elements deal with aquatic resources, and could also be considered as both potential corridors of migration or barriers to dispersal, depending on the geographic location and the considered period.

Vegetation
Estimating prehistoric HG densities in various environments is difficult. Attempts to use densities of archaeological artefacts at a continental scale have been restricted to North America (Steele *et al.* 1998). At the Old World scale, we have used reviews of ethnographic density data in contemporary HG groups.

The synthetic work of Kelly (1995) gives estimation of population densities on more than 100 ethnic groups. More recently, Binford (2001) listed the demographic and environmental variables of 390 HG ethnical groups. These two studies, along with a few other data sets, were summarized by Marlowe (2005).

By using these data, one implicitly assumes that contemporary estimates of HG demographic parameters can be extrapolated to past populations, which may be abusive since virtually all HG in the ethnographic record have complex technologies compared to early Palaeolithic groups. Moreover, they are also all (to a certain degree) in contact with agricultural or industrialized societies (Blurton Jones *et al.* 2002; Marlowe 2005; Spielmann & Eder 1994). This can positively affect their efficiency in extracting resources, and therefore their demography. Contrastingly, a majority of remaining HG populations are confined to unfavourable environments where carrying capacities are obviously limited. Uncertainties around estimations of HG population densities are therefore important. The consequences of these uncertainties on the output statistics our simulations can be studied within the framework of a sensitivity analysis.

By assuming that the type of vegetation determines the quantity of food resources that can be extracted, we can make the hypothesis that similar vegetation categories will harbour similar carrying capacities. Areas for which no empirical estimates of HG densities exist can therefore be attributed carrying capacity values which are taken from areas of similar vegetation for which data do exist. Getting maps of vegetation coverage at continental scales has therefore been an important step. Since no vegetation map was available for the Last Glacial Maximum period (see Ray 2003b for a discussion), we constructed one based on a several sources (Ray & Adams 2001). A similar map for the present climate but without significant human impacts (about 4000 years ago), so-called 'present potential', was also produced and made available online (Ray & Adams 2002). These two maps (presented in Fig. 11.1) take into account altitudinal zones and are therefore more realistic than previous similar maps (e.g. Adams & Faure 1997). Carrying capacity estimates for the various types of vegetation of these maps are found in Excoffier *et al.* (this volume).

Topography
Mountainous regions may have greatly impacted human migrations at the continental scale. High-altitude mountain chains such as the Alps or the Himalayas have certainly acted as strong barriers to migration, which has sometimes been taken into account in previous simulation studies (Barbujani *et*

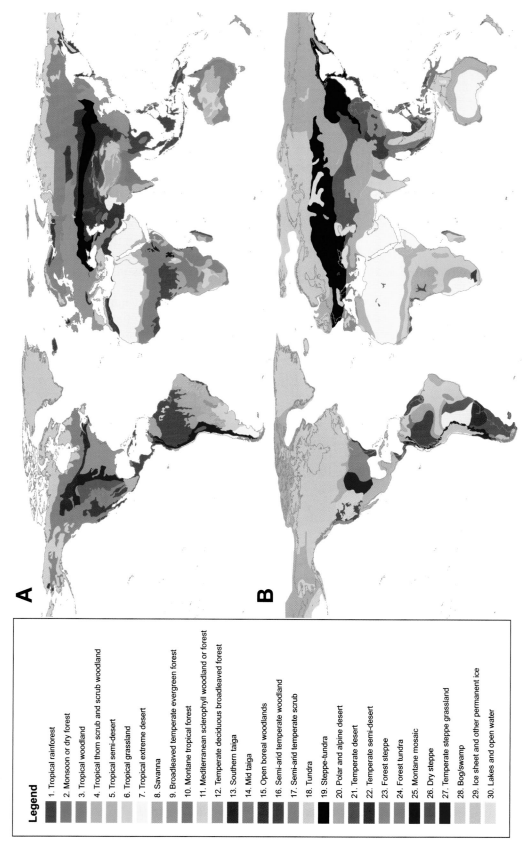

Figure 11.1. *GIS-based vegetation maps for the present potential period (around 4000 BP) (A) and the Last Glacial Maximum (between 25,000 and 15,000 BP) (B). For (B) a sea-level drop of 120 metres is taken into account.*

Legend

1. Tropical rainforest
2. Monsoon or dry forest
3. Tropical woodland
4. Tropical thorn scrub and scrub woodland
5. Tropical semi-desert
6. Tropical grassland
7. Tropical extreme desert
8. Savanna
9. Broadleaved temperate evergreen forest
10. Montane tropical forest
11. Mediterranean sclerophyll woodland or forest
12. Temperate deciduous broadleaved forest
13. Southern taiga
14. Mid taiga
15. Open boreal woodlands
16. Semi-arid temperate woodland
17. Semi-arid temperate scrub
18. Tundra
19. Steppe-tundra
20. Polar and alpine desert
21. Temperate desert
22. Temperate semi-desert
23. Forest steppe
24. Forest tundra
25. Montane mosaic
26. Dry steppe
27. Temperate steppe grassland
28. Bog/swamp
29. Ice sheet and other permanent ice
30. Lakes and open water

al. 1995; Mithen & Reed 2002). Other areas with less pronounced topography may also have been avoided by past populations, which may have favoured flatter areas. However, medium- or low-altitude mountains may also contain food resources of interest, as well as shelters not found in plains. In certain areas, an intermediate topography might therefore be favoured over flatter areas. It is very difficult to estimate to which degree and at what period the different range of topographic features have affected the directions of movements of past populations. In the absence of evidence, we have therefore made the hypothesis that the choice of movement depends on altitudinal gradients perceive by the migrants, and that they prefer moving in directions that minimize this gradient.

The consideration of topography in the modelling of the demography of past human populations can be approached in two ways: (1) mountainous regions susceptible to have played a role can be considered as non-crossable or with limited gene flow (e.g. Barbujani et al. 1995); (2) slope indexes can be calculated and used as a surrogate for the friction. Using standards GIS tools, these slopes are easily derived from a Digital Elevation Model (DEM) using the average maximum technique (Burrough 1986).

Once the slopes are obtained, a function linking slope index to the cost of movement must be defined. The energy cost linked to human walking has been studied by many authors in a physiological context (see Marble 1996). There are several applications of these cost relationship in archaeological studies, notably at regional scale to find ancient pathways linking villages (e.g. Bellavia 2001; Kantner 1996). At the scale of North America, Anderson & Gillam (2000) have used the squared slope index as an inversely proportional measure of movement preference for colonizing hunter-gatherers. However, one of the difficulties in using slope indexes is the resolution of the underlying DEM. It has been shown that extreme altitudinal gradients are rapidly erased by increasing the resolution of the data set (Gao 1998). At the continental scale, with typical deme size of 100 × 100 km, it becomes obvious that a single slope index summarizing the overall topography of the deme is meaningless, although it might pick up the steepest gradients of the major mountainous regions (see Fig. 11.2A). An alternative and more informative way of summarizing the topography of the landscape is to consider a 'roughness index' that represents the changes in altitude values within a given surface (a deme). We have therefore used here the standard deviation of the altitudes within a deme. This roughness value increases with both the degree of variation of the altitudes within a deme, and the mean altitude

of the deme. We assume here that human movements will preferentially be directed toward areas of low roughness. Another advantage of roughness indexes is that the range of values is much wider than with slopes, which gives a more discriminating measure among regions with very different topographic patterns (see Fig. 11.2B).

Streams

Riparian resources are made up of elements that can be directly extracted from streams (e.g fish, fresh water) and from their immediate environment, which is usually rich in plant species and which attracts various terrestrial animal species. This type of environment is therefore usually considered to sustain a relatively higher human density than surrounding terrestrial environments (e.g. Meltzer 1999). However, as pointed by Binford (2001, 167), the rare data on stream and river production do not allow one to get sound estimates of the quantity of resources available for past HG populations. Binford has nevertheless summarized his data on mean HG density per type of exploited resources. By only considering HG ethnic groups with a high degree of mobility, and a subsistence based only on hunting and gathering, the mean density for coastal and riparian groups is 2 to 5 times higher than that of groups exploiting terrestrial plants or animals (Binford 2001, 214–15). When these data are further stratified by climatic type, the same tendency is found for each climate type, with population densities increasing towards the equator. These results therefore justify to give a higher carrying capacity to coastal and riparian environments. Note however that these results are only trends that have a variance in certain regions, and that they do not allow one to get distinct estimates for marine, riparian and lake-side environments.

Rivers can not only increase carrying capacities, but they can also be considered as migration corridors. By acting as a linear landscape element with larger resources, a barrier to migration, or a fluvial transport, streams may have facilitated the dispersal of individuals over large distances (e.g. Anderson & Gillam 2000; Krings et al. 1999; Misra 2001; Tolan-Smith 2003).

The ArcWorld data set (ESRI 1992) provides us with hydrographical data at a 1:25 million-scale (see Fig. 11.2A). At the continental scale, we have chosen to only consider the major streams that probably had the most significant impact on human migrations. However, the choice of current stream configuration may not always be a good representation of the past configuration, but palaeohydrographic data are presently too scarce to take into account temporal changes in stream configuration. In practice, SPLATCHE

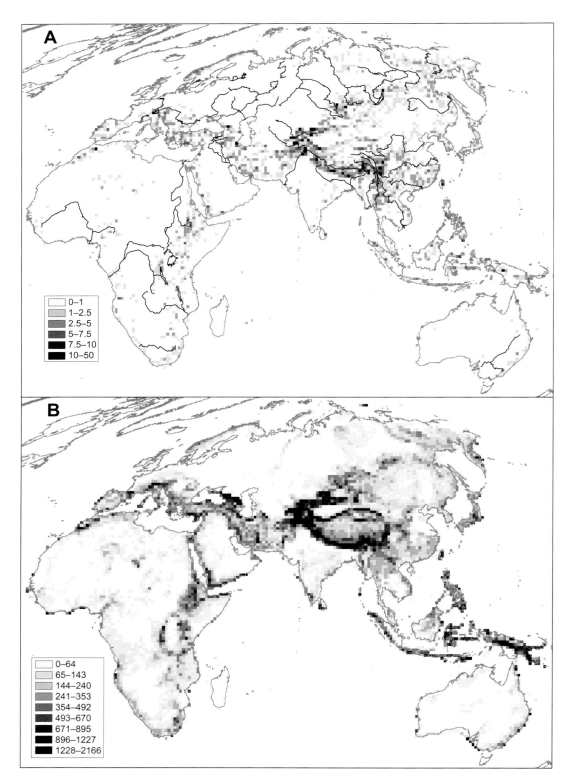

Figure 11.2. *Slopes (A) and roughness (B) maps. Slopes are expressed in degrees, and roughness legend represents the standard deviation of altitudes within each 100 × 100 km deme. The resolution of the underlying digital elevation model is 4 km. Black lines in (A) represents the major stream network. The map extent is that at the Last Glacial Maximum, while grey lines are current coastlines. The terrestrial and bathymetric data set ETOPO2 (NOAA 2001) was used for these calculations. Maps are projected in the Hammer projection (standard meridian: 80°).*

allows one to automatically adjust the K and F values to account for the higher carrying capacity and lower friction of streams. This is done by modifying the carrying capacity (K) and friction (F) values initially attributed to the vegetation categories. Usually, one multiplies K and divides F by an arbitrary factor, typically set between 2 and 5.

Coastlines

Aquatic resources along coastlines are numerous, and many archaeological studies suggest that they have been exploited in the Late Pleistocene and the Holocene (for a review, see Mannino & Thomas 2002). Binford's (2001, 214–15) contemporary data set complements these findings with observed higher population density of HG groups exploiting this resources. Even during glacial periods, when hyper-arid conditions were found in many places, it is likely that the emerged landmasses (due to sea-level drop) still contained a large vegetal and animal biomass, and therefore could have facilitated the survival and the dispersal of human populations (Faure *et al.* 2002). During our period of interest, we can therefore reasonably postulate that the carrying capacity of the coastline environment has been relatively higher than the inland environment.

Coastlines may have also played a major role as corridors of migrations, as the linear structure of coastlines can favour long-distance migrations, due to constantly accessible resources that do not require the use of new technologies or social adaptations to exploit these resources (Mannino & Thomas 2002). The combined corridor function and relatively higher carrying capacity of coastlines are at the root of the theories stipulating an initial global human dispersal through coastlines between Africa and Australia (Stringer 2000), or during the colonization of the Americas (Mandryk *et al.* 2001).

Incorporation of dynamic environmental heterogeneity

So far we discussed how to incorporate environmental spatial heterogeneity, but climate has greatly fluctuated during our period of interest, with a last glacial maximum (LGM) episode around 20,000 BP and an interglacial period about 120,000 BP. These climatic fluctuations have lead to continental changes in vegetation patterns, and one therefore expects that human densities and carrying capacities have varied accordingly. Sea water frozen in icecaps during that period also had a major impact on the relative sea level. This level has varied to a great extent, with a maximum relative drop of 120 metres (compared to

contemporary sea level) during the LGM (Lambeck & Chappell 2001). In certain areas, the associated emergence of land masses had a profound impact on coastline delineation, which could have impacted human migrations.

Dynamic vegetation

In order to model temporal fluctuations in vegetation patterns, one would ideally require a series of surface vegetation maps. Palaeobotanical data are unfortunately very scarce before the LGM, with only very localized pollen cores allowing inference of past vegetation at a very local scale (e.g. Chepstow-Lusty *et al.* 2005; Peyron *et al.* 2000; Zheng & Li 2000). In order to simulate a temporal fluctuation of the vegetation, we used an interpolation mechanism based on variations of global temperatures. Several palaeobotanical studies have indeed shown a connection between temperature changes at the continental scale and vegetation shifts (e.g. Dorale *et al.* 1998; Shi *et al.* 2000), even though other factors such as humidity, type of substrate and inter-specific competition are also influencing vegetation cover (Spikins 2000). We have thus used the record average global temperature inferred from the ice cores of lake Vostok in Antarctica (Petit *et al.* 1999) as a proxy for vegetation changes, and therefore of variations in K and F values (Fig. 11.3). Figure 11.3D indeed shows that temperatures have widely fluctuated between the two extreme climatic states which are the LGM and the last interglacial (127–110 kya). This last interglacial period can actually be considered as climatically similar to the current interglacial (Rioual *et al.* 2001). Moreover, the high correlation between palaeotemperatures recorded in Antarctica and in Greenland suggests a certain homogeneity of these changes at the global scale, even though there is sometimes a time lag of several hundreds, or even thousand of years for these variations in the two hemispheres (Blunier & Brook 2001).

Nevertheless, we can obtain the carrying capacity K_t of a deme at any time t by a simple linear interpolation between the carrying capacities of the deme inferred from the two extreme vegetation states, as

$$K_t = K_P + \frac{V_t(K_{LGM} - K_P)}{V_{LGM}}$$

where K_P and K_{LGM} are the carrying capacities of the present potential and the LGM, respectively, V_t is the change in temperature (compared to contemporary measure) at time t on the Vostok curve, and V_{LGM} is the maximum change in temperature during the LGM. Friction values are interpolated similarly.

We are aware that using a mean global temperature as a proxy for change in vegetation, and further

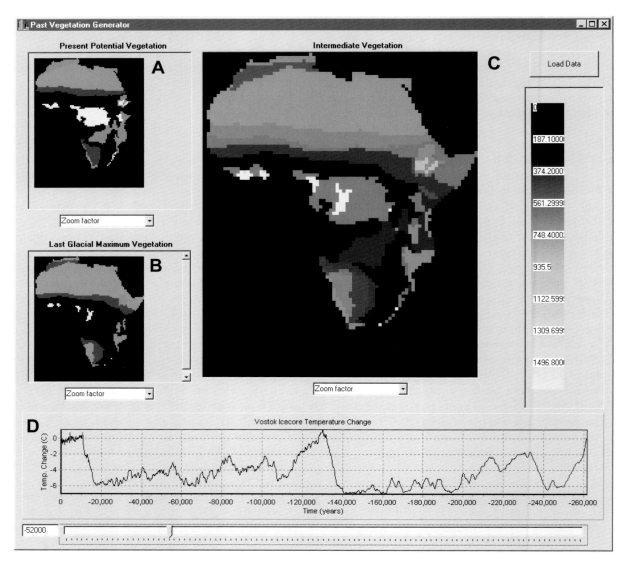

Figure 11.3. *SPLATCHE module for the dynamic vegetation change. The present potential map at continental scale (here Africa) and the same map at the Last Glacial Maximum (B) are used to generate an intermediary map (C) of carrying capacities at any period in the past (here 52,000 BP). The Vostok ice core temperature curve (D) is used as a proxy for the level of intermediacy between the two extreme vegetation states. The legend on the right represents carrying capacities.*

assuming that carrying capacity of humans is proportional to the vegetation biomass, are simplistic assumptions (see e.g. Binford 2001, chap. 4). However, in this exploratory phase of the impact of temporal heterogeneity on patterns of genetic diversity, it remains a meaningful way to model smooth changes in carrying capacities through time. To our knowledge, there are indeed currently no other simple methods to obtain similar changes in human carrying capacities at our temporal scale. We have therefore implemented this dynamic module in a modified version of SPLATCHE (Fig. 11.3). Figure 11.4 shows the effects of the tem-

poral change of vegetation on the deme sizes at different locations. Figures 11.4A and 11.4B illustrate the large density fluctuations in demes where the vegetation was very different during the LGM compared to the present potential state. Figure 11.4C shows size changes in a deme where these fluctuations are much less pronounced.

Dynamic coastlines
To obtain estimates of emerged land masses, we used the bathymetric data set ETOPO2 (NOAA 2001) describing the topography of the sea floor, as well as

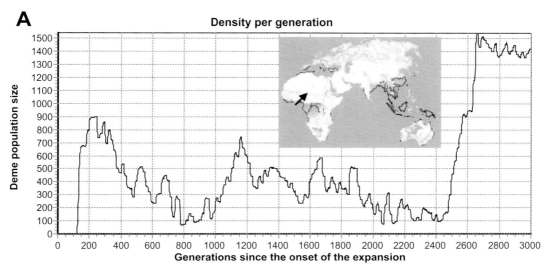

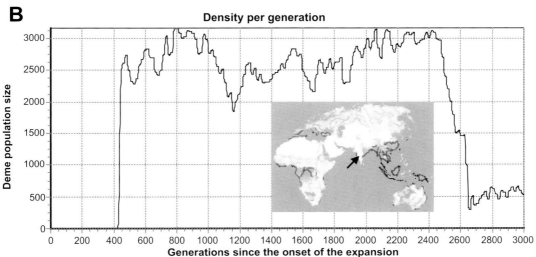

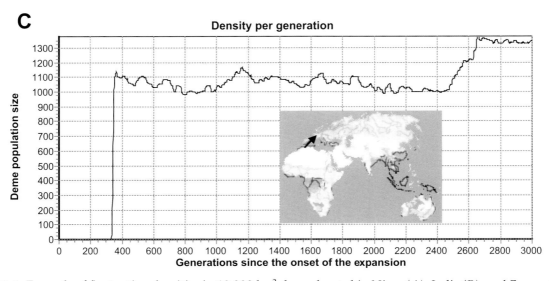

Figure 11.4. *Example of fluctuating densities in 10,000 km² demes located in Niger (A), India (B), and France (C). Arrows in each map inset show the exact location of the demes.*

111

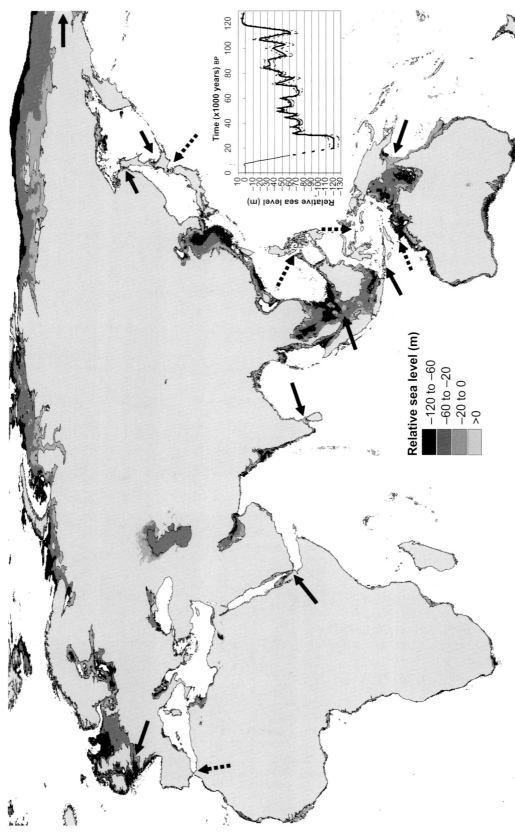

Figure 11.5. *Areas of emerged landmasses for various relative sea levels. Solid arrows indicate terrestrial bridges at the lowest level (−120 m), and dashed arrows indicate a lack of such bridges. The graph shows sea level variations at the Huon Peninsula (New Guinea) relative to actual level (data obtained from Lambeck & Chappell 2001). The mean level is in bold, and dashed lines indicate upper and lower limits of measurements. The bold dashed line on the right part of the graph is inferred from data from northern Australia.*

a temporal series of relative sea-level drop through time (Lambeck & Chappell 2001). In Figure 11.5, we show a representation of these sea-level changes in a GIS. However, this simple technique does not consider post-glacial isostatic rebound (rise of land masses previously depressed by the weight of ice sheets) that may have particularly affected northern Europe and northern America following the retreat of glaciers. During the LGM, the relative sea-level drop was at its minimum of about –120 m, and large areas in Southeast Asia (see also Voris 2000), northern Australia, and northern Europe were emerged, while other continent margins (e.g. Africa) were much less affected. We implemented these dynamic coastlines by updating the state of the coastline demes, and by allowing submerged individuals to move to emerged neighbouring demes.

Impact on genetic diversity

A modelling framework incorporating past environmental heterogeneity is certainly more realistic than its uniform alternative. Because variations of carrying capacities and frictions affect the demography of individual demes, they will also affect the genetic structure of sampled genes. Our simulation of the genealogies of a set of sampled genes is based on the coalescent theory, which defines probabilities of coalescent events (i.e. probability that two genes have a common ancestor in the previous generation) as a function of deme densities and immigration rates. When many genes aggregate in the same deme, the number of potential coalescence events increases. For a given number of genes, it is expected that there will be relatively less coalescence events in a large size deme than in a small size deme, because the probability of a coalescent event is inversely proportional to the population size. We show in Figure 11.6 how the level of heterogeneity and the consideration of dynamic environment affect the spatial densities of coalescence events. For this example, we first simulated a demographic expansion from East Africa 120,000 years ago (4000 generations assuming a 30-year generation time), followed by 5000 coalescent simulations of 24 samples composed of 30 genes. The technical details of the simulations are found in Excoffier *et al.* (this volume) and Ray *et al.* (2005).

In a uniform environment (Fig. 11.6A), we observe that there are three main regions with a high density of coalescent events: (i) in and around the sampled demes (white squares), (ii) in areas of 'spatial bottlenecks' (geographic constraints canalizing lineages, such as the region of the Levant), and (iii) around the origin of the expansion (white arrow). This is due to

the high density of genes in these regions (for details, see Currat & Excoffier 2005; Ray 2003b).

When heterogeneity of K is allowed in the simulations (Fig. 11.6B and C), regions with high densities of coalescent events become more restricted to areas with low number of immigrants (i.e. small $N \times m$ values: see Ray *et al.* 2003), even though spatial bottlenecks still play a similar role than in the uniform environment. For the scenario with temporal heterogeneity (Fig. 11.6D), patterns of densities are somewhat blurred compared to the low and high heterogeneity scenarios. This is due to the temporal variations of carrying capacities and frictions, which translate to complex spatial and temporal changes in coalescent probabilities. Moreover, the emerged areas in Southeast Asia allow for the movements of lineages over a much larger surface than in the other scenarios. More lineages are therefore likely to escape coalescence when migrating through the spatial bottleneck of Southeast Asia. In any case, we can see that various degrees of environmental heterogeneity significantly affect patterns of genetic diversity. We have further investigated this issue in the context of the recovery of the geographic origin of an expansion (see Excoffier *et al.* this volume).

Limitations and perspectives

In our view, the use of a simulation framework incorporating some of the environmental constraints that have impacted on past human demography is a necessary step toward a better understanding of the patterns of human genetic diversity. Although a complete sensitivity analysis remains to be done to better understand the effects of these additional levels of complexity, it is important to discuss the limitations of our model and the perspectives for incorporations of additional realism.

The choice of carrying capacity (K) and friction (F) values for a given environment is central to our model, because it will dictate simulated patterns of demography and genetic diversity. We used an approach that attributes identical K and F values to similar vegetation patterns in our vegetation map. African, Southeast Asian and South American rainforests are an example of comparable vegetation that may not necessarily show identical population densities, due to continental or regional specificities in exploiting resources. A thorough investigation of these specificities may therefore lead to better K and F maps. Although scarce, archaeological data may also help in certain locations to get estimates of K through artefact densities (e.g. Steele *et al.* 1998) or to get estimates of F from temporal patterns inferred from radiocarbon

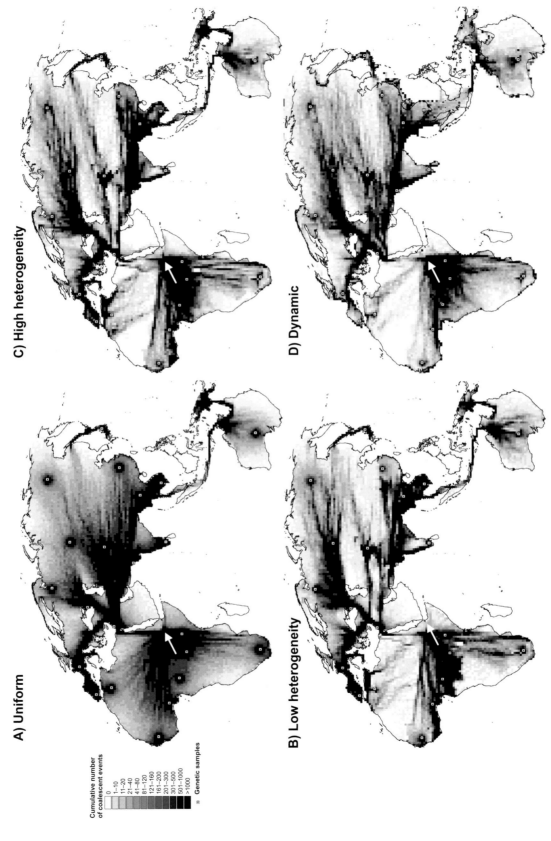

Figure 11.6. *Density of coalescent events over 5000 coalescent simulations of 24 samples (visible in panel A as small white squares). The white arrow indicates the origin of the expansion.*

dates (e.g. Gkiasta *et al.* 2003). An alternative way is to directly estimate these parameters by integrating our simulations into an Approximate Bayesian Computation (ABC: Beaumont *et al.* 2002) framework, which is a planned improvement of our inferential framework. We have also seen that more realistic alternative models to the simple logistic *K* model exist. Even though calibrating these multi-parameter models is extremely difficult at our spatial and temporal scales of interest, it would be important to compare the effects of considering these models on simulated genetic diversity. For example, Read & Leblanc (2003) suggest that populations with low carrying capacity suffer less from demographic crashes that population with high carrying capacity, which is the opposite case in the stochastic version of the logistic growth model. Implementing Read & Leblanc's suggestion into our model could allow one to test for significant departure from the expectation of the standard model, in term of genetic diversity. If significant, more effort could then be dedicated to the implementation of more realistic demographic models.

An additional difficulty of our simulations is the somewhat unrealistic uniform representation of desert or semi-desert areas, such as the Saharan region. We have so far used a very low carrying capacity for this type of environment, which translates into a very low but uniform density over the whole Sahara. In reality, these environments show patches of high-quality resources that are scattered and prone to spatial and temporal variations in a metapopulation context. In a recent work, Wegmann *et al.* (2006) have implemented an innovative way to model stochastically patchy environments. Their main results show that patterns of genetic diversity are greatly affected by the spatial heterogeneity of the environment, and, to a lesser extent, by their temporal heterogeneity.

The realism of dynamic changes of vegetation as we proposed it could also be improved. We have so far considered a global temperature measure as a proxy for changes in carrying capacities. Alternatives to that approach could use more detailed past climate reconstructions and their use to infer past vegetation dynamics at continental scale (e.g. Brovkin *et al.* 2002; Dupont *et al.* 2000). This approach may be more accurate in the way vegetation may change at certain locations, but their use at global scale for our period of interest remains difficult due to a very coarse grid resolution, and a link between climate data and potential carrying capacities which is not straightforward. Before contemplating additional and more realistic approaches to the putatively important process of past vegetation dynamism, we need an in-depth study of the consequences of our simple dynamism of carry-

ing capacities on genetic diversity. This should be the subject of a forthcoming investigation.

Another limitation of our model is the absence of long-distance dispersal, defined as migrations over more than one deme in a single generation. Long-distance dispersal is in fact what is expected along migration corridors such as streams or coastlines. In our current model, demes adjacent to these corridors are always colonized rapidly, because they still receive a small number of immigrants. We therefore cannot fully implement their role of corridor, because migrations are not strictly restricted to the demes belonging to the corridors. A model incorporating long-distance dispersal events and restricting them to known landscape features might greatly affect the simulated patterns of genetic variations (Ibrahim *et al.* 1996; Nichols & Hewitt 1994). It is therefore important to develop such alternative models and compare them to current ones.

Finally, if population expansions have occurred throughout human evolution, population contractions have also certainly been very frequent (e.g. at the onset of glacial periods). An example is the potential retreats to refuges in southern Europe and the consequent recolonization of northern Europe (Bocquet-Appel & Demars 2000; Housley *et al.* 1997). Due to isolation and founder effects, the contraction/recolonization dynamics has certainly greatly affected patterns of genetic diversity at certain locations. Implementing this type of dynamism into our current model would be important, but the dynamics of a contraction seems more difficult to implement than that of an expansion in an empty area. Coupled to the possibility of simulating several waves of migrations and interactions between species or subpopulations (see Currat *et al.* this volume), these more complex models should pave the way to extremely interesting studies allowing one to better understand the genetic signature left by climatic changes, not only in human populations, but in other animal (Taberlet *et al.* 1998) or plant (Petit *et al.* 2004) species.

Acknowledgements

We are grateful to Shuichi Matsumura and an anonymous reviewer for helpful comments on an earlier draft. This work was made possible thanks to Swiss NFS grants nos. 31-054059-98 and 3100A0-100800 to LE.

References

Adams, J.M. & H. Faure, 1997. Preliminary vegetation maps of the world since the last glacial maximum: an aid to archaeological understanding. *Journal of Archaeological Science* 24, 623–47.

Anderson, D.G. & J.C. Gillam, 2000. Paleoindian colonization of the Americas: implications from an examination of physiography, demography, and artifact distribution. *American Antiquity* 65, 43–66.

Barbujani, G., R.R. Sokal & N.L. Oden, 1995. Indo-European origins: a computer-simulation test of five hypotheses. *American Journal of Physical Anthropology* 96, 109–32.

Baumhoff, M.A., 1958. Ecological determinants of population. *University of California Archaeological Survey Reports* 48, 32–65.

Baumhoff, M.A., 1963. Ecological determinants of Aboriginal California populations. *University of California Archaeological Survey Reports* 49, 155–236.

Beaumont, M.A., W.Y. Zhang & D.J. Balding, 2002. Approximate Bayesian computation in population genetics. *Genetics* 162, 2025–35.

Bellavia, G., 2001. Extracting «natural pathways» from a Digital Elevation Model — applications to landscape archaeological studies, in *Computer Applications and Quantitative Methods in Archaeology: Proceedings of the 29th Conference*, ed. G. Burenhult. (BAR International Series.) Gotland: BAR, 5–12.

Belovsky, G.E., 1988. An optimal foraging-based model of hunter-gatherer population dynamics. *Journal of Anthropological Archaeology* 7, 329–72.

Binford, L.R., 2001. *Constructing Frames of Reference: an Analytical Method for Archaeological Theory Building using Hunter-gatherer and Environmental Data Sets*. Berkeley (CA): University of California Press.

Blunier, T. & E.J. Brook, 2001. Timing of millennial-scale climate change in Antarctica and Greenland during the last glacial period. *Science* 291, 109–12.

Blurton Jones, N.G., K. Hawkes & J.F. O'Connell, 2002. Antiquity of postreproductive life: are there modern impacts on hunter-gatherer postreproductive life spans? *American Journal of Human Biology* 14, 184–205.

Bocquet-Appel, J.-P. & P.Y. Demars, 2000. Population kinetics in the upper Palaeolithic in western Europe. *Journal of Archaeological Science* 27, 551–70.

Brovkin, V., J. Bendtsen, M. Claussen, *et al.*, 2002. Carbon cycle, vegetation, and climate dynamics in the Holocene: Experiments with the CLIMBER-2 model. *Global Biogeochemical Cycles* 16, 1139.

Burrough, P.A., 1986. *Principles of Geographical Information Systems for Land Resources Assessment*. New York (NY): Oxford University Press.

Chepstow-Lusty, A., M.B. Bush, M.R. Frogley, P.A. Baker, S.C. Fritz & J. Aronson, 2005. Vegetation and climate change on the Bolivian Altiplano between 108,000 and 18,000 yr ago. *Quaternary Research* 63, 90–98.

Currat, M. & L. Excoffier, 2004. Modern humans did not admix with Neanderthals during their range expansion into Europe. *PLoS Biology* 2, e421.

Currat, M. & L. Excoffier, 2005. The effect of the Neolithic expansion on European molecular diversity. *Proceedings of the Royal Society London, Biological Science* 272, 679–88.

Currat, M., N. Ray & L. Excoffier, 2004. SPLATCHE: a program to simulate genetic diversity taking into account environmental heterogeneity. *Molecular Ecology Notes* 4, 139–42.

Dewar, R.E., 1984. Environmental productivity, population regulation, and carrying capacity. *American Anthropologist* 86, 601–14.

Dorale, J.A., R.L. Edwards, E. Ito & L.A. Gonzalez, 1998. Climate and vegetation history of the Midcontinent from 75 to 25 ka: a speleotherm record from Crevice Cave, Missouri, USA. *Science* 282, 1871–4.

Dupont, L.M., S. Jahns, F. Marret & S. Ning, 2000. Vegetation change in equatorial West Africa: time-slices for the last 150 ka. *Palaeogeography, Palaeoclimatology, Palaeocology* 155, 95–122.

Eller, E., 2001. Estimating relative population sizes from simulated data sets and the question of greater African effective size. *American Journal of Physical Anthropology* 116, 1–12.

ESRI, 1992. *ArcWorld. A Comprehensive GIS Data Base for Use with Arc/Info and Arc/view. User's Guide and Data Reference.*

Excoffier, L., 2002. Human demographic history: refining the recent African origin model. *Current Opinion in Genetics and Development* 12, 675–82.

Faure, H., R.C. Walter & D.R. Grant, 2002. The coastal oasis: ice age springs on emerged continental shelves. *Global and Planetary Change* 33, 47–56.

Gao, J., 1998. Impact of sampling intervals on the reliability of topographic variables mapped from grid DEMs at a micro-scale. *International Journal of Geographic Information System* 12, 875–90.

Gkiasta, M., T. Russell, S. Shennan & J. Steele, 2003. Origins of European agriculture — the radiocarbon record revisited. *Antiquity* 77, 45–62.

Harpending, H.C., M.A. Batzer, M. Gurven, L.B. Jorde, A.R. Rogers & S.T. Sherry, 1998. Genetic traces of ancient demography. *Proceedings of the National Academy of Sciences of the USA* 95, 1961–7.

Housley, R., C. Gamble, M. Street & P. Pettit, 1997. Radiocarbon evidence for the late glacial human recolonisation of northern Europe. *Proceedings of the Prehistoric Society* 63, 25–54.

Ibrahim, K.M., R.A. Nichols & G.M. Hewitt, 1996. Spatial patterns of genetic variation generated by different forms of dispersal during range expansion. *Heredity* 77, 282–91.

Kantner, J., 1996. An evaluation of Chaco Anasazi roadways, in *Proceedings of the Society for American Archeology Annual Meeting*. New Orleans (LA), Society for American Archeology, 22.

Kelly, R.L., 1995. *The Foraging Spectrum: Diversity in Hunter-gatherer Lifeways*. Washington (DC): Smithsonian Institution Press.

Krings, M., A. Salem, K. Bauer, *et al.*, 1999. MtDNA analysis of Nile river valley populations: a genetic corridor or a barrier to migration? *American Journal of Human Genetics* 64, 1166–76.

Lambeck, K. & J. Chappell, 2001. Sea level change through the last glacial cycle. *Science* 292, 679–86.

Mandryk, C.A.S., H. Josenhans, D.W. Fedje & R.W. Mathewes, 2001. Late Quaternary paleoenvironments of northwestern North America: implications for inland versus coastal migration routes. *Quaternary Science Reviews* 20, 301–14.

Mannino, M.A. & K.D. Thomas, 2002. Depletion of a resource? The impact of prehistoric human foraging on intertidal mollusc communities and its significance for human settlement, mobility and dispersal. *World Archaeology* 33, 452–74.

Marble, D.F., 1996. The Human Effort Involved in Movement Over Natural Terrain. Part I of the final report submitted under National Park Service contract 6115-4-8031. Unpublished report, Ohio State University, Columbus, Ohio.

Marlowe, F.W., 2005. Hunter-gatherers and human evolution. *Evolutionary Anthropology* 14, 54–67.

Meltzer, D.J., 1999. Human responses to Middle Holocene (altithermal) climates in the North American great plains. *Quaternary Research* 52, 404–16.

Misra, V.N., 2001. Prehistoric human colonization of India. *Journal of Bioscience* 26, 491–531.

Mithen, S. & M. Reed, 2002. Stepping out: a computer simulation of hominid dispersal from Africa. *Journal of Human Evolution* 43, 433–62.

Nichols, R.A. & G.M. Hewitt, 1994. The genetic consequences of long-distance dispersal during colonization. *Heredity* 72, 312–17.

NOAA, 2001. ETOPO2, topographic and bathymetric surface of the earth at 2 min resolution. National Geophysical Data Center, Boulder, Colorado.

Petit, J.R., J. Jouzel, D. Raynaud, *et al.*, 1999. Climate and atmospheric history of the past 420,000 years from the Vostok ice core, Antarctica. *Nature* 399, 429–36.

Petit, R.J., R. Bialozyt, P. Garnier-Géré & A. Hampe, 2004. Ecology and genetics of tree invasions: from recent introductions to Quaternary migrations. *Forest Ecology and Management* 197, 117–37.

Peyron, O., D. Jolly, R. Bonnefille, A. Vincens & J. Guiot, 2000. Climate of east Africa 6000 14C yr BP as inferred from pollen data. *Quaternary Research* 54, 90–101.

Ray, N., 2003a. Comment on 'Population growth, carrying capacity, and conflict'. *Current Anthropology* 44, 77–8.

Ray, N., 2003b. Modélisation de la démographie des populations humaines préhistoriques à l'aide de données environnementales et génétiques, in *Département d'anthropologie et d'écologie*. Genève: Université de Genève, 331.

Ray, N. & J.M. Adams, 2001. A GIS-based vegetation map of the world at the Last Glacial Maximum (25,000–15,000 BP). *Internet Archaeology* 11.

Ray, N. & J. Adams, 2002. Present-potential vegetation maps of the world. A GIS-based reconstruction using altitudinal zones. Available online at http://cmpg.unibe.ch/people/ray/ppveg.

Ray, N., M. Currat & L. Excoffier, 2003. Intra-deme molecular diversity in spatially expanding populations. *Molecular Biology and Evolution* 20, 76–86.

Ray, N., M. Currat, P. Berthier & L. Excoffier, 2005. Recovering the geographic origin of early modern humans by realistic and spatially explicit simulations. *Genome Research* 15, 1161–7.

Read, D.W. & S.A. LeBlanc, 2003. Population growth, carrying capacity, and conflict. *Current Anthropology* 44, 59–76.

Rioual, P., V. Andrieu-Ponel, M. Rietti-Shati, *et al.*, 2001. High-resolution record of climate stability in France during the last interglacial period. *Nature* 413, 293–6.

Rogers, E., 1969. Natural environment — social organization — witchcraft: Cree versus Ojibway — a test case, in *Contributions to Anthropology: Ecological Essays*, ed. D. Damas. (Bulletin 230.) Ottawa: National Museum of Canada, 24–39.

Shi, N., L.M. Dupont, H. Beug & R. Schneider, 2000. Correlation between vegetation in southwestern Africa and oceanic upwelling in the past 21,000 years. *Quaternary Research* 54, 72–80.

Slatkin, M. & R.R. Hudson, 1991. Pairwise comparisons of mitochondrial DNA sequences in stable and exponentially growing populations. *Genetics* 129, 555–62.

Spielmann, K.A. & J.F. Eder, 1994. Hunters and farmers: then and now. *Annual Review of Anthropology* 23, 303–23.

Spikins, P., 2000. GIS models of past vegetation: an example from northern England, 10,000-5,000 BP. *Journal of Archaeological Science* 27, 219–34.

Steele, J., J. Adams & T. Sluckin, 1998. Modelling Paleoindian dispersals. *World Archaeology* 30, 286–305.

Stringer, C., 2000. Coasting out of Africa. *Nature* 405, 24–7.

Stringer, C., 2002. Modern human origins: progress and prospects. *Philosophical Transactions of the Royal Society of London B* 357, 563–79.

Taberlet, P., L. Fumagalli, A.G. Wust-Saucy & J.F. Cosson, 1998. Comparative phylogeography and postglacial colonization routes in Europe. *Molecular Ecology* 7, 453–64.

Thompson, H., 1966. A technique using anthropological and biological data. *Current Anthropology* 7, 417–24.

Tolan-Smith, C., 2003. The social context of landscape learning and the late glacial-early postglacial recolonization of the British Isles, in *Colonization of Unfamiliar Landscapes: the Archaeology of Adaptation*, eds. M. Rockman & J. Steele. London: Routledge, 116–29.

Tsoularis, A. & J. Wallace, 2002. Analysis of logistic growth models. *Mathematical Biosciences* 179, 21–55.

Voris, H.K., 2000. Maps of Pleistocene sea levels in Southeast Asia: shorelines, river systems and time durations. *Journal of Biogeography* 27, 1153–67.

Wegmann, D., M. Currat & L. Excoffier, 2006. Molecular diversity after a range expansion in heterogeneous environments. *Genetics* 174, 2009–20.

Zheng, Z. & Q. Li, 2000. Vegetation, climate, and sea level in the past 55,000 Years, Hanjiang Delta, southeastern China. *Quaternary Research* 53, 330–40.

Chapter 12

Extreme Population Genetics on Islands

Daniel Falush

This paper attempts to articulate a particular vision of how reconstruction of demographic history should be performed. A realization of this vision in its purest form would be 'extreme population genetics' in which sequence data from a set of individuals is analysed without regard to the species involved, where the samples are collected, the fossil record or what particular demographic scenarios are plausible at the outset. Interpretation would only begin once analysis is completed. Some of the elements required for extreme population genetics are already in place. Others may never be.

In each field of academic study, the literature has its own peculiar set of unfortunate tendencies. Within anthropological genetics, a familiar problem is over-interpretation. A pattern in DNA sequence data is noticed which is in some way analogous to a particular historical event. The event is then assumed to have caused the pattern without any analysis of whether the pattern could equally well reflect an entirely different event, or indeed be an artefact of the random sampling of genes as they are passed from generation to generation. Details relating to the pattern are then used to embellish the history of the event concerned, without taking account of the ascertainment effect caused by noting the pattern in the first place.

'Extreme population genetics' aims to make over-interpretation more difficult, or at least more transparent, by divorcing analysis from interpretation. As the name is intended to suggest, extreme population genetics is hard, if not impossible. Indeed it is diametrically opposed to the sensible Bayesian credo of making full use of prior information in statistical analysis. Nevertheless, we will argue that the ideal represents a valuable counterpoint to prevailing tendencies within the field and in particular provides an approach to ensuring that genetic data is used to *reliably* tell us something *that we did not already know* about the historical events in question.

In order to outline how extreme population genetics might work, and in keeping with the theme of this volume, we focus on the case of island colonization. Islands are discrete entities which typically

lack meaningful spatial structure within them. This feature reduces the space of possible demographic histories considerably. Colonization can in many cases be thought of as occurring in a relatively small number of discrete events, for example corresponding to the arrival of specific groups of boats, another useful simplification. Our job is to use genetic data to reconstruct the most important of the events.

Extreme population genetics requires an informative data set. This means data from many individuals from each island. The pattern of variation at any particular locus is affected to a large extent by random sampling so many loci are needed to give multiple independent realizations of the underlying demographic process in order that random sampling effects can be abstracted from. The data set needs to be large but ideally should also be informative about events that occur on different timescales. Temporal information can be provided by the molecular clock of new mutations in sequence data or by the decay of linkage disequilibrium with time between genetically linked markers. The data set needs to be informative, because the first step in extreme population genetics is to throw away all of the information external to the genetic data set. This includes the labels telling us which individuals come from which island and whatever historical information we might have.

In its purest form, extreme population genetics is done by a machine. Sequence data is put in and a partial or complete historical narrative is output. Only once the machine has done its work does interpretation in the light of external evidence begin. No such machine has yet been constructed but parts of it have. With some human intervention and the right data set, it is now possible to do something approximating extreme inference, especially in contexts where there are discrete demes, such as on islands.

This paper will describe how extreme population genetics might be performed, point out some gaps in existing machinery and make the argument that the approach is a good one. While being as concrete as possible, the aim of the article is to outline an idea, rather than to provide a comprehensive review of the machinery or practice of inference. The fact that most of the examples are taken from the author's own work or that of his immediate collaborators should therefore not be taken to imply that these are the only examples the author has regard for.

Step 1: run STRUCTURE

Extreme sports are often characterized by the participants making the activity as difficult and dangerous as possible. Extreme inference is similar in that the first, apparently perverse, step is to throw out the labels indicating which individual originated from which island and to attempt to reconstruct them based on the genetic data. For typical multilocus data sets, this can be done using the program STRUCTURE (Pritchard *et al.* 2000; Falush *et al.* 2003a). In its simplest version, STRUCTURE assumes that each individual in the sample comes from one of K populations. The populations are each characterized by a set of allele frequencies at each locus. Under the assumption that the loci are genetically unlinked to each other and provide independent information, STRUCTURE uses Markov chain Monte Carlo in order to simultaneously estimate both the frequency of each allele in each of the K populations and the posterior probability (the probability after having looked at the data) that every individual comes from population 1,2… or population K. Heuristic methods can be used to try and choose the most appropriate value of K by comparing the output of runs with different values of K (Evanno *et al.* 2005).

STRUCTURE has proved to be popular, with 611 citations to date for Pritchard *et al.* (2000), because it often does the job of recreating the labels well. In what is probably the best known of the 611 papers, Rosenberg *et al.* (2002) showed that it is possible to group humans from 52 ethnic groups into continental clusters and regional sub-clusters based on genotypes from 377 microsatellite loci.

A cynical observer might claim that the large number of citations for STRUCTURE reflects its util-

ity in producing minimal publishing units. In the past researchers genotyped markers from two or more locations and reported a positive value of F_{ST} between the locations as if this was news. Running STRUCTURE and reproducing the labels undoubtedly represents a greater achievement. As well as showing that the populations are differentiated, the researcher can use this to effectively distinguish individuals from different locations and genotype without getting their samples mixed up. But what else does it tell us? And what did Rosenberg *et al.* tell us about human population structure that we did not already know?

In fact, redefining the labels represents a key first step in demographic analysis. If the labels defined based on genetics match up with the original labels, it shows that the person who collected the samples has understood the basic features of population structure well enough to choose the labels appropriately. The continental clustering observed by Rosenberg *et al.* demonstrates that despite the complexity of human migratory history, most of the individuals in the study carry a distinct genetic signature of their continent of origin. In the context of islands, finding one population for each island would demonstrate firstly that there is no strong hidden population structure such as the presence of two populations on the same island. Secondly it would show that there has been no recent genetic exchange between the islands. Thirdly, since enough markers were typed to detect the differentiation, there would be some hope of elucidating the demographic events that caused it.

Step 2: run STRUCTURE again and again

In discussing the comparison of the populations that are defined based on STRUCTURE with the populations defined based on labels, we are getting ahead of ourselves. Under the rules of extreme population genetics, we should finish the analysis before performing biological interpretation of the results. How then do we decide that the labels defined by STRUCTURE are meaningful and correspond to the most interesting and appropriate biological units that the data set can be split into?

A first characteristic of genuine population subdivision is that it should be reproducible with different sets of loci taken from the same individuals. So one way to check that subdivisions are genuine is to split the loci into two and examine whether the same ones are found using each half of the loci. This is a good idea in principle but might be arduous in practice. For example, quite frequently subdivision will be detectable based on the entire data set but not one half or another. A simple explanation for this pattern would be a lack of statistical power. So the committed extreme population geneticist will genotype additional markers until two randomly chosen halves of the data set can be used to detect the same subdivisions. They might then find that additional subdivision was detectable using the whole data set, requiring the typing of yet more markers. Although this process might seem unprofitable, the most interesting result would be to establish that there was unexpected but entirely genuine subdivision in the data set. This finding would be a good example of genetic data telling us something that we did not already know.

Understanding the cause of the subdivision is potentially even harder. STRUCTURE assumes that within each of the K populations individuals are randomly mating and at Hardy-Weinberg equilibrium. Even on an idealized small island, this will not be true exactly because individuals have relatives who they share large proportions of their ancestry with. In the worst case, some sub-populations detected by STRUCTURE might consist of clusters of individuals from the same family or extended family. Some effort should therefore be made to detect patterns of allele sharing that indicate immediate familial relationships in the sample, with full siblings for example sharing 50 per cent of their genes on average. This type of analysis can be done for example using the program PARENT-AGE (Emery *et al.* 2001). Genes obtained from close relatives do not provide independent information about historical demographic processes, as opposed to recent ones and should be removed from the data set, although of course the presence of relatives does tell us something important about the nature of the sample.

Ultimately, if STRUCTURE finds populations of individuals which are well supported and reproducible, contain more than 3 or 4 individuals each and are not obviously relatives, then it is possible to be reasonably confident they are genuine, differentiated populations that do not mate randomly with each other. These populations putatively represent islands with significant barriers to gene flow and distinct demographic histories. Although this will not be confirmed until the code is broken at the end of the analysis, the extreme population geneticist now hopes that he or she has reached the starting point for demographic analysis.

There are in fact many reasons why this process may not work. STRUCTURE may fail to distinguish between two populations if the differentiation between them is too subtle to be detectable given the number of markers and numbers of individuals that are genotyped. In extreme inference, what one gets out is proportional to what one puts in. If one genotypes

few markers, one gets a simple history. With very few markers, STRUCTURE would give $K = 1$ corresponding to all the individuals belonging to a single population and the diagnosis would be that Nothing (detectable) Happened. More markers lead to higher values of K and progressively more complex histories. This proportionality is a healthy feature of extreme population genetics but when interpreting the history it is necessary to bear in mind the size of the data set and the power of the analysis to detect demographic events of different magnitudes.

Even if populations are differentiated and detectable in principle, STRUCTURE may fail for reasons that are related to the algorithm it uses to search for the solution. STRUCTURE starts with a random configuration of individuals into populations and finds progressively better clusters. In certain circumstances it may fail to 'mix' which in this context means to tend towards the most appropriate solution in a reasonable time.

STRUCTURE is more likely to mix badly and to fail to reproducibly identify the correct populations if:

i. some of the populations have much larger numbers of individuals in the sample than others;
ii. there are more than about 8 distinct populations in the data set;
iii. genetic distances between the populations are skewed, with some pairs of populations being similar to each other but highly distinct from others;
iv. diversity within one or more of the populations is a subset of that found in another population.

These issues are worth mentioning because they illustrate the limits on what extreme population genetics can practically achieve. It simply is not feasible to distinguish between every possible scenario, involving arbitrary numbers of populations with arbitrary numbers of individuals in each one. For example, it is often possible to address problems (ii) and (iii) by using STRUCTURE to first define populations, and then to define sub-populations within each population, as has been done for example by Rosenberg *et al.* (2001; 2003) for humans and chickens and (Falush *et al.* 2003b) for the bacterium *Helicobacter pylori*. However, sub-clustering presupposes hierarchical population splits, which may be an oversimplification that misses some of the most interesting details of the history being investigated, for example if a population is founded by the fusion of two others.

Step 3: run STRUCTURE with admixture

Finally we come to the most anthropologically (or biologically) interesting reason why labels may fail to correspond to populations, which is recent migration, leading to genetic exchange between them. Detecting and classifying migrants and hybrids is a matter of model choice. Does a model where each individual receives all of its ancestry from one population provide a better fit to the data than a model allowing mixed ancestry? And if there is mixed ancestry, what information can we deduce about when the migration occurred? Has migration occurred in a small number of discrete events, or has it been continuous?

As with the problem of defining the number of genuine populations, the easiest way of deciding about admixture is to use the labels, in this case to identify individuals that do not belong in the location they are currently found. But again, this represents a shortcut that will in some cases limit the information that genetic data can provide. A better signature of genetic exchange is to identify hybrid individuals.

STRUCTURE provides some useful tools for detecting and categorizing genetic exchange. Its admixture model assumes that instead of coming from one or other of the K populations, each individual has an ancestry vector q, with q_i corresponding to the proportion of ancestry from population i. In principle, it is possible to formally test for the presence of admixture without using the individual labels by comparing the model probabilities under the admixture model with those obtained assuming no admixture. However, comparing models which differ substantially in their number of parameters is a notoriously difficult problem in statistical inference. Here, the admixture model may give a better fit to data sets which depart from the model assumptions, even if those departures are not caused by recent admixture. For example if gene frequencies form a continuum instead of being naturally divisible into K populations, the admixture model with a small value of K is likely to give quite a good fit.

When run on data sets with a large number of hybrids, the admixture model is likely to give a higher model probability than the no admixture model, occurs for example in the African-American and *Helicobacter pylori* data sets described by Falush *et al.* (2003a,b). For both data sets, STRUCTURE can identify admixed individuals, which allows it for example to show that the majority of African-Americans have some European ancestry, while most West Africans do not. The distribution of ancestry proportions from a large number of individuals provides information about both the extent and timing of admixture, although the statistical apparatus to exploit this distribution has not been developed. Additional information on timing of admixture comes from the size distribution of the chunks of DNA inherited from the ancestral populations. For example, the distribution of chunk sizes has been used to estimate that for African-Americans, admixture took place on average 6–7 generations ago, which is consistent with most of them arriving in America in the eighteenth century (Falush *et al.* 2003a; Smith *et al.* 2004).

Note that models involving admixture typically require many more loci to investigate than those simply involving population subdivision. If populations are weakly differentiated, it becomes particularly difficult to establish the extent of admixture between them. The admixture model of STRUCTURE can assign hybrid origins (but with high confidence limits) simply through lack of statistical power to assign the individual to one population or another. Therefore, care should be taken that the data does in fact contain a genuine signature of hybrid origins. For example, using the MIGRATION model of STRUCTURE, the user can specify the origin of each individual. Individuals are only assigned partial or full ancestry to another population if there is good statistical evidence supporting ancestry from another population (see Pritchard *et al.* 2000). This model breaks the rules of extreme population genetics by using labels, but it is also possible to envisage a model in without labels which assumes with high probability as having complete ancestry to one population or another and only assigns individuals as admixed if there is an appropriate signal to indicate that they really do have a mixed genotype rather than a difficult to call one.

Despite this gloomy list of potential pitfalls, it is remarkable what can be achieved with an appropriate data set. The best example of this is in *H. pylori* (Falush *et al.* 2003b) where we were able to infer a complex and multi-layered history involving a hierarchical pattern of population splits and both recent and ancient admixture, with none of the analysis depending on labels. This analysis was as informative as it was because of the nature of the data set, with highly differentiated populations, a large number of polymorphic sites, with high recombination rates between them.

Step 4: infer demographic relationships between populations (possibly by running STRUCTURE)

Detecting populations and identifying and classifying recent hybrids between them represent the first steps in extreme analysis. Unfortunately, statistical methods for the later steps, in which the process by which the populations diverged from each other is inferred, are less well developed. Particularly vexing is the question of model choice. There are many different ways in which populations can have become differentiated, and, as yet, few methods for testing between them.

Figure 12.1 shows eight different historical scenarios involving three observed populations. Many additional scenarios are also possible. Scenarios 6 and 7 involve a forth unobserved population which needs to be proposed in order to provide an appropriate history of the observed populations. The eight scenarios are:

1. the independent colonization of two islands from a first;
2. sequential hopping from one island to the next;
3. one island is colonized from two different sources;
4. constant migration between all islands; and
5. independent colonization of two islands from a first followed by recent admixture;
6. each of the three populations is founded independently from an unobserved population;
7. two of the populations are founded independently from an unobserved population, with one of the two observed populations going on to found the third observed population.

Scenarios involving recent admixture can be distinguished from those without mixing by the absence of hybrid individuals but further classification and parameter estimation is more challenging.

For example, if hybrid individuals are found, then by assuming migration-drift equilibrium, it is possible to use LAMARC to or GENETREE to estimate migration rates and population sizes of each of the populations (Bahlo & Griffiths 2000; Beerli & Felsenstein 2001) see also the contribution of R.C. Griffiths in this volume). However, for human populations in particular, change has been the normal state of affairs and it in most cases it will be unreasonable to assume that equilibrium has been reached, making it difficult to interpret quantities estimated under the equilibrium assumption. After new islands are colonized exponential population growth is the norm and in many cases gene frequencies will not have changed substantially after the initial colonization event. Therefore if admixture is detected, it may actually be more reasonable to think that the past differs from the present and to decompose the historical scenario into recent and ancient time periods. This kind of decomposition was assumed, for example in the analysis of *H. pylori*, where there is evidence for substantial gene frequency change leading to distinct ancestral populations, followed by admixture of these populations in several different parts of the world (Falush *et al.* 2003b).

In the absence of recent admixture, the situation is similar; under particular scenarios it may be possible to estimate some of the demographic quantities of interest but these scenarios are not necessarily the most likely ones *a priori* and formal statistical methods have yet to be developed to test between scenarios.

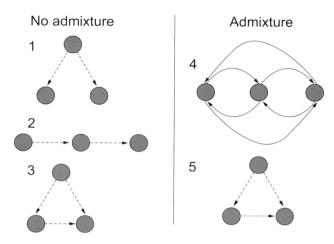

No admixture and an unobserved population

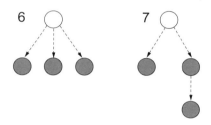

Figure 12.1. *Some historical scenarios for migration between three observed island populations. Filled lines indicate continous migration, dashed lines ancient migration and dotted lines recent migration. Filled circles indicate populations present in the sample while open circles indicate unobserved populations.*

Nevertheless, using more informal methods it is possible to exploit existing tools to build up a reasonable picture of the demographic history in question.

For example, Falush *et al.* (2003a) fit a model in which the populations diverged by genetic drift from a common ancestor (the 'F model') to populations of *Drosophila melanogaster* from Tasmania, Australia and Israel. The model infers the genetic composition of the ancestral population and estimates a value of *F* for each population, which indicates the amount of drift since divergence took place. We estimated *F* values in pairwise analyses, with one of the three populations excluded in each comparison. A high divergence value was always estimated for the Tasmanian population. By contrast the Australian population was found to have diverged by a very small amount since it diverged from the Tasmanian population but by a greater amount since it diverged from the Israeli one. The Israeli population showed intermediate divergence levels in each pairwise analysis. Informally, we can use these results to accept a model, corresponding to scenario 7 in Figure 12.1, in which the *Drosophila* population first split into two with one population going to Australia and the other going to Israel. The Australian population giving rise to the Tasmanian one with a substantial genetic bottleneck occurring as it was founded. This model is highly plausible on biogeographical grounds but of course glosses over many details of the early history of the spread *Drosophila*, which are unlikely to have taken place either in Israel or in Australia. In the spirit of extreme inference, it was possible to reconstruct this history without making use of population labels, although not all individuals are assigned to the correct population based on the available 48 microsatellite loci (Falush *et al.* 2003a).

In principle it should be possible to extend the technology of the *F* model, to estimate drift parameters where populations have diverged from each other hierarchically, as implied by the scenarios 2 and 7 in Figure 12.1. If the models are comparable, it may be possible to use statistical tests, rather than the kind of *ad hoc* reasoning described above, to decide which of the different possible scenarios is most appropriate. Moreover, it may also be possible to separately estimate the time of divergence and the amount of genetic drift since divergence (see e.g. Hey 2005 & refs. therein) and build demographic histories that incorporate population expansions as well as bottlenecks. Slowly but surely, more and more of the technology of extreme inference will come into place.

Why be extreme?

Extreme population genetics is arduous and unforgiving and the rewards can be meagre. Even if the data set is excellent, the history that it tells will inevitably be broad brush. It is unlikely, for example, tell you the exact number of boats that arrived on a particular island or identify Genghis Kahn's exceptional genetic contribution to modern populations. It certainly will not identify who are the seven (nodal) daughters of Eve or where they lived.

The broad brush history should not be underestimated. Firstly, it may contain some surprises; hitherto unexpected major migrations that will initiate a complete re-evaluation of the archaeological record. Second, even if the events that are inferred are all known, it may be quite salutary to see what is left out. Migrations that for whatever reason are archeologically fascinating may turn out to be demographically inessential.

Extreme population genetics is essentially a (small c) conservative proposition. It emphasizes how little we know not how much. Population genetics has made some real progress but we are still crawling rather than walking or running. We can typically only make inferences by assuming that human populations evolve as discrete entities most of the time, while the reality for most populations, even most island populations, is of constant — and complex — mixture with surrounding populations. No matter. There is still likely to be something that we can reliably infer. Let's start from there.

References

Bahlo, M. & R.C. Griffiths, 2000. Inference from gene trees in a subdivided population. *Theoretical Population Biology* 57, 79–95.

Beerli, P. & J. Felsenstein, 2001. Maximum likelihood estimation of a migration matrix and effective population sizes in *n* subpopulations by using a coalescent approach. *Proceedings of the National Academy of Sciences of the USA* 98, 4563–8.

Emery, A.M., I.J. Wilson, S. Craig, P.R. Boyle & L.R. Noble, 2001. Assignment of paternity groups without access to parental genotypes: multiple mating and developmental plasticity in squid. *Molecular Ecology* 10, 1265–78.

Evanno, G., S. Regnaut & J. Goudet, 2005. Detecting the number of clusters of individuals using the software STRUCTURE: a simulation study. *Molecular Ecology* 14, 2611–20.

Falush, D., M. Stephens & J.K. Pritchard, 2003a. Inference of population structure using multilocus genotype data: linked loci and correlated allele frequencies. *Genetics* 164, 1567–87.

Falush, D., T. Wirth, B. Linz, *et al.*, 2003b. Traces of human migrations in Helicobacter pylori populations. *Science* 299, 1582–5.

Hey, J., 2005. On the number of New World founders: a population genetic portrait of the peopling of the Americas. *PLoS Biology* 3, e193.

Pritchard, J.K., M. Stephens & P. Donnelly, 2000. Inference of population structure using multilocus genotype data. *Genetics* 155, 945–59.

Rosenberg, N.A., T. Burke, K. Elo, *et al.*, 2001. Empirical evaluation of genetic clustering methods using multilocus genotypes from 20 chicken breeds. *Genetics* 159, 699–713.

Rosenberg N.A., J.K. Pritchard, J.L. Weber, *et al.*, 2002. Genetic structure of human populations. *Science* 298, 2381–5.

Rosenberg, N.A., L.M. Li, R. Ward & J.K. Pritchard, 2003. Informativeness of genetic markers for inference of ancestry. *American Journal of Human Genetics* 73, 1402–22.

Smith, M.W., N. Patterson, J.A. Lautenberger, *et al.*, 2004. A high-density admixture map for disease gene discovery in African Americans. *American Journal of Human Genetics* 74, 1001–13.

Chapter 13

Ancestral Inference from Microsatellite Data by Sequential Importance Sampling in Subdivided Population Models

Robert C. Griffiths & Yvonne J. Griffiths

Ancestral inference about migration rates and other demographic features in a population genetics model where mutation is according to a stepwise mutation model can be made by a computationally intensive method of importance sampling on coalescent histories. In this paper such methods are described and applied to a classical data set of dinucleotide microsatellite frequencies from Pygmy populations.

1. Introduction

There has been much research into computation methods of ancestral inference from samples of genes conditional on their observed type configuration using importance sampling (IS), Markov Chain Monte Carlo (MCMC) and Bayesian techniques. In the simplest stepwise mutation model, inference involves finding a maximum likelihood estimate of θ, the mutation parameter.

We focus here on ancestral inference from microsatellite loci in subdivided populations using importance sampling methods developed initially by Griffiths & Tavaré (1994), greatly improved by Stephens & Donnelly (2000), and generalized by De Iorio & Griffiths (2004a,b). De Iorio et al. (2005) in a recent paper extended the theory of De Iorio & Griffiths (2004b), developed methods for ancestral inference from microsatellite loci in subdivided populations, and illustrated them by an analysis of microsatellite data from two Australian populations of the red fox (*Vulpes vulpes*). We refer the reader to this paper for a full description of importance sampling in the model considered here, and for references to other computational methods of ancestral inference.

Estimating migration rates by maximum likelihood is optimal in a frequentist setting in that the approach uses the full information in the data. Bayesian methods have been used to estimate migration rates and could be used here instead of likelihood methods making use of the IS algorithm to evaluate the posterior distribution of parameters given the data,

with suitable priors for mutation and migration rates. F_{ST} statistics have been used extensively to estimate migration rates (Hartl & Clark 1997; Schneider et al. 2000) but a likelihood or Bayesian approach should give better parameter estimates with smaller variances.

The ancestry of a sample of n genes is described by a coalescent tree (Kingman 1982), where pairs of ancestral lines coalesce at unit rate within subpopulations forming a tree back in time to the ancestor of the sampled genes. Mutations occur at rate $\theta/2$ along the edges of the coalescent tree according to a Poisson process.

In the stepwise mutation model, the allele type space is the set of integers $\{\ldots, -2, -1, 0, 1, \ldots\}$. Transitions of allele type when a mutation occurs are made according to a random walk from state j to a state $j + Z$, where Z is an integer-valued random variable. In the simplest case studied by Ohta & Kimura (1973), Moran (1975) and Moran (1976), $Z = \pm 1$ with probability 1/2. There is a distribution of the configuration of types in a sample with positions measured relative to the most recent common ancestor of the sample, which could be taken without loss of generality to be 0. The distribution is shift invariant, only depending on the relative positions of the types on a line.

In this paper importance sampling algorithms for computing the likelihood of a sample of genes at loci under a stepwise mutation model in a subdivided population are discussed. Analyses of dinucleotide repeat data for several pairs of human populations from the classical Marshfield microsatellite data set are made for illustration. Although our analyses do not consider all 377 loci in this data set, the results are of genuine anthropological interest.

Maximum likelihood estimates of mutation rates and migration rates between subpopulations are obtained based on multiple independent loci. The time to the most recent common ancestor (TMRCA) is calculated conditional on the data configuration for each locus. The technique uses an approximate stochastic process for coalescent evolution back in time, then corrects the approximate process by sequential importance sampling on the coalescent sample paths. The full likelihood of observed data can be computed by repeated simulation. Parameters in the model are then varied to find their maximum likelihood estimates. The technique is more sophisticated than simply simulating coalescent trees with mutations and migration and observing the outcome, because it simulates coalescent histories consistent with the data automatically. For example, the mean time to the most recent common ancestor can be estimated by taking the mean over the observed histories. Importance sampling on coalescent histories is discussed in more detail in the Appendix.

In the current pairwise subpopulation analyses, the two subpopulations are assumed to exchange genes with each other and no other subpopulations. The migration rates are an approximation to path rates through all possible subpopulation routes between the two subpopulations. A model which jointly includes all subpopulations with recurrent migration is straightforward to formulate but the matrix of migration rates is difficult to estimate by likelihood methods. To acccommodate the effect of unknown subpopulations, Beerli (2004) considers data with two subpopulations and a *ghost* subpopulation. He finds that the migration rate between the subpopulations is robust to the addition of the ghost subpopulation, but that effective subpopulation sizes change. Slatkin (2005) considers ghost subpopulations furthur and concludes that when a ghost subpopulation is present, there is no way to define a matrix of migration rates that predicts all features of the coalescent process for the true migration matrix.

Hey *et al.* (2004) and Hey (2005) analyse data from two subpopulations which contain linked microsatellite loci and SNP data. Their model is the *Isolation with Migration* (IM) model introduced by earlier authors (Nielsen & Wakeley 2001; Hey & Nielsen 2004), where recurrent migration occurs back to a point in time, then prior to this time subpopulations are isolated. A full likelihood analysis is made using an MCMC approach to compute genealogies conditional on the observed data set. The IM model has isolation back

in time, compared to our model which assumes there has always been recurrent migration. The method we use here and that used by Hey (Hey *et al.* 2004; Hey 2005) belong to the same family of computational approaches in that they generate genealogies conditional on the data. The IS algorithm in this paper could be used instead of the MCMC method in the IM model to generate genealogies for microsatellite data.

2. Subdivided populations

As the model with only two subpopulations is applied in the illustrative examples given in this paper, mathematical notation in the Appendix has been simplified in the following sections. Subscripts 1 and 2 are used to label the two subpopulations.

The total effective population size N (haploid genomes) for a pair of subpopulations is estimated by the relationship $\theta = 2Nu$, where u is the mutation rate per gene per generation. Individual effective subpopulation sizes are $N_1 = q_1N$, $N_2 = q_2N$, where q_1 and q_2 are the relative sizes of subpopulations 1 and 2 ($q_1 + q_2 = 1$). The total scaled mutation parameter for a pair of subpopulations is θ and those for the individual subpopulations are $\theta_1 = q_1\theta$ and $\theta_2 = q_2\theta$.

The migration parameters are:
(a) v_1 and v_2, the probabilities per lineage per generation that an offspring from subpopulation 1 had a parent in subpopulation 2, and that an offspring from subpopulation 2 had a parent in subpopulation 1.
(b) m_1 and m_2, the backward migration rates from subpopulation 1 to subpopulation 2 and from subpopulation 2 to subpopulation 1. $m_1 = 2Nv_1$ and $m_2 = 2Nv_2$.
(c) $\tilde{v}_1$ and $\tilde{v}_2$, the probabilities per lineage per generation that an offspring from a parent in subpopulation 1 migrates to subpopulation 2, and that an offspring from a parent in subpopulation 2 migrates to subpopulation 1.
(d) $\tilde{m}_1$ and $\tilde{m}_2$, the forward migration rates from subpopulation 1 to subpopulation 2 and from subpopulation 2 to subpopulation 1. $\tilde{m}_1 = 2N\tilde{v}_1$ and $\tilde{m}_2 = 2N\tilde{v}_2$.

The mean number of emigrant genes from subpopulation 1 to subpopulation 2 per generation is $N_1\tilde{v}_1$, equal to the mean number of immigrant genes in subpopulation 2 from subpopulation 1, N_2v_2; with a similar argument reversing the subpopulations. Therefore, relationships are

$$N_1\tilde{v}_1 = N_2v_2, \quad N_2\tilde{v}_2 = N_1v_1, \quad q_1\tilde{m}_1 = q_2m_2, \quad q_2\tilde{m}_2 = q_1m_1.$$

In our parameter scaling if the subpopulations are of

equal size and migration is symmetric ($m_1 = m_2 = m$, $v_1 = v_2 = v$), the theoretical value of $F_{ST} = (1 + 2\,m)^{-1}$. Notation for migration rates varies between authors. Unlike our notation, m is often used for the fraction of the population that migrates (e.g. Hartl & Clark 1997; Slatkin 1995; Schneider *et al.* 2000). When there are only two subpopulations $F_{ST} = (1 + 8N'm')^{-1}$ (Schneider *et al.* 2000; Slatkin 1995), where the diploid population size in each subpopulation is N', and m' is the proportion of diploid immigrants per generation. The average number of immigrants into a subpopulation per generation is then $N'm'$ and an identification with our parameters is that $N' = N/4$, $m' = 2v$, and $N'm' = m/4$.

3. Analysis of human microsatellite frequencies

3.1. Data

To illustrate the inference procedures described in this paper, published data for 21 autosomal, dinucleotide microsatellite loci, typed by the Mammalian Genotyping Service, Center for Medical Genetics, Marshfield Clinic Research Foundation, were analysed. The data were extracted from the Marshfield Screening Set 10 data set, available online as the file `DiversityFrequencies` at URL 1.

The Marshfield short tandem repeats (STRs) data set contains genotypes for 377 dinucleotide, trinucleotide and tetranucleotide STRs, from more than 1000 human DNA samples from 51 populations distributed throughout the world and has been used in several previous studies of human evolution and genetic diversity (Zhivotovsky *et al.* 2003; Rosenberg *et al.* 2002; Ramakrishnan & Mountain 2004; Storz *et al.* 2004).

In selecting the dinucleotide microsatellites for the analysis, loci were excluded if they had a very small number of repeats (<10), if there was evidence that they occur on chromosomal regions subject to selection (Storz *et al.* 2004), if the lengths of the PCR products included both odd and even numbers of base pairs, and if more than three genotypes were missing in the smaller samples. To avoid possible bias due to overrepresentation of individual chromosomes, a maximum of two loci were included per chromosome and these were chosen to have very different linkage map distances. The loci used were: D1S235, D1S2682, D3S1262, D3S1560, D4S403, D4S408, D5S408, D6S305, D7S2477, D8S261, D9S1779, D9S1838, D11S969, D12S1638, D13S285, D14S1007, D15S128, D16S516, D17S784, D20S851 and D22S1169. Details of these and other STR loci are available online at URL 2.

The populations examined were: Mbuti Pygmies from the Ituri rainforest region of the Democratic Republic of the Congo (sub-Saharan Africa); Biaka

Table 13.1. *Location, haploid sample size (n) and mean Expected Heterozygosity (H) of the populations analysed.*

Population	Latitude/Longitude	n	H
Mbuti Pygmies (sub-Saharan Africa)	1°N, 29°E	30	0.816
Biaka Pygmies (sub-Saharan Africa)	4°N, 17°E	68	0.807
Yorubans (sub-Saharan Africa)	6–10°N, 2–8°E	50	0.796
Palestinians (central Israel)	32°N, 35°E	102	0.785
Makrani (Pakistan)	26°N, 62–66°E	50	0.791
Han (China)	26–39°N, 108–120°E	90	0.704
French (Europe)	46°N, 2°E	58	0.762

H was calculated as the average over all 21 loci of $n(1 - \sum p_i^2)/(n-1)$, where $\{p_i\}$ are the allele frequencies at a locus (Jobling *et al.* 2004).

Pygmies from the Central African Republic (sub-Saharan Africa): Yorubans from Nigeria (sub-Saharan Africa); Palestinians from Central Israel; Makrani from coastal Pakistan; Han from China; and French from Europe (see Table 13.1).

The analyses were initially carried out with the data set as published on the Marshfield Center for Medical Genetics web site. However, a recent publication (Ramachandran *et al.* 2005) reported problems with the genotypes of two Biaka samples. One (sample 981) is a duplicate of another Biaka sample whilst the genotype of the second (sample 980) indicates that the sample is contaminated or wrongly labelled or the individual is a very recent immigrant to the population. For the 21 loci we studied, sample 980 had five alleles that were not present in other individuals in the Biaka sample. One of these five alleles was not present in any sub-Saharan African sample but rela-

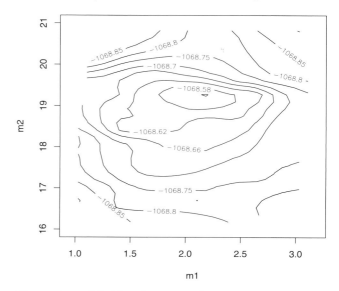

Figure 13.1. *Likelihood contours for migration rates.*

tively common worldwide. Samples 980 and 981 were thus deleted from the Biaka sample and a second set of analyses carried out for the Biaka population. The results presented in Tables 13.1 to 13.4 and Figures 13.1 and 13.2 for the Biaka Pygmies were obtained with this second, corrected data set of 34 diploid individuals. The results for the two Biaka data sets will be compared briefly later.

3.2. Analysis
A program stepsim which implements the IS algorithm described in the Appendix was used to analyse the data as pairs of subpopulations. In each run, a three-dimensional matrix of values for the scaled mutation parameter (θ), the backward migration rates from subpopulation 1 back to subpopulation 2 (m_1) and from subpopulation 2 back to subpopulation 1 (m_2) was generated and the program stepsim run for 10,000 iterations for each of the 21 loci for each point in this matrix.

For each combination of θ and migration rates, the joint likelihood across all 21 loci was calculated and these joint likelihoods used to find maximum likelihood estimates of θ, m_1, m_2. The Krig function from the R Statistics software, in the fields package, fits a multivariate normal shaped density to a data set consisting of a response to a set of parameters. It was used to calculate and visualize the likelihood surface with respect to the migration rates m_1 and m_2. Figure 13.1 is the output of likelihood contours from Krig used in maximum likelihood estimation of m_1 = 2.2, m_2 = 19.3 with θ = 18.7 for the Mbuti and Biaka populations.

For each pair of subpopulations, this process of estimation was repeated for a number of combinations of relative effective subpopulation sizes (q_1, q_2).

Values ranging from 1.0×10^{-3} (Weissenbach *et al.* 1992) to 6.2×10^{-4} (Ellegren 2000; Zhivotovsky *et al.* 2000) have been found for the mutation rate per locus per meiosis for dinucleotide microsatellites. An estimate of the effective mutation rate per locus per generation for dinucleotide microsatellite loci is u = 1.52×10^{-3} (Zhivotovsky *et al.* 2000; 2003) and we use this estimate in calculating effective subpopulation sizes.

Illustrative pairs of human populations were used for the analyses with the results shown in Tables 13.2 and 13.3. Our estimates of the scaled mutation parameter θ are comparable with the mean value of 9.94 calculated by Valdes *et al.* (1993) for 108 dinucleotide loci from the Marshfield set of markers using the variance of the distribution of allele sizes.

The value of θ was assumed to be constant across loci. The mutation rate is known to vary among loci

Table 13.2. *Estimates of relative sizes (q_1, q_2), mutation rates (θ_1, θ_2), and haploid effective population sizes (N_1, N_2) for pairs of populations.*

Populations	q_1, q_2	θ_1, θ_2	N_1, N_2
Mbuti	0.725	13.56	4459
Biaka	0.275	5.14	1692
Mbuti	0.55	9.90	3257
Yorubans	0.45	8.10	2664
Mbuti	0.65	11.77	3870
Palestinians	0.35	6.33	2084
Mbuti	0.65	10.85	3570
Makrani	0.35	5.85	1924
Mbuti	0.725	11.89	3911
Han	0.275	4.51	1484
Mbuti	0.725	12.32	4054
French	0.275	4.68	1538
Biaka	0.3	4.35	1431
Yorubans	0.7	10.15	3339
Biaka	0.5	7.15	2352
Palestinians	0.5	7.15	2352
Biaka	0.5	7.20	2368
Makrani	0.5	7.20	2368
Biaka	0.65	7.73	2544
Han	0.35	4.17	1370

(Ellegren 2000), however, so the model is approximate. Higher variation at some loci due to a larger than average mutation rates could be mistaken for population isolation, or lower variation due to smaller mutation rates could be mistaken for higher levels of migration. Our decision to only use dinucleotide microsatellites and to only choose those with 11 to 21 steps separating the shortest and longest alleles reduces the variability of mutation rates among loci. Because of the computation needed, it would be difficult to perform a likelihood analysis with each locus having a separate mutation rate. A Bayesian approach of having mutation priors for each individual locus would be an approach that could be followed to deal with variation in θ.

An advantage of the current analysis is that it does not assume the same effective population size for all populations nor symmetric migration rates. The results in Tables 13.2 and 13.3 indicate that these populations do have different effective population sizes and that gene flow is not symmetric.

The hunter-gatherer Mbuti Pygmies consistently have the highest estimates of effective population size with a mean of 3854 haploid genomes (1927 diploid individuals). This mean is higher than that for the other Pygmy population, the Biaka, whose mean is only 2077 haploid genomes (1039 diploid individuals). The mean for the Biaka is also lower than the mean of 3002 haploid genomes (1501 diploid individuals) for the Yorubans, the third sub-Saharan population examined. The lowest estimates were for the Han, with a mean of 1427 haploid genomes (714 diploid individuals). Our values are lower than most previous estimates of effective population sizes for these populations. Jin *et al.* (2000, table 4) using a set of 64 dinucleotide microsatellite loci and an effective mutation rate of 1.52×10^{-3} obtained estimates of 2792, 2312 and 2526 diploid individuals for Mbuti, Biaka and Chinese samples. Zhivotovsky *et al.* (2003, table 2), using 271 tetranucleotide microsatellite loci from the Marshfield data set, suggest an effective population size of 2609 diploid individuals for the sub-Saharan hunter-gatherer populations before a possible recent (4.3 kya) growth phase, and estimates of 1883 and 1688 diploid individuals, respectively, for the African farming populations and East Asian populations before population growth commencing 35.3 kya and 17.6 kya. Considering the ancient sub-Saharan African population that was a common ancestor of all modern humans, however, Zhivotovsky *et al.* (2003) suggest that its effective population size before differentiation and expansion may have been as low as 700 diploid individuals.

The values in Table 13.2 suggest the effective population sizes for both the Biaka Pygmies and the Han (Chinese) samples are lower than those for both the Mbuti Pygmy and Yoruban populations. Analyses using a different set of loci, and a larger number of loci, are needed to determine whether our low values for the Biaka and Han populations are genuine or due to the particular loci chosen for these illustrative analyses.

The two Pygmy populations also differ in their patterns of migration. The Biaka population generally has the higher backward migration rate in a pair of populations, consistent with being a recipient of lineages from other populations. The Mbuti population, in comparison, generally has the lower backward migration rate, suggesting it has been a source of ancestor lineages. These results are consistent with the suggestion that the Mbuti may represent a very ancient African lineage (Zhivotovsky *et al.* 2003; Cavalli-Sforza *et al.* 1994) and with the extensive hybridization of the Biaka with non-Pygmy populations described by Cavalli-Sforza *et al.* (1994).

Our analyses suggest that gene flow between the Biaka and the Yorubans has been greater than that between the Biaka and Mbuti. The analysis of Rosenberg *et al.* (2002, fig. 2) using the Structure software package (Pritchard *et al.* 2000) and the multidimensional scaling analysis of Zhivotovsky *et al.* (2003), also indicate that the Biaka Pygmies share more alleles with non-Pygmy sub-Saharan African populations such as the Yorubans than they do with the Mbuti Pygmies.

Table 13.3. *Estimates of the migration parameters for the pairs of populations.*

Populations	q_1, q_2	m_1, m_2	v_1, v_2	$\tilde{m}_1, \tilde{m}_2$	$\tilde{v}_1, \tilde{v}_2$
Mbuti	0.725	2.2	0.00018	7.3	0.00068
Biaka	0.275	19.3	0.00157	5.8	0.00047
Mbuti	0.55	10.0	0.00084	7.4	0.00062
Yorubans	0.45	9.0	0.00076	12.2	0.00103
Mbuti	0.65	2.5	0.00021	4.3	0.00036
Palestinians	0.35	7.9	0.00066	4.6	0.00039
Mbuti	0.65	4.1	0.00037	4.2	0.00038
Makrani	0.35	7.8	0.00071	7.6	0.00069
Mbuti	0.725	2.1	0.00019	2.7	0.00025
Han	0.275	7.0	0.00065	5.5	0.00051
Mbuti	0.725	1.6	0.00014	3.3	0.00030
French	0.275	8.7	0.00078	4.2	0.00038
Biaka	0.3	43.9	0.00460	31.0	0.00325
Yorubans	0.7	13.3	0.00139	18.8	0.00197
Biaka	0.5	6.6	0.00070	5.7	0.00061
Palestinians	0.5	5.7	0.00061	6.6	0.00070
Biaka	0.5	6.6	0.00070	4.4	0.00046
Makrani	0.5	4.4	0.00046	6.6	0.00070
Biaka	0.65	4.5	0.00057	3.4	0.00044
Han	0.35	6.4	0.00082	8.4	0.00107

The migration rates with a number of populations at increasing distance from the current location of the Mbuti and Biaka Pygmies were estimated. Although, the model makes the assumption that migration is only between the two populations being considered, which would not be true in practice, the results are of interest. The sets of migration estimates (Table 13.3) do not show a close relationship between migration rate and geographic distance. The backward migration rate for the Mbuti population in the Mbuti and Biaka analysis is low whereas the migration rates between the Han and the Biaka are relatively high. This apparently high migration with the Han may be a reflection of higher growth in this Chinese population and analyses using the model with exponential growth or an *Isolation with Migration* (IM) model may lead to different conclusions.

The migration rates estimated for these populations using the Arlequin software (Schneider *et al.* 2000) and assuming that the two populations exchange genes with each other and no other populations, are given for comparison in Table 13.4. These estimates are based on the R_{ST} genetic distance measure developed for microsatellite loci and a stepwise mutation model by Slatkin (1995). Only one migration parameter (designated here by M'_{Arl}) is estimated as the model assumes that a constant proportion (m_{Arl}) migrates each generation and that each population has the same constant population size (N_{Arl}). The migration rates in Table 13.4 also do not show a close relationship with geographic distance. The highest values are for the two Pygmy populations with the Yorubans but the migration rate for the two Pygmy populations with each other is quite small, lower than that between the Biaka and the Han and not markedly greater than that between the Mbuti and the Han.

Where migration is symmetric and the two populations are of equal size, the parameters, N_{Arl} (haploid genomes), m_{Arl}, $M'_{Arl} = N_{Arl}m_{Arl}$, in the model used in the Arlequin software are related to the parameters in our model as follows: $N_{Arl} = N_1 = N_2 = N/2$; $m_{Arl} = v_1 = v_2 = \tilde{v}_1 = \tilde{v}_2$; $4M'_{Arl} = m_1 = m_2 = \tilde{m}_1 = \tilde{m}_2$.

Where the migration rates are asymmetric and the two subpopulation differ in size, exact comparisons of our migration estimates and M'_{Arl} are not possible. An approximate comparison can be made, however, by defining a parameter $M'' = (q_1m_1 + q_2m_2)/4$ based on our backward migration and relative population size parameters. Values of M'' are given in Table 13.4 and most are similar to the corresponding M'_{Arl} values. The M'' are lower, however, for the Mbuti with the Yorubans and both Pygmy populations with the Han.

Table 13.4. *The migration rates estimated using the Arlequin software* (M'_{Arl}) compared with $M'' = (q_1m_1 + q_2m_2)/4$.

Populations	With Biaka M'_{Arl}	With Mbuti M'_{Arl}	With Biaka M''	With Mbuti M''
Mbuti	1.93		1.73	
Yorubans	6.25	6.18	5.62	2.39
Palestinians	2.20	2.21	1.54	1.10
Makrani	1.40	0.95	1.38	1.35
Han	2.27	1.61	1.29	0.86
French		0.89		0.89

As noted in Section 3, the analyses for the Biaka population were carried out using the original data on the Marshfield Center web site and also when samples 980 and 981 were excluded. The results presented and discussed are for this second corrected Biaka data set. Biaka sample 981 was a duplicate of another Biaka sample whilst sample 980 was believed to be mislabelled, contaminated, or from a very recent immigrant to the population. For the 21 loci we studied, individual 980 had five alleles that were not not present in other individuals in the Biaka sample. Four of these alleles only differed by one step from other alleles present in the Biaka population but the fifth was six steps below the next Biaka allele at the locus (D6S305). Furthermore, this allele was present in every population except the sub-Saharan African populations and the Yizu and was, moreover, relatively common outside sub-Saharan Africa, having a worldwide frequency of 0.151. Comparing the two

sets of analyses, the major effect of excluding these two Biaka individuals was not on the migration rates but on the relative population sizes and the mutation parameter, θ. The relative population size of the Biaka Pygmy populations decreased in the analyses with the Mbuti Pygmies and the Yorubans but did not change in the analyses with the non-African populations. For all analyses the θ estimate for the Biaka population and hence its effective population size decreased, consistent with the reduced number of alleles in the corrected data set. The mean and range of θ for the Biaka population using the corrected and original data sets, respectively, were 6.3 (4.2–7.7) and 6.7 (4.9–8.1). The backward migration estimates, with those for the corrected data set given first and the rate for the Biaka population being the first value in each pair, were: Biaka and Mbuti 19.3 & 2.2, 12.5 & 3.2; Biaka and Yorubans 43.9 & 13.3, 37.0 & 13.4; Biaka and Palestinians 6.6 & 5.7, 8.0 & 5.7; Biaka and Makrani 6.6 & 4.4, 8.0 & 4.9; Biaka and Han 4.5 & 6.4, 5.5 & 6.6.

The estimates of the time to the most recent common ancestor (TMRCA) for the 21 loci, computed with 700,000 runs for each locus, are plotted for the population pairs in Figure 13.2. These estimates are based on an average effective mutation rate of 1.52×10^{-3} and a generation time of 25 years. The TMRCA of a locus is the time to the most recent common ancestor of the segment of DNA where that locus is located. The 21 loci were chosen to be independent and, as anticipated, they differ in their TMRCAs. We have assumed the same mutation rate per locus, whereas in practice there may be variability of rates, which would lead to different TMRCA estimates.

The loci are plotted in increasing order of the number of dinucleotide steps between the shortest and longest allele at the locus. There is a trend for the TMRCA estimates to increase as the number of steps increases. The TMRCA estimates (in years) ranged from 86,700±46,337 to 210,444±82,548. Those involving the Biaka population (closed symbols in Fig. 13.2) are generally lower than for the Mbuti population (open symbols). Our TMRCA estimates for the DNA sequences are compatible with the population divergence times estimated using 45 dinucleotide microsatellite loci from the Marshfield data set by Zhivotovsky *et al.* (2003) for the earliest of the four major separation events in their human evolutionary tree (Zhivotovsky *et al.* 2003, figs. 5&6, table 3). The upper and lower bounds they give, based on a generation time of 25 years, for the time of this ancient African divergence event are 69.8±11.0 and 142.9±17.4 kya. Our TMRCA for the DNA segments are, as expected, somewhat greater than the times they suggest for this divergence of ancient sub-

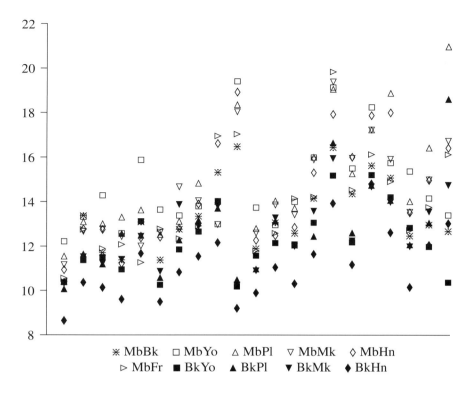

Figure 13.2. *Time to the most recent common ancestor (TMRCA). Time units in 10^4 years. Loci in increasing order of range of allele size.*

Saharan hunter-gatherers from the common ancestral human population.

These illustrative analyses suggest that the Mbuti and Biaka Pygmies have very different histories. The effective population sizes estimated for the Mbuti Pygmies are higher that those for the Biaka Pygmies which are similar to those of the non-African populations studied. The pattern of migration is also different with higher levels of admixture suggested for the Biaka. Further analyses need to be carried out using different loci and a larger number of loci to examine whether the present results apply generally for these populations or whether they are a product of the particular loci chosen. Such further analyses are possible as the the Marshfield data set contains genotypes for 377 dinucleotide, trinucleotide and tetranucleotide microsatellite loci.

URL for web addresses
1. http://www2.marshfieldclinic.org/RESEARCH/ GENETICS/Freq/FreqInfo.htm.
2. http://www.broad.mit.edu/cgi-bin/contig/phys_ map.

4. Appendix

4.1. Coalescent histories and importance sampling

Let E be the set of possible types of a gene. Denote the sample configuration of the numbers of different types as $\boldsymbol{n} = (n_j, j \in E)$, and $p(\boldsymbol{n})$ the probability of obtaining a sample $\boldsymbol{n}$. $\boldsymbol{e}_j$ will denote the jth unit vector. A coalescent history $\{H_k, k = 0, -1, \ldots, -m\}$ is defined as the set of ancestral configurations at the embedded events in the Markov process where coalescence, mutation or other events take place. H_0 denotes the current state, and H_{-m} the state when a singleton ancestor is reached. The Markov nature of the process implies that

$$p(H_k) = \sum_{\{H_{k-1}\}} p(H_k \mid H_{k-1}) p(H_{k-1}). \quad (4.1)$$

$p(H_k)$ and $\{p(H_{k-1})\}$ are unknown, whereas the probabilities $p(H_k \mid H_{k-1})$ are easily derived from the distribution of the coalescent tree. In (4.1) history probabilities are evaluated in the direction from the ancestor type to the sample data configuration. However a reverse history process from the sample data to the ancestor is required to efficiently evaluate the sample likelihood. A sequential importance sampling representation is based on an approximation $\hat{p}(H_{k-1} \mid H_k)$ to the unknown reverse probabilities $p(H_{k-1} \mid H_k)$. In one step

$$p(H_k) = \sum_{\{H_{k-1}\}} \frac{p(H_k \mid H_{k-1})}{\hat{p}(H_{k-1} \mid H_k)} p(H_{k-1}) \hat{p}(H_{k-1} \mid H_k)$$

$$= \mathbb{E}_{\hat{p}} \sum_{\{H_{k-1}\}} \left[\frac{p(H_k \mid H_{k-1})}{\hat{p}(H_{k-1} \mid H_k)} p(H_{k-1}) \mid H_k \right]. \quad (4.2)$$

The full sequential importance sampling representation from continuing (4.2) over states $H_0, H_{-1}, \ldots, H_{-m}$ is

$$p(H_0) = \mathbb{E}_{\hat{p}} \left[\frac{p(H_0 \mid H_{-1})}{\hat{p}(H_{-1} \mid H_0)} \cdots \frac{p(H_{-m+1} \mid H_{-m})}{\hat{p}(H_{-m} \mid H_{-m+1})} p(H_{-m}) \right]$$
$$(4.3)$$

where $\mathbb{E}_{\hat{p}}$ is taken over histories $H_{-1}, \ldots, H_{-m}$ with $\hat{p}(\cdot \mid \cdot)$ being the reverse chain transition probabilities. Probabilities of a history sample path $\mathcal{H}$ are evaluated in forward and reverse directions in the numerator and denominator of (4.3). The likelihood of the data can be evaluated by repeated simulation of sample histories in a reverse direction from the current sample configuration H_0 to H_{-m} under $\hat{p}(\cdot)$ with transition probabilities $\hat{p}(H_{k-1} \mid H_k)$, then averaging the sequential importance sampling weights

$$\frac{p(H_0 \mid H_{-1})}{\hat{p}(H_{-1} \mid H_0)} \cdots \frac{p(H_{-m+1} \mid H_{-m})}{\hat{p}(H_{-m} \mid H_{-m+1})} p(H_{-m}) \quad (4.4)$$

obtained on each run to obtain an estimate of the likelihood. The importance sampling construction actually holds for general Markov chains with an absorbing state, as well as in population genetics. Times between events can be included allowing ancestral inference about the TMRCA conditional on the observed samples. In r replicate IS runs there are r (likelihood, tmrca) pairs returned of $(l_1, t_1), \ldots, (l_r, t_r)$ giving an empirical distribution $t_1, \ldots, t_r$ with probabilities $l_1 / \sum_{k=1}^r l_k, \ldots, l_r / \sum_{k=1}^r l_k$ and a mean estimate $\bar{t} = \sum_{k=1}^r t_k l_k / \sum_{k=1}^r l_k$.

In a panmictic model if a historical configuration is $H_k = \mathbf{n}$ then either $H_{k-1} = \mathbf{n} - \mathbf{e}_j$ for some $j \in E$ corresponding to coalescence of two type j genes, or $H_{k-1} = \mathbf{n} + \mathbf{e}_i - \mathbf{e}_j$ for some $i, j \in E$ corresponding to mutation forward in time from i to j chosen with transition probability matrix P. The simplest microsatellite model is when $j = \pm 1$ and then $P_{i\,i+1} = P_{i\,i-1} = \frac{1}{2}$.

Proposal distributions $\hat{p}(H_{k-1} \mid H_k)$ can be found by an approximation in the coalescent process. Let B_j be the event that a gene of type $j \in E$ is the first type to be involved in either a coalescent or mutation event back in time in a sample of n genes with type configuration $\mathbf{n}$. The approximation assumes that $\hat{p}(B_j \mid \mathbf{n}) = n_j/n$, with the heuristic argument that (P_{ij}) has a stationary distribution (P_j) so $p(B_j) = P_j$, and the sample frequency approximates the true probability (De Iorio & Griffiths 2004a). The coalescent approximation turns out to be equivalent to a diffusion process generator approximation (De Iorio & Griffiths 2004a).

Define $\pi(i \mid \mathbf{n})$ as the probability that an additional type chosen from the population is of type i, given a sample configuration of $\mathbf{n}$. These are important quantities because reverse chain transition probabilities can be expressed in terms of them. The proposal distributions in the notation of Stephens & Donnelly (2000) are

$$\hat{p}(H_{k-1} \mid H_k) = \begin{cases} \dfrac{n_j - 1}{n + \theta - 1} \times \dfrac{n_j}{n} \times \dfrac{1}{\hat{\pi}(j \mid \mathbf{n} - \mathbf{e}_j)} \\ \qquad\qquad \text{if } H_{k-1} = \mathbf{n} - \mathbf{e}_j \\[2ex] \dfrac{\theta}{n + \theta - 1} \times \dfrac{n_j}{n} \times P_{ij} \times \dfrac{\hat{\pi}(i \mid \mathbf{n} - \mathbf{e}_j)}{\hat{\pi}(j \mid \mathbf{n} - \mathbf{e}_j)} \\ \qquad\qquad \text{if } H_{k-1} = \mathbf{n} + \mathbf{e}_i - \mathbf{e}_j \end{cases}$$

with importance weight for a single transition of

$$\begin{cases} \dfrac{n}{n_j} \times \hat{\pi}(j \mid \mathbf{n} - \mathbf{e}_j) & \text{if } H_{k-1} = \mathbf{n} - \mathbf{e}_j \\[2ex] \dfrac{n_i + 1 - \delta_{ij}}{n_j} \times \dfrac{\hat{\pi}(j \mid \mathbf{n} - \mathbf{e}_j)}{\hat{\pi}(i \mid \mathbf{n} - \mathbf{e}_j)} & \text{if } H_{k-1} = \mathbf{n} + \mathbf{e}_i - \mathbf{e}_j, \end{cases}$$

Stephens & Donnelly (2000) approximate π by $\hat{\pi}$, defined by

$$\hat{\pi}(j \mid \mathbf{n}) = \sum_{i \in E} \frac{n_i}{n} \sum_{l=0}^{\infty} \left(\frac{\theta}{n + \theta} \right)^l \frac{n}{n + \theta} P_{ij}^l.$$

De Iorio & Griffiths (2004a) approximate the diffusion process generator describing the distribution of population frequencies, giving a general way to obtain $\hat{\pi}(j \mid \mathbf{n})$ in more complex systems, extending the technique to subdivided populations in De Iorio & Griffiths (2004b).

The *parent independent mutation* model has a mutation matrix P with rows $(p_1, \ldots, p_d)$, and

$$\pi(j \mid \mathbf{n}) = \hat{\pi}(j \mid \mathbf{n}) = \frac{n_j}{n + \theta} + \frac{\theta}{n + \theta} p_j.$$

The *stepwise mutation* model in its simplest form has a mutation matrix $P_{ij} = 1/2$ if $|i - j| = 1$, and

$$\hat{\pi}(j \mid \mathbf{n}) = \sum_{i \in E} \frac{n_i}{n} Q_{ij},$$

where

$$Q_{ij} = \frac{1 - \rho}{\sqrt{1 - \rho^2}} \times \left[\frac{\rho}{1 + \sqrt{1 - \rho^2}}\right]^{|j - i|},$$

with $\rho = \theta/(n + \theta)$. The jump $Z = j - i$ is distributed as a two-sided geometric for $Z > 0$ with an additional atom at 0 (De Iorio *et al.* 2005).

4.2. Subdivided populations

In a subdivided population model with g subpopulations let S be the subpopulation type space. A gene's type is then indexed by $S \times E$, the subpopulation it is in, and its allele type. Possible transitions back in time to a sample of genes at a prior history event to a gene type (α, j) are: coalescence of a pair of genes of type (α, j); mutation forward in time from type (α, i) to (α, j) with rate $\theta/2$ and transition probability P_{ij}; and migration back in time of a type j gene from subpopulation α to β at rate $m_{\alpha\beta}/2$. Let $m_\alpha = \sum_{\beta \neq \alpha} m_{\alpha\beta}$, and denote $(q_\alpha, \alpha \in S)$ as relative subpopulation sizes. A Wright-Fisher model in discrete time gives rise to this model as subpopulation sizes tend to infinity. Let $(N_\alpha)_{\alpha \in S}$ be the subpopulation sizes, $N = \sum_{\alpha \in S} N_\alpha$, $q_\alpha = N_\alpha/N$, $\alpha \in S$, and $v_{\alpha\beta}$, $\alpha, \beta \in S$ be the probability that the parent of an offspring in subpopulation α is from subpopulation β in the previous generation. The backward migration rates are defined as $m_{\alpha\beta} = 2N v_{\alpha\beta}$, $\alpha, \beta \in \Gamma$, $\alpha \neq \beta$ with the overall rate $m_\alpha = \sum_{\beta \neq \alpha} m_{\alpha\beta}$. If $(\tilde{m}_{\beta\alpha})$ are the forward migration rates then $\tilde{m}_{\beta\alpha} = q_\alpha m_{\alpha\beta}/q_\beta$. The model considered here is the usual coalescent time scaled model where time is measured in units of N generations, and $N \to \infty$ while migration and mutation rates are kept constant. The same principles are used to construct importance sampling proposal distributions in subdivided population models as in a single population, leading to the following table for the reverse transition probabilities $H_k \to H_{k-1}$ and

Table 13.5. *Importance sampling distribution. D($\mathbf{n}$) is a scale constant.*

H_{k-1}	Proposal distribution	Importance weight
$\mathbf{n} - \mathbf{e}_{\alpha j}$	$\dfrac{n_{\alpha j}(n_{\alpha j} - 1)q_\alpha^{-1}}{\hat{\pi}(j \mid \alpha, \mathbf{n} - \mathbf{e}_{\alpha j})D(\mathbf{n})}$	$\dfrac{n_\alpha}{n_{\alpha j}} \times \hat{\pi}(j \mid \alpha, \mathbf{n} - \mathbf{e}_{\alpha j})$
$\mathbf{n} - \mathbf{e}_{\alpha j} + \mathbf{e}_{\alpha i}$	$\dfrac{n_{\alpha j}\theta P_{ij}\hat{\pi}(i \mid \alpha, \mathbf{n} - \mathbf{e}_{\alpha j})}{\hat{\pi}(j \mid \alpha, \mathbf{n} - \mathbf{e}_{\alpha j})D(\mathbf{n})}$	$\dfrac{n_{\alpha i} + 1 - \delta_{ij}}{n_{\alpha j}} \times \dfrac{\hat{\pi}(j \mid \alpha, \mathbf{n} - \mathbf{e}_{\alpha j})}{\hat{\pi}(i \mid \alpha, \mathbf{n} - \mathbf{e}_{\alpha j})}$
$\mathbf{n} - \mathbf{e}_{\alpha j} + \mathbf{e}_{\beta j}$	$\dfrac{n_{\alpha j}m_{\alpha\beta}\hat{\pi}(j \mid \beta, \mathbf{n} - \mathbf{e}_{\alpha j})}{\hat{\pi}(j \mid \alpha, \mathbf{n} - \mathbf{e}_{\alpha j})D(\mathbf{n})}$	$\dfrac{n_\alpha(n_{\beta j} + 1)}{n_{\alpha j}(n_\beta + 1)} \times \dfrac{\hat{\pi}(j \mid \alpha, \mathbf{n} - \mathbf{e}_{\alpha j})}{\hat{\pi}(j \mid \beta, \mathbf{n} - \mathbf{e}_{\alpha j})}$

importance weights. $\hat{\pi}(i \mid \alpha, \mathbf{n})$ is the probability that an additional gene taken from subpopulation α is of type i, given a sample configuration of $\mathbf{n}$. Details are in De Iorio & Griffiths (2004b).

A system of equations that the distributions $\hat{\pi}$ satisfy is

$$\left[n_\alpha q_\alpha^{-1} + m_\alpha + \theta\right]\hat{\pi}(j \mid \alpha, \mathbf{n}) =$$
$$n_{\alpha j}q_\alpha^{-1} + \theta \sum_{i \in E} P_{ij}\hat{\pi}(i \mid \alpha, \mathbf{n}) + \sum_{\beta \neq \alpha} m_{\alpha\beta}\hat{\pi}(j \mid \beta, \mathbf{n})$$

These equations have a matrix algebra solution, which in general needs evaluating numerically. Special cases do have explict solutions, including the stepwise mutation model with two sub-populations (De Iorio & Griffiths 2004b; De Iorio *et al.* 2005).

References

Beerli, P., 2004. Effect of unsampled populations on the estimation of population sizes and migration rates between sampled populations. *Molecular Ecology* 13, 827–36.

Cavalli-Sforza, L.L., P. Menozzi & A. Piazza, 1994. *The History and Geography of Human Genes.* (Abridged Paperback Edition). Princeton (NJ): Princeton University Press.

De Iorio, M. & R.C. Griffiths, 2004a. Importance sampling on coalescent histories. I. *Advances in Applied Probability* 36, 417–33.

De Iorio, M. & R.C. Griffiths, 2004b. Importance sampling on coalescent histories. II Subdivided population models. *Advances in Applied Probability* 36, 434–54.

De Iorio, M., R.C. Griffiths, R. Lebois & F. Rousset, 2005. Stepwise mutation likelihood computation by sequential importance sampling in subdivided population models. *Theoretical Population Biology* 68, 41–53.

Ellegren, H., 2000. Microsatellite mutations in the germline: implications for evolutionary inference. *Trends in Genetics* 16, 551–8.

Griffiths, R.C., 2001. Ancestral inference from gene trees, in *Genes, Fossils, and Behaviour: an Integrated Approach to Human Evolution*, eds. P. Donnelly & R. Foley. (NATO Science Series, Series A: Life Sciences 310.) Amsterdam: IOS Press, 137–72.

Griffiths, R.C. & S. Tavaré, 1994. Simulating probability distributions in the coalescent. *Theoretical Population Biology* 46, 131–59.

Hartl, D.L. & A.G. Clark, 1997. *Principles of Population Genetics.* 3rd edition. Sunderland (MA): Sinauer Associates, 190.

Hey, J., 2005. On the number of New World founders: a population genetic portrait of the peopling of the Americas. *PLoS Biology* 3, 965–75.

Hey, J. & R. Nielsen, 2004. Multilocus methods for estimating population sizes, migration rates and divergence time, with applications to the divergence of *Drosophila pseudoobscura* and *D. persimilis*. *Genetics* 167, 747–60.

Hey, J., Y.-J.Won, A. Sivasundar, R. Nielsen & J.A. Markert, 2004. Using nuclear haplotypes with microsatellites to study gene flow between recently separated *Cichlid* species. *Molecular Ecology* 13, 909–19.

Jin L., M.L. Baskett, L.L. Cavalli-Sforza, L.A. Zhivotovsky, M.W. Feldman & N.A. Rosenberg, 2000. Microsatellite evolution in modern humans: a comparison of two datasets from the same populations. *Annals of Human Genetics* 64, 117–34.

Jobling, M.A., M.E. Hurles & C. Tyler-Smith, 2004. *Human Evolutionary Genetics: Origins, Peoples & Disease*. New York (NY): Garland Science.

Kingman, J.F.C., 1982. The coalescent. *Stochastic Processes and Applications* 13, 235–48.

Moran, P.A.P., 1975. Wandering distributions and the electrophoretic profile, I. *Theoretical Population Biology* 8, 318–30.

Moran, P.A.P., 1976. Wandering distributions and the electrophoretic profile, II. *Theoretical Population Biology* 10, 145–9.

Nielsen, R. & J. Wakeley, 2001. Distinguishing migration from isolation: a Markov chain Monte Carlo approach. *Genetics* 158, 885–96.

Ohta, T. & M. Kimura, 1973. A model of mutation appropriate to estimate the number of electrophoretically detectable alleles in a finite population. *Genetical Research* 22, 201–4.

Pritchard, J.K., M. Stephens & P. Donnelly, 2000. Inference of population structure using multilocus genotype data. *Genetics* 155, 945–59.

R Development Core Team, 2004. *R: a Language and Environment for Statistical Computing*. Vienna: R Foundation for Statistical Computing.

Ramachandran S., O. Deshpande, C.C. Roseman, N.A. Rosenberg, M.W. Feldman & L.L. Cavalli-Sforza, 2005. Support from the relationship of genetic and geographic distance in human populations for a serial founder effect originating in Africa. *Proceedings of the National Academy of Sciences of the USA* 102(44), 15,942–7.

Ramakrishnan, U. & J.L. Mountain, 2004. Precision and accuracy of divergence time estimates from STR and SNPSTR variation. *Molecular Biology and Evolution* 21, 1960–71.

Rosenberg N.A., J.K. Pritchard, J.L. Weber, *et al.*, 2002. Genetic structure of human populations. *Science* 298, 2381–5.

Schneider, S., D. Roessli & L. Excoffier, 2000. *Arlequin ver. 2000. A Software for Population Data Analysis*. Geneva: Genetics and Biometry Laboratory, University of Geneva, Switzerland.

Slatkin, M., 1995. A measure of population subdivision based on microsatellite allele frequencies. *Genetics* 139, 457–62.

Slatkin, M., 2005. Seeing ghosts: the effect of unsampled populations on migration rates estimated for sampled populations. *Molecular Ecology* 14, 67–73.

Stephens, M. & P. Donnelly, 2000. Inference in molecular population genetics. *Journal of the Royal Statistical Society* Series B 62, 605–55.

Storz, J.F., B.A. Payseur & M.W. Nachman, 2004. Genome scans of DNA variability in humans reveal evidence for selective sweeps outside of Africa. *Molecular Biology and Evolution* 21, 1800–11.

Valdes, A.M., M. Slatkin & N.B. Freimer, 1993. Allele frequencies at microsatellite loci: the stepwise mutation model revisited. *Genetics* 133, 737–49.

Weissenbach, J., G. Gyapay, C. Dib, *et al.*, 1992. A second-generation linkage map of the human genome. *Nature* 359, 794–801.

Zhivotovsky, L.A., L. Bennett, A.M. Bowcock & M.W. Feldman, 2000. Human population expansion and microsatellite variation. *Molecular Biology and Evolution* 17, 757–67.

Zhivotovsky, L.A., N.A. Rosenberg & M.W. Feldman, 2003. Features of evolution and expansion of modern humans, inferred from genomewide microsatellite markers. *American Journal of Human Genetics* 72, 1171–86.

Chapter 14

Joint Determination of Topology, Divergence Time and Immigration in Population Trees[1]

Mark A. Beaumont

It is often hoped that population genetics will be a strong partner in archaeological and linguistic analysis of human prehistory. There are, however, many challenges, not least because there is rather little information in most data with which to draw strong conclusions. Computer-intensive statistical methods have been developed to extract as much information from the data as possible, and to provide a flexible framework within which complex models of population history can be handled. To be able to advance further, we need to analyse autosomal DNA variation at many loci. Current computer-intensive methods that aim to analyse the data fully and accurately begin to fail when faced with many loci and complex models. There has been a move towards the development of more approximate computer-intensive methods. This paper describes a particular class of models that has wide applicability, where populations diverge genetically though time, influenced by random genetic drift and migration. I describe an approximate Bayesian method that uses summary statistics measured from microsatellite loci to make inferences about demographic parameters in two- and three-population models. The method can be used to infer effective sizes of current and ancestral populations, immigration rates, splitting times and tree topology (in the three-population case). A novel method, based on categorical regression, for model selection is introduced, and used to infer tree topologies. Comparisons are made with a full-likelihood method for two populations developed by Hey and Nielsen, and it appears that the method gives comparable results. Multiple simulated test data sets are analysed with the three-population model, and it is concluded that in the presence of immigration the ability to make strong inferences about the population tree topology is quite weak. The categorical regression method for model selection is demonstrated to be substantially more efficient than simple rejection. I analyse data sets of 19 microsatellite loci from Channel Island foxes, and 329 microsatellite loci from three human populations. In the case of the foxes no strong conclusions about population tree topology can be made. With the human data, much stronger inferences about topology can be made. Overall, however, there appears to be little scope for accurate inference of demographic parameters with microsatellite data in the face of immigration, even when large numbers of microsatellite loci are used.

1. Introduction

Population genetic analysis has long held out the prospect that it can greatly enhance and complement the insights into human prehistory gleaned from archaeological and linguistic studies. Although there have been some successes, particularly with respect to the support given for the idea that modern humans emerged from Africa relatively recently, with hindsight we can see that current studies represent the steady trudge up the foothills of a mountain whose grand vistas are yet to open up. There are a number of reasons for this. Most pertinent is that there is actually rather little information, at least of the kind relevant to archaeologists, in much of the genetic material typically analysed. Secondly, those data that are of potential value, such as autosomal SNPs and multilocus autosomal sequences, are currently very hard to analyse effectively.

Although population genetics has a rich history of statistical analysis, most of the methods originally developed were of limited application, and not designed for the revolution in molecular genetics underway throughout the 1980s. The conceptual framework for analysing molecular genetic data as efficiently as possible was laid down in the 1990s, when computer-intensive statistical methods, originating in physics, were first applied to population genetic problems (Griffiths & Tavaré 1994; Kuhner et al. 1995; Wilson & Balding 1998). It became clearer how to probabilistically model genetic data, taking both Bayesian and likelihood-based frequentist approaches. These methods have an inherent flexibility, not readily accessible in the moment-based statistical techniques that had traditionally been used, and potentially allow for highly complex demographic and evolutionary scenarios to be modelled.

One goal of these recent techniques is to try to better understand the demographic prehistory of human populations by inferring the parameters in specific models. One particular class of models has been motivated by the idea that, if different geographic regions have been populated relatively recently from a common ancestral stock, the genetic differences between populations may tell us something about the time since the regions were colonized, the rate of migration between the populations, their sizes, and changes in population size associated with colonization. More concretely, when, for example, one group of humans from a certain population colonizes another region it is as if the original population has split into two. Initially the gene frequencies may be similar, depending on the size of the founding group, but then, due to random changes in gene frequency from generation to generation (random genetic drift) the gene frequencies in the populations will steadily diverge through time. Migration between the two populations may keep the gene frequencies similar. After a while, depending on the rate of migration and population sizes, the gene frequencies become independent of the time of the colonization event, and the populations are said to be in immigration-drift balance. In this case we can no longer say anything about the time of population divergence or ancestral population size, but can still say something about migration rates and population sizes. These processes can be encapsulated in a population genetic model, and we can then, given some data, try to infer the parameters of the model.

The genetic analysis of geographically structured populations has tended to be influenced by the two underlying conceptual models alluded to above. In one scenario the observed pattern of genetic variation arises from a process of immigration, mutation, and random genetic drift at equilibrium (Wright 1931; 1937). In the other, the pattern is generated by transient historical phenomena such as the splitting of populations and their subsequent genetic divergence. For this latter case, typically, moment-based methods have been used to obtain estimates of the time of population divergence. The topology of the population tree has often been obtained from ordination methods, such as neighbour-joining (Saitou & Nei 1987).

Since the middle of the 1990s microsatellites have often been used to infer population topologies, and moment-based methods that incorporated appropriate mutational models were developed to infer times of population divergence (e.g. Goldstein et al. 1995). A comparison of these methods on simulated data sets was carried out by Takezaki & Nei (1996), and they concluded that many hundreds of loci would be needed to infer parameters with any certainty. They also noted that drift-based estimators were better at recovering the topology of the population tree, while estimators based on a mutation model were better at obtaining the times of population divergence.

Ideally, likelihood-based procedures should be more efficient in extracting the information in the data available to infer topologies and branch lengths. Models in which populations diverge through time have been the subject of early attempts at likelihood-based analysis to infer demographic parameters (Cavalli-Sforza & Edwards 1967). A Bayesian method has been developed for single or linked microsatellite loci, and single locus sequence data modelled through the infinite-sites approximation (the program BATWING: Wilson et al. 2003). In BATWING, Bayesian computation is performed via Markov chain Monte Carlo (MCMC) simulation, and, in principle, the procedure can be used for any number of populations, although in practice convergence of the MCMC restricts the range of application of this approach.

A useful advance has been the introduction of probabilistic models that combine both equilibrium and non-equilibrium features (Nielsen & Wakeley 2001; Hey & Nielsen 2004). As with the method of Wilson et al. (2003), inference under this model is performed via MCMC to obtain relative likelihoods for different parameter values. This approach can infer immigration rates, times of population splitting, and population sizes for a pair of populations. The recent improvement described in Hey & Nielsen (2004), implemented in the IM ('Isolation with Migration') program, allows the analysis of multi-locus data evolving under a number of different mutational models (sequences, SNPs, microsatellites).

A natural extension of the method is to consider larger numbers of populations that can diverge in a bifurcating way (as in Wilson et al. 2003), in the presence of gene flow. However, while very powerful, it has to be recognized that, as with many MCMC-based genealogical methods, convergence can be quite slow, particularly for large data sets, and it may be difficult to extend the computational approach in Hey & Nielsen (2004) to consider larger numbers of populations. There has been a general recognition (Li & Stephens 2003) that methods of genealogical analysis based on MCMC or importance sampling (IS) are typically restricted to small data sets. The reason for this is that the likelihoods can only be written down for a single genealogical history, but many histories are compatible with any given data set. Thus the dimensionality of the problem is already very large for even a small amount of data, and MCMC or importance sampling methods struggle to sample from the even vaster space associated with larger data sets.

In recognition of this, various other approximate methods have been suggested that allow the flexibility of Bayesian and likelihood-based inference, while at the same time allowing for larger data sets to be considered (Hudson 2001; McVean et al. 2002; Li & Stephens 2003).

Given the weak relationship between the patterns found in population genetic data, and the evolutionary and demographic history we typically wish to uncover, the future of these methods surely lies in analysis of multiple nuclear sequences. Such data sets are becoming more widely available in a wide variety of organisms (Jennings & Edwards 2005). However, it is evident from these data that the effect of recombination is ubiquitous, and this vitiates the assumptions inherent in the use of the IM program, and may necessitate discarding significant amounts of sequence data (Hey & Nielsen 2004). Ideally, recombination needs to be included in the model, but this would greatly increase the dimensionality of the problem, and, realistically, can probably only be practicably addressed using approximate likelihood-based methods.

It seems apparent that, after the first flush of promise of MCMC and IS approaches in the late 1990s, the future of population genetic data analysis lies in the exploration and development of alternative, approximate, statistical methods that also have the flexibility found in Bayesian and likelihood-based analysis. The motivation of this paper is to explore how easy it is to tackle similar problems to those considered by Hey & Nielsen (2004) using an approximate method based on summary statistics. This approach, first proposed in population genetics context by Pritchard et al. (1999), has come to be called 'Approximate Bayesian Computation' (ABC) (Beaumont et al. 2002; Marjoram et al. 2003). The aim of this study is to compare the method with that of Hey & Nielsen (2004) on a pair of populations, and then to examine the behaviour of an extension of the method to three populations. In this latter case the tree topology becomes a parameter that also needs to be inferred.

2. Models and methods

The ABC approach to statistical inference does not require an explicit likelihood function. All that it requires is a probabilistic simulation program that can generate data sets with the same attributes as those found in the 'real' data set, obtained from nature. The goal is to capture these attributes via summary statistics and thereby make inferences about parameters in the simulation model. A good description of the method is in Excoffier et al. (2005). Below, I first describe the demographic and genetic models whose parameters we wish to infer; I then describe the ABC method; and finally describe the summary statistics that are calculated from the real and simulated data.

2.1. The demographic and genetic model
The models described here are of two or three populations. Data were simulated using a coalescent simulation, modified from the method described in Beaumont & Nichols (1996). A single-step microsatellite mutation model was used for these simulations, although the method allows for more general mutation models to be considered (Pritchard et al. 1999).

In the case of two populations the model was identical to that in, for example, Nielsen & Wakeley (2001) and Hey & Nielsen (2004). The treatment in these papers is in terms of scaled parameters. Here I describe the model in terms of the natural parameters (Fig. 14.1), but in comparisons between the ABC method and the IM program will also give the scaled parameters below. This is a model of an ancestral population of size N_A that splits at some time T in the past to give two populations of size N_1 and N_2. Since the time of splitting (looking forward in time) there has been immigration at rates m_1 and m_2, where immigrants into one population are drawn from the other population.

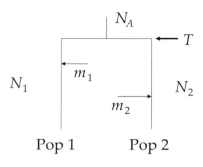

Figure 14.1. *Illustration of the two-population model. See text for description of parameters.*

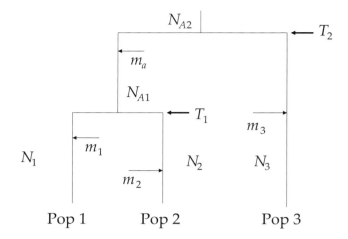

Figure 14.2. *Illustration of the three-population model. See text for description of parameters.*

Variation in mutation rate among loci was modelled in a hierarchical way following Storz & Beaumont (2002). The mutation rates at each locus are assumed to be drawn from a lognormal distribution with (on the $\log_{10}$ scale) mean of μ and standard deviation σ. Inference were made on these parameters rather than the mutation rates at individual loci. Note, this is somewhat different from the method of modelling variation in mutation rates among loci adopted by Hey & Nielsen (2004). The scaled parameters in Hey & Nielsen (2004) are $t = \mu T$, $\theta_1 = 2N_1\mu$, $\theta_2 = 2N_2\mu$, $\theta_A = 2N_A\mu$, $\mathcal{M}_1 = m_1/\mu$, $\mathcal{M}_2 = m_2/\mu$.

In the case of three populations we have parameters N_1, N_2, and N_3 for the sizes of the current populations, N_{A1} for the size of the most recent ancestral population, and N_{A2} for the common ancestral population size (Fig. 14.2). The time of the most recent split is T_1 and the time of the most ancient split is T_2. The immigration rates for the current populations are m_1, m_2, and m_3. The immigration rate for the most recent ancestral population is m_a. When there are three populations (i.e. in the interval between the most recent split and the current time) the immigrants into one population are drawn with equal probability from the other two populations (thus an island model is assumed). Variation in mutation rate among loci was modelled as for the two-population case. In addition for three populations there are 3 possible tree topologies, given indicators (1, 2, 3) for ordered populations ((POP1, POP2), POP3), ((POP1, POP3), POP2), ((POP2, POP3), POP1). Thus, overall, for the two-population case there are 8 parameters that can be inferred, and for the three-population case there are 14 parameters. Further parameters could be included in the three-population case. For example, immigration rate and effective size could change at the time of the most recent split for the population not involved in the split (i.e. N_{A3} and M_3 could change at the time of the split: see Fig. 14.2), which might be reasonable if this vicariance event also had an effect on the other population.

Also, a migration matrix could be used during the period of three populations, instead of assuming an island model. These enhancements would then lead to a 19 parameter model.

2.2. ABC approach to genealogical inference
In the simplest Bayesian calculation we have a probabilistic model that gives the joint distribution of an (unobserved) parameter Φ and some measurement that could be obtained from the data, S. Typically we make this calculation via the likelihood $P(S|\Phi)$, which gives the probability distribution of any value of S, given a value of Φ, and prior distribution for the parameter, $P(\Phi)$. The product of these gives the joint distribution $P(S, \Phi)$. If we have a specific observation, s, we then want to know the distribution of parameter values given this observation, $P(\Phi | S = s)$. This is the posterior distribution and can, in principle be computed as $P(\Phi, S)/P(S)$. The ABC approach simply involves simulating parameters from the joint distribution, $P(\Phi, S)$, and then using some density estimation method to obtain an approximation to this conditional distribution (Fig. 14.3). Simulation from the joint distribution can be done in two steps: first simulate a parameter values from the prior distribution, and then, using this value, simulate from the likelihood; repeat as many times as needed. One aspect, which makes the method attractive and flexible, is that there is no need to have (or manipulate in any way) explicit analytical expressions for $P(\Phi, S)$, $P(\Phi)$, or $P(S|\Phi)$. One simply needs some method of simulating from these distributions. Typically the data will be summarized not by one value, but by a number of summary statistics. The general idea is to use as many summary statistics as possible, so that it is possible to replace the data with these summaries

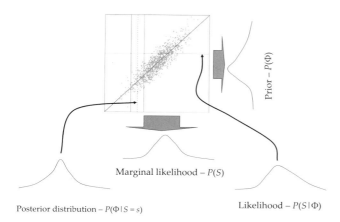

Figure 14.3. *This figure illustrates the basic ABC approach. The points in the figure are simulated from the joint distribution of parameter values and data. The aim of the ABC approach is to take a 'slice' through the distribution at a point corresponding to the measurement obtained from the real data, and thereby compute the conditional distribution of parameter values.*

and still obtain similar posterior densities to those that would be obtained with a method that could use all the data (i.e. the summary statistics are 'sufficient' in the statistical sense).

In the original specification of Pritchard *et al.* (1999), the conditional distributions were calculated by simply taking all the points simulated from the joint distribution that had summary statistics within some narrow interval around those observed in the data (as illustrated in Fig. 14.3). As pointed out in Beaumont *et al.* (2002), there are other potentially more efficient methods of conditional density estimation, and they proposed a method based on local linear regression. The main difference between the two methods is that, with the earlier method, if the interval for accepting the points (the region within the two lines on either side of the dotted line in Fig. 14.3) is made large enough the prior will then be recovered (since the parameter values are drawn from the prior). This is not the case for the regression method, and if the joint distribution is multivariate normal, as illustrated in the figure, then a good estimate of the true posterior distribution will be recovered by accepting all the points. The analysis presented in this paper is based on the regression method, which is summarized in Appendix 14.1.

2.3. Summary statistics

A weakness of ABC methods is that there is currently no objective 'rule' for choosing summary statistics, and therefore the eventual choice is somewhat arbitrary. Another problem to consider is the explosion

of summary statistics that can potentially occur as one considers an increasing number of populations. The summary statistics described here were chosen primarily because of their history of use in previous (moment-based) studies of microsatellite data (e.g. Takezaki & Nei 1996; King *et al.* 2000):

1. heterozygosity in each population $n/(n-1)(1 - \sum x_i^2)$;
2. sample variance of allele length in each population;
3. number of alleles in each population;
4. heterozygosity for each pair of populations pooled together;
5. variance for each pair of populations pooled together;
6. number of alleles for each pair of populations pooled together.

These were measured for each locus and then averaged. If, for any locus, the sample size in a population was ≤ 1 for any population, the summary statistics for that locus were not included in the average for the population, or pair of populations. In total, for two-population models there were 9 summary statistics, and for three-population models there were 18.

2.4. Model selection

Making inferences about the posterior probability of particular models, poses some challenges for computational methods such as MCMC, although the use of reversible-jump MCMC has proved very useful (Green 1995). As pointed out in Pritchard *et al.* (1999), it is relatively straightforward in principle to estimate the posterior probability of particular models using approximate methods based on summary statistics: we estimate the marginal probability of the summary statistics under model M_1, $\pi_{M1}(S = s)$, by simply counting up the proportion of simulated points that are within our tolerance region of the target summary statistics $\| S_i - s \| < \delta$. Two models can then be compared as

$$\frac{\hat{\pi}_{M1}(S = s)}{\hat{\pi}_{M2}(S = s)}.$$

However, as with parameter estimation, the use of straightforward rejection is potentially inefficient, and may be improved with kernel-based methods for estimation of the density.

However, another alternative, explored for the first time in this article, is to directly estimate the posterior probability of a model itself rather than to do so indirectly via comparison of estimates of $\pi_{Mi}(S = s)$. This can be straightforwardly achieved in the regression framework by treating the model indicator as a categorical variable Y that can take values from

$(1, \cdots, n_M)$. We can then estimate the coefficients β in a multinomial logit model in which

$$P(Y = j \mid S) = \frac{\exp(\beta_j^T S)}{\sum_{i=1}^{M} \exp(\beta_i^T S)}$$

and thereby obtain an estimate of $P(Y = j \mid S = s)$. This can be performed using weighted regression, as described above. The method used in this paper is implemented in the VGAM package by Thomas Yee under R (http://www.stat.auckland.ac.nz/~yee).

2.5. Comparison with IM
The IM package was used to compare posterior distributions from a full-data method with those obtained under the ABC method for 5 test simulations. Simulated data sets consisted of samples of size 50 chromosomes in each population scored for 10 microsatellite loci. The parameters used to simulate the data sets were $t = 4$, $\theta_1 = 0.5$, $\theta_2 = 2$, $\theta_A = 10$, $\mathcal{M}_1 = 4$, $\mathcal{M}_2 = 1$.

For the simulations described here the IM version of (11/12/04) was used. Priors for θ_1, θ_2 and θ_A were chosen to be uniform on the range (0,30), for $\mathcal{M}_1$ and $\mathcal{M}_2$ uniform (0,10), and for t uniform (0,8). Two independent simulations were run, each for 5×10^7 updates after an initial discarded burn-in of 500,000 updates. The Metropolis-coupling option was not used.

In order to make comparisons between methods, for the ABC simulations μ was given a point prior of 5×10^{-4}, and the priors for the other parameters chosen so that the priors on the scaled parameters were identical to those of IM. Variability in mutation rate could not be matched identically, because of the different method used to represent this. In the ABC analysis the prior for σ was a normal distribution (as in Storz & Beaumont 2002), truncated at 0, with mean 0 and standard deviation 0.1 (compatible with up to a 100-fold variation in mutation rates among loci).

The ABC analysis of the data was similar to that described in Beaumont *et al.* (2002) except that, since the parameters are distributed along uniform bounds, a logistic transformation was used prior to the regression adjustment, and then the regression-adjusted parameter values were back-transformed. Five hundred thousand points from the joint distribution of parameters and summary statistics were simulated, and the 2000 points closest to each target set of summary statistics were used for regression-adjustment ($P_\delta = 0.004$) (see Appendix 14.1).

2.6. Simulations for three populations
Two sets of test data was generated, consisting of 100 independent simulations of respectively 50 and

500 loci with a sample size of 50 chromosomes per population. For ease of exposition, because scaling of parameters can be confusing in complex demographic models, in the description below I fix the mutation rate at a notional $\mu = 5 \times 10^{-4}$ both in the generation of test data sets and in the analysis. To generate the test data the following parameters were used: $\sigma = 0$ (i.e. no variation in mutation rate among loci), $N_1 = 1000$, $N_2 = 1000$, $N_3 = 1000$, $N_{A1} = 1000$, $N_{A2} = 1000$, $T_1 = 100$, $T_2 = 1100$, $m_1 = m_2 = m_3 = m_a = 0.0005$.

For the ABC analysis, three different sets of prior distributions were used to analyse the test data with 50 loci. Each of these was replicated twice, leading to six independent sets of 500,000 points. Of these, the 10,000 points with the shortest Euclidean distance to each target set of summary statistics were used in the regression adjustment ($P_\delta = 0.02$). In the first set of replicates a point prior equal to that in the simulated data was set for the divergence times; in the second set, the immigration rates were fixed at the 'true' values; and in the third set the demographic parameters were free to vary. When not fixed, the following priors were used: a uniform prior on (0, 10,000) for N_1, N_2, N_3, N_{A1}, and N_{A2}, a uniform prior on (0, 10,000) for T_1 and $T_2 - T_1$, a uniform prior on (0, 0.005) for the mutation rates, and a uniform prior on the three different topologies. The mean mutation rate was fixed at $\mu = 5 \times 10^{-4}$, with standard deviation among loci at $\sigma = 0.1$, as for the two-population case. For the simulation tests with 500 loci, the same settings were used to simulate and analyse the data as for 50 loci, but in this case only the scenario without point priors for immigration or divergence time was studied.

3. Results

3.1. Two populations: a comparison of ABC and MCMC
Visual inspection of the output from the IM analysis suggested that reasonable convergence had been achieved, although mixing for t was relatively poor, and there was some variation in the two independent chains. It is possible that improved performance could have been obtained by choosing the Metropolis-coupling option, but earlier tests using Metropolis-coupling with 5 parallel chains were not encouraging. This is not to conclude that Metropolis-coupling is not useful, but it would appear that some effort is needed in optimizing the heating-parameters and numbers of chains. Each IM simulation took around 45 hours to run on a Xeon 3.2Ghz (Nocona) computer (maximally optimized using an Intel compiler under Linux). In the ABC analysis the 500,000 points were simulated in 20 minutes, and the same set was then used in the analysis of all simulated data sets.

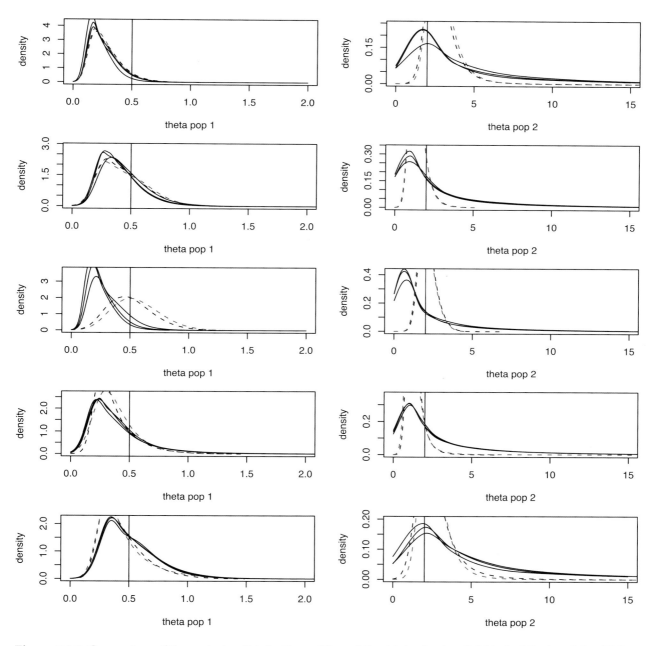

Figure 14.4. *Comparison of the posterior distributions of* θ_1 *and* θ_2 *obtained using IM (dashed line) and the ABC method on 5 different data sets.*

The posterior distributions of the six parameters computed for the five different simulated data sets are illustrated in Figures 14.4, 14.5 and 14.6. In general there is quite good agreement between the two approaches. The inferences from IM appeared substantially better only in the case of θ_2, where in four out of five cases the posterior density at the true parameter value was greater for IM than the ABC method. Agreement was best for θ_1 and $\mathcal{M}_2$. Neither method was able to make good inferences about θ_A,

$\mathcal{M}_1$, or t. Overall, although caveats about convergence must be borne in mind, it would appear that the ABC method is competitive with a full-data likelihood method, and is substantially faster to run.

3.2. Three populations

A summary of the ability of the method to recover the true tree topology is given in Table 14.1. It can be seen that when divergence times are fixed, very strong inferences are made about the topology. When immi-

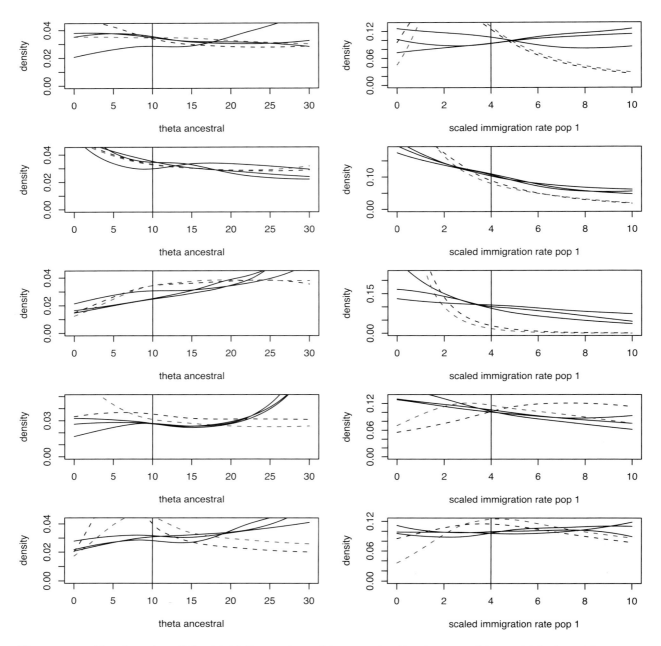

Figure 14.5. *(Continuation of Fig. 14.4.) Comparison of the posterior distributions of* θ_A *and* $\mathcal{M}_1$ *obtained using IM (dashed line) and the ABC method on 5 different data sets.*

gration rates are fixed the mean posterior probability of the true topology is around 0.8. This reduces to only 0.6 when all parameters have wide priors. Increasing the number of loci to 500 only increases the posterior probability to around 0.75. When the posterior probability of the true topology is high, the replicates agree very well, with correlation coefficients near to 1. The fact that the correlation coefficient is only 0.76 when there are wide priors on both immigration and diver-

gence time reflects that the standard error of the logit proportion is proportionately much higher in this case. These standard errors appear to give a good reflection of the reliability of the ABC regression adjustment.

When the other parameters are analysed (Tables 14.2, 14.3 & 14.4) it can be seen that it is in general very difficult to make strong statements about the parameter values, particularly when the prior bounds are as broad as used here. When the

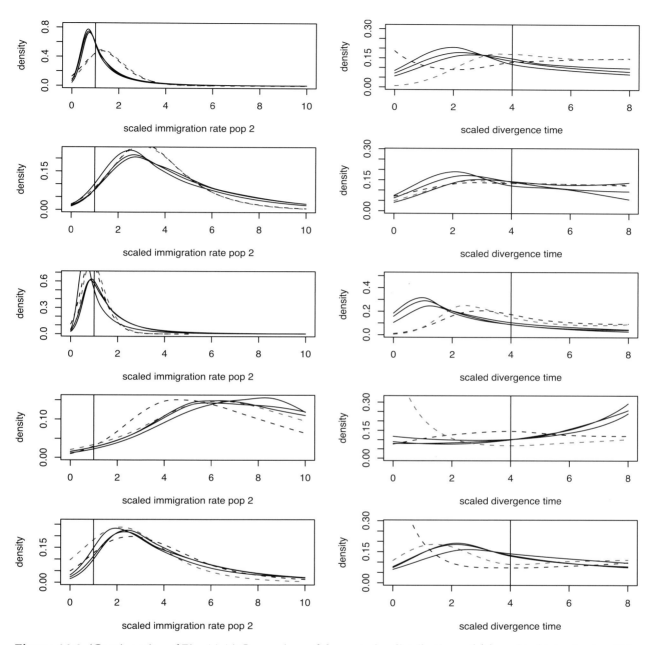

Figure 14.6. *(Continuation of Fig. 14.4.) Comparison of the posterior distributions of* M_2 *and* t *obtained using IM (dashed line) and the ABC method on 5 different data sets.*

Table 14.1. *Summary of inferences of topology.* $P_{CR}(\cdot)$: *the probability of a topology estimated using categorical regression;* $P_{rej}(\cdot)$: *the probability of a topology estimated using rejection;* $L(\cdot)$: $(\log P_{CR}(\cdot))/(\log P_{CR}(3))$; SE: *standard error; cor: Pearman's correlation coefficient between the two replicates in estimates of* $L(1)$. *Other than the correlation coefficient, the results presented are means over the 100 simulated data sets. All results are rounded to two digit precision.*

		$P_{CR}(1)$	$P_{CR}(2)$	$P_{CR}(3)$	$P_{rej}(1)$	$P_{rej}(2)$	$P_{rej}(3)$	$L(1)$	$L(2)$	SE $L(1)$	SE $L(2)$
Fixed T	cor	1									
	rep1		1	2.4e-06	2.9e-05	0.35	0.32	0.32	18	−1.5	0.68	0.77
	rep2		1	4.4e-06	3.6e-05	0.35	0.32	0.33	18	−1.3	0.67	0.76
Fixed m	cor	1									
	rep1		0.81	0.10	0.089	0.34	0.33	0.33	2.3	0.16	0.15	0.15
	rep2		0.82	0.094	0.082	0.33	0.33	0.33	2.4	0.16	0.15	0.15
Free	cor	0.76									
	rep1		0.6	0.19	0.21	0.33	0.34	0.33	1.1	−0.10	0.16	0.16
	rep2		0.57	0.22	0.21	0.32	0.33	0.34	1.0	0.065	0.15	0.16
Free 500	cor	0.95									
	rep1		0.74	0.12	0.15	0.32	0.33	0.35	1.6	−0.21	0.19	0.20
	rep2		0.72	0.11	0.17	0.32	0.33	0.34	1.4	−0.47	0.19	0.20

Table 14.2. *Summary of inferences of demographic parameters with splitting times fixed at true values. Definitions of parameters given in the text. cor: Pearson correlation coefficient of estimated modes in the two replicates; RRMSE: square root of the relative mean square error; lo, hi: respectively lower and upper 0.95 HPD intervals; cov: proportion of simulations in which the true value is found within the HPD intervals. Other than the correlation coefficient, the results presented are means over the 100 simulated data sets. All results are rounded to two digit precision. Note that for the summaries for the prior, when the prior is uniform there is no mode (and corresponding RRMSE), and, in this case, the bounds of the uniform distribution are given instead of the HPD interval.*

		cor	mean	mode	RRMSE mean	RRMSE mode	lo	hi	cov
N_1	rep1	1	1863	731	1.1	0.44	82	5773	1
	rep2		1946	758	1.1	0.43	93	5983	1
	prior		5000		4		0	10,000	
N_2	rep1	1	1900	741	1.1	0.42	92	5787	1
	rep2		1839	699	1.0	0.43	81	5674	1
	prior		5000		4		0	10,000	
N_3	rep1	1	514	121	0.55	0.88	0.17	1834	0.79
	rep2		519	121	0.55	0.88	0.17	1843	0.78
	prior		5000		4		0	10,000	
N_{A1}	rep1	1	2746	1165	1.9	0.64	119	7640	0.99
	rep2		2766	1183	1.9	0.66	124	7699	0.97
	prior		5000		4		0	10,000	
N_{A2}	rep1	1	1175	793	0.56	0.59	0	2666	1
	rep2		1156	769	0.55	0.59	0	2626	1
	prior		5000		4		0	10,000	
m_1	rep1	0.94	0.0017	8.7e-05	2.6	1.0	0	0.0044	1
	rep2		0.0017	7.1e-05	2.5	1	0	0.0043	1
	prior		0.0025		4		0	0.005	
m_2	rep1	0.76	0.0018	3.0e-05	2.7	1.1	0	0.0044	1
	rep2		0.0019	9.1e-05	2.8	1.1	2.7e-06	0.0045	1
	prior		0.0025		4		0	0.005	
m_3	rep1	0.74	0.00078	1.5e-05	0.92	0.97	0	0.0028	0.99
	rep2		0.00078	3.3e-06	0.93	1	0	0.0028	0.99
	prior		0.0025		4		0	0.005	
m_a	rep1	1	0.0016	5e-05	2.4	1.3	0	0.0042	1
	rep2		0.0016	5e-05	2.4	1.3	0	0.0041	1
	prior		0.0025		4		0	0.005	
$N_1 m_1$	rep1	1	2.4	1.1	4.1	1.4	0	7	1
	rep2		2.3	1.0	4.1	1.4	0	7	1
	prior		13	0	24	1	0	35	
$N_2 m_2$	rep1	1	2.5	1.2	4.3	1.6	0	7.3	1
	rep2		2.6	1.2	4.5	1.6	0	7.6	1
	prior		13	0	24	1	0	35	
$N_3 m_3$	rep1	1	0.28	0.11	0.58	0.8	0	0.83	0.64
	rep2		0.28	0.10	0.58	0.8	0	0.83	0.64
	prior		13	0	24	1	0	35	
$N_{A1} m_a$	rep1	1	4.3	0.61	8.4	0.74	0	17	1
	rep2		4.3	0.54	8.4	0.65	0	17	1
	prior		13	0	24	1	0	35	

divergence times are fixed (Table 14.2) the square root of the relative mean square error (RRMSE) is typically not substantially above 1 for modes, but somewhat higher for means. In general the means tend to overestimate parameter values, and modes tend to underestimate them. The confidence interval is given by the 0.95 highest posterior density (HPD) limits. These enclose a region within which the parameter value is found with probability 0.95, and in which the probability density is always greater than or equal to the probability density at the limits. The coverage (proportion of simulations where the true value is within the chosen confidence interval), based on 0.95 HPD intervals, is generally quite good, apart from that for N_3 and $N_3 m_3$. However, the HPD intervals for immigration rates are not substantially different from the prior bounds (or HPD intervals in the case of scaled immigration rates). The correlation in modal estimates between the two replicates are generally good. In the case of immigration rates they are lower. However, here the posterior distributions are almost rectangular, following the priors, and modes would be poorly estimated by any sampling method. Estimates based on the means are generally much better correlated, but the modes have been chosen to illustrate the repeatability of the procedure because they are more sensitive to the shape of the posterior distributions.

Table 14.3. *Summary of inferences of demographic parameters with immigration rates fixed at true values. Details as for Table 14.2. An estimate of the correlation coefficient when a standard deviation is 0 is given as NA.*

		cor	mean	mode	RRMSE mean	RRMSE mode	lo	hi	cov
T_1	rep1	1	527	70	4.4	0.39	0	1898	1
	rep2		517	68	4.3	0.41	0	1863	1
	prior		5000		49		0	10,000	
T_2	rep1	1	2682	1023	1.5	0.21	0	7001	1
	rep2		2644	1000	1.5	0.22	0	6893	1
	prior		10,000	10,000	8.1	8.1	2236	17,764	
N_1	rep1	1	2519	1897	1.6	1	547	5051	0.98
	rep2		2578	1946	1.6	1.0	588	5123	0.97
	prior		5000		4		0	10,000	
N_2	rep1	0.99	2452	1903	1.5	1	536	4988	0.99
	rep2		2482	1892	1.5	1	561	4988	0.98
	prior		5000		4		0	10,000	
N_3	rep1	1	1735	1160	0.83	0.35	295	3758	1
	rep2		1775	1184	0.87	0.37	305	3909	1
	prior		5000		4		0	10,000	
N_{A1}	rep1	1	3468	313	2.5	1.6	0	6841	1
	rep2		3415	444	2.5	1.5	0	6980	1
	prior		5000		4		0	10,000	
N_{A2}	rep1	NA	2231	0	1.3	1	0	7655	1
	rep2		2242	0	1.3	1	0	7620	1
	prior		5000		4		0	10,000	

When the immigration rates are fixed (Table 14.3), the point estimates of divergence times based on the mode are quite good, although the HPD limits tend to be wide. Estimates of population sizes tend to be worse than in Table 14.2, and the modal estimates are biased high for current populations, and low for ancestral populations, with wide HPD limits. The correlation coefficient of modal estimates is generally very good.

When all parameters (other than mutation rate) are free to vary, the quality of inferences falls. The correlation between replicates in estimates of the mode are often quite low, but in these cases, as noted above, the posterior distributions are very similar to the flat priors, and modes would be difficult to estimate under any method, and more likely reflect problems in density estimation than problems in the regression/rejection procedure itself. Relevant to this argument is the observation of a very high correlation in the case of the scaled immigration rates and T_2, which have priors that have a mode — essentially, the posterior distribution follows the prior. The results for T_1, where the correlation is low, and the relatively small bias of the modal estimate appears at variance with the very high RRMSE is explained by the observation that the mode is generally estimated at 0, with respectively 2 and 5 cases out of 100 where the mode is at 10,000 in the two replicates. The population sizes and scaled immigration rates are generally the best-estimated of the parameters. Coverage is poor for T_2 and immigration rates. It is particularly bad for the latter parameters, and may reflect poor behaviour

of the regression adjustment, but, again, it should be noted that the posterior distributions tend to be very broad, and these results may also reflect problems in density estimation. With 500 loci the inferences are similar to those from 50 loci, with somewhat narrower HPD limits and lower RRMSEs (results not shown). In particular the coverage for T_2 is similar to that for the 50 locus case, but for m_1 and m_2 it is zero, with the mean lower HPD limit at around 0.001, and never lower than the true value of 0.0005.

Overall, although a much wider set of scenarios needs to be investigated, and conclusions are necessarily tentative, it would appear that there is little scope, without more informative priors, for making strong statements about demographic history using even large numbers of microsatellite loci. Other analyses (not reported here) based on sets of 100 simulated data sets, as here, but under different scenarios (e.g. no immigration, non-identical parameter values) tend to back up this conclusion. Current population sizes and N_{A2} are quite well estimated, but once immigration is included in the prior the population tree topology is very difficult to infer with certainty.

3.3. Analysis of Channel Island fox data

As an example application of the ABC approach, part of a data set on Californian Channel Island foxes has been used, previously analysed in Goldstein *et al.* (1999). The populations chosen for study were those from mainland California (M) ($n = 15$), the island of Santa Cruz (SCR) ($n = 29$), and the island of San Clemente (SCL) ($n = 30$). Nineteen microsatellite loci

Table 14.4. *Summary of inferences of demographic parameters when there are no point priors on times or immigration rates. Details as for Tables 14.2 and 14.3.*

		cor	mean	mode	RRMSE mean	RRMSE mode	lo	hi	cov
T_1	rep1	0.44	3749	100	37	10	0	8248	1
	rep2		3954	500	39	22	0	7768	1
	prior		5000		49		0	10,000	
T_2	rep1	0.95	9000	8657	7.2	7	1016	16,600	0.6
	rep2		9256	9473	7.4	7.7	1170	16,985	0.43
	prior		10,000	10,000	8.1	8.1	2236	17,764	
N_1	rep1	1	1155	543	0.38	0.5	111	3015	1
	rep2		1168	545	0.39	0.5	123	3040	1
	prior		5000		4		0	10,000	
N_2	rep1	0.98	1102	529	0.32	0.51	104	2824	1
	rep2		1095	538	0.32	0.5	98	2862	1
	prior		5000		4		0	10,000	
N_3	rep1	1	1036	459	0.34	0.58	74	2878	1
	rep2		967	429	0.33	0.6	69	2631	1
	prior		5000		4		0	10,000	
N_{A1}	rep1	0.31	3588	102	2.6	1.3	0	7633	1
	rep2		4059	1015	3.1	3	0	6918	1
	prior		5000		4		0	10,000	
N_{A2}	rep1	NA	4375	204	3.4	1.6	0	8815	1
	rep2		4214	0	3.2	1	0	9152	1
	prior		5000		4		0	10,000	
m_1	rep1	0.9	0.0031	0.0043	5.2	8	0.00065	0.005	0.24
	rep2		0.0032	0.0045	5.4	8.3	0.00076	0.005	0.12
	prior		0.0025		4		0	0.005	
m_2	rep1	0.67	0.003	0.0041	5.1	7.5	0.00064	0.005	0.28
	rep2		0.0032	0.0046	5.4	8.4	0.00074	0.005	0.12
	prior		0.0025		4		0	0.005	
m_3	rep1	0.97	0.00083	0.00024	0.99	0.6	0	0.0028	0.98
	rep2		0.00082	2e-04	1	0.67	0	0.0028	0.98
	prior		0.0025		4		0	0.005	
m_a	rep1	0.4	0.0027	0.0047	4.3	8.7	1.6e-05	0.0011	0.62
	rep2		0.0027	0.0049	4.4	9	0.00029	0.0047	0.99
	prior		0.0025		4		0	0.005	
$N_1 m_1$	rep1	0.99	3	1.6	5.4	2.5	0	7.7	1
	rep2		3.1	1.7	5.6	2.7	0	8	1
	prior		13	0	24	1	0	35	
$N_2 m_2$	rep1	0.99	2.9	1.5	5	2.2	0	7.4	1
	rep2		3	1.7	5.3	2.6	0	7.7	1
	prior		13	0	24	1	0	35	
$N_3 m_3$	rep1	1	0.7	0.33	0.79	0.48	0	1.8	0.98
	rep2		0.65	0.32	0.72	0.49	0	1.7	0.97
	prior		13	0	24	1	0	35	
$N_{A1} m_a$	rep1	NA	9.8	0	19	1	0	33	1
	rep2		11	0	22	1	0	36	1
	prior		13	0	24	1	0	35	

were scored. In the analysis by Goldstein *et al.* (1999) the UPGMA (Unweighted Pair Group Method with Arithmetic mean) consensus tree based on $(\delta\mu)^2$ suggested a grouping of ((SCL, SCR), M), but the bootstrap support given for each clade was around 50%, consistent with a probability of each possible tree topology of around (1/3, 1/3, 1/3). The aim of the analysis was to try to resolve this tree better, and to obtain parameter estimates.

A point prior of 1.5 years was chosen for the generation time. The priors for the divergence times were based on information in Goldstein *et al.* (1999).

There was much uncertainty about value of N_e, and I chose generalized gamma distributions with thick upper tails and the bulk of the density towards values <2000, with a lower limit of 20 for the island populations and the first ancestral population and 200 for the mainland and the common ancestral population. A Beta (1, 1000) prior was used for immigration rate in all populations. Densities and summaries of these priors are listed in Figures 14.7, 14.8, and Table 14.5, along with the results.

It can be seen that the effective size of the mainland population is much higher than suggested by the priors. This probably also pulls the mutation rate towards high values, but this remains to be tested. The effective size of the island populations are smaller than suggested by the priors. There appears to be little or no information in the data on the splitting times (marginal to topology). The point estimate for the probability of ((M, SCR), SCL) is 0.23, that of ((M, SCL), SCR) is 0.26, and that of ((SCR, SCL), M) is 0.52. The log of the ratio of the first two probabilities over the last is respectively –0.822 (0.4 s.e.) and –0.701 (0.41 s.e.). Thus there is slightly stronger evidence in favour of the Mainland population being the outgroup than in the analysis of Goldstein *et al.* (1999), but there is no strong support for any particular topology, and there is some error in these estimates. In addition it should be noted that quite informative priors have been used. The priors on the splitting times were based on the assumption of a ((SCR, SCL), M) topology, which will have some influence on the inferred topology. The immigration rate into the mainland population is inferred to be much lower than suggested by the priors. There is a fair amount of support for zero immigration rates in all the populations (the 0.05 HPD limits include 0 in all cases). Further analyses need to be carried out conditioning on zero migration, and examining the influence of the priors.

3.4. Analysis of San, French, and Orcadian microsatellite data
The study by Rosenberg *et al.* (2002) has provided gene frequency information on microsatellite variation at 377 microsatellite loci surveyed from 52 worldwide human populations. This provides a valuable down-loadable resource (http://rosenberglab.bioinformatics. med.umich.edu/datasets.html). From this data set I chose to analyse 3 samples: French (29 individuals), San (7), Orcadians (16). In these samples, 329 loci showed perfect repeats, and the remainder were discarded.

For effective population sizes a gamma prior was used with shape parameter 1.5. In the case of the French and San populations a scale parameter of 20,000 was used, 1000 was used for Orcadians, and 50,000 for N_{A1} and N_{A2}. For the current populations 10 was added to the simulated random variables, and for the ancestral populations 100 was added. For the time to the first split (back in time) the prior was also gamma. In this case the scale was 2000 with shape 2, and 1000 was added to the simulated random variables. For $T_2 - T_1$ a gamma prior was used with scale 10,000 and shape 4. For the immigration rate, a prior was put on the number of immigrants (e.g. $N_1 m_1$ etc.). This was a generalized gamma distribution ($a = 0$; $b = 2.0$; $c = 1.1$; $k = 0.8$). The shapes of these priors are illustrated in Figures 14.9–14.11. The prior for the

Table 14.5. *Summary of analysis of Channel Island fox data. The posterior modes and 0.95 HPD limits are shown. The equivalent summaries for the priors are shown underneath. These latter were estimated from simulated data, and are not obtained analytically, and therefore there is some minor variation in estimates for identical prior distributions.*

parameter	mode	HPD lo	HPD hi
μ	–3.07	–3.37	–2.74
	–3.50	–4.09	–2.92
σ	0.00	0.00	0.275
	0.00	0.00	0.196
T_1	10,900	3250	14,200
	5140	3210	14,200
T_2	12,600	11,100	17,000
	12,600	11,000	16,700
N_1	2670	984	7420
	350	200	2770
N_2	41.7	13.2	146
	142	20	2000
N_3	34.3	8.81	96.8
	145	20	2010
N_{A1}	205	0	2310
	181	20	2560
N_{A2}	424	102	3180
	356	200	2730
m_1	0.0000984	0	0.000324
	0	0	0.0149
m_2	0.000576	0	0.00462
	0	0	0.0149
m_3	0.000871	0.00	0.00518
	0	0	0.0152
m_a	0	0	0.0126
	0	0	0.0147

mutation rate was lognormal with mean on a log 10 scale of –3.5 and standard deviation of 0.2, the prior for was a normal distribution with mode at 0 and standard deviation of 0.1, truncated at 0.

For the analysis two replicate samples of 500,000 were taken from the joint distribution of priors and summary statistics. The closest 10,000 points were used in the analysis. Inferences about the topology were very strong. From the categorical regression method the estimated log odds ratios of probability of a ((French, Orcadian), San) and a ((French, San), Orcadian) topology versus a ((San, Orcadian), French) topology were respectively 20.6 (s.e.: 0.64) and –5.7 (0.84) for the first replicate and 19.5 (0.60) –5.2 (0.77) for the second. These translate to estimated posterior probabilities for the 3 topologies (in the order given above) of respectively, (~ 1, 3.8×10^{-12}, 1.1×10^{-9}) and (~ 1, 1.6×10^{-11}, 3.0×10^{-9}). For comparison, the estimates that come from the rejection method are (0.35 0.30 0.35) in both replicates. The difference here (and in the test simulations above) may seem surprising, but it is worth noting that in the first replicate the 10 'nearest' simulated points (in terms of Euclidean distance) all have the ((French, Orcadian), San) topology and in the second replicate this figure is 25.

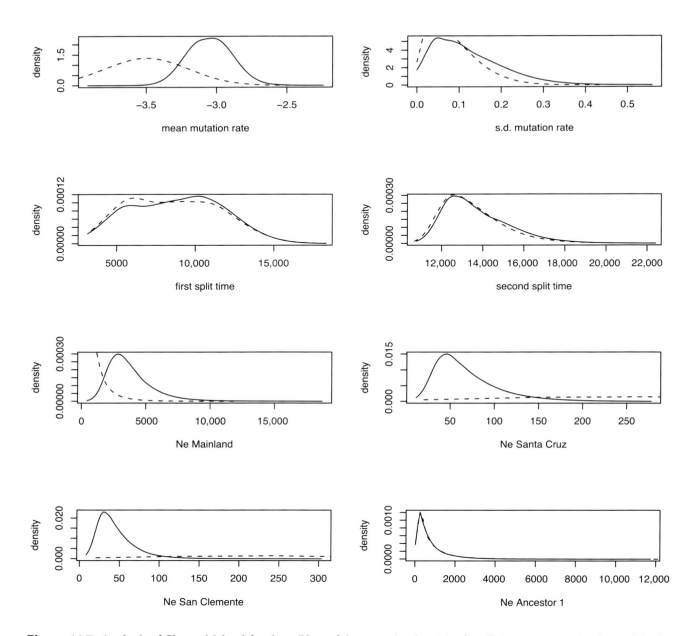

Figure 14.7. *Analysis of Channel Island fox data. Plots of the posterior densities for all the parameters in the model. The prior distribution is shown as a dotted curve. See text for details.*

Inferences about the other parameters are relatively weak. Of the population sizes (Fig. 14.9), the posterior estimates are typically around the 10,000 figure observed in many studies (Harpending *et al.* 1998), although with mutation rate prior used, the mode is somewhat lower than this. There is no strong evidence of any major demographic changes since the populations split. The estimates for the San, and the common ancestor are the most strongly distinguishable from the priors. The modal estimate for the San is around 4000 and around 6000 for the common ancestor.

There appears to be almost no information (in addition to that provided by the priors) on divergence times (Fig. 14.10). The divergence time for the most recent common ancestor is increased somewhat relative to the prior. The immigration rates follow the prior (Fig. 14.10). The estimates for the scaled immigration rates suggest (Fig. 14.11) that immigration into the San is reduced relative to the prior, and increased in the case of the Orcadians, with a mode at around 2 immigrants per generation.

regression. Errors in the regression adjustment may well explain, for example, the relatively poor performance in comparison with IM for 2 (Fig. 14.4), and the poor coverage noted for some immigration rates in Table 14.4. A more efficient approach might be to sample from a distribution that is closer to the posterior distribution and then reweight the simulated points by the ratio of the probability density of the parameter values under the prior to that under the sampling distribution. An iterative, adaptive, scheme may be useful in this regard.

The analysis of microsatellite data is only one part of the IM program (Hey & Nielsen 2004), which is primarily designed to analyse sequences, and can also work with microsatellites linked to short sequences. Different types of markers can be mixed together in the same analysis. These aspects should not be problematic to implement in an ABC approach, which will also be able to incorporate recombination. The only way to try to overcome the difficulties posed by the relatively low information content of markers such as microsatellites is through the analysis of multilocus nuclear sequence data. Since recombination will need to be included in such a model, it is likely that only approximate methods will be feasible with such data, and this represents a suitable future goal in the development of the ABC approach described here.

5. Appendix

5.1. Regression-based method for conditional density estimation

In this method we assume that we have measured a d dimensional vector of summary statistics s from a data set. We have n random draws of a (scalar) parameter $\Phi_{1,...,n}$ and corresponding summary statistics $S_{1,...,n}$ simulated from the joint distribution of parameters and summary statistics $P(S, \Phi)$. (The model may have any number of parameters, which can be considered jointly, but the regression adjustment described here is applied to one parameter at a time.) We scale s and S so that each summary statistic in S has unit variance.

We use the method of local-linear regression to compute the posterior mean $E(\Phi \mid S = s)$ (see, for example, Ruppert & Wand (1994), for background to the approach). In this method we want to minimize

$$\sum_{i=1}^{n} \{\Phi_i - \alpha - \beta^T(S_i - s)\}^2 K_\delta(\| S_i - s \|)$$

where

$$\alpha = E(\Phi \mid S = s),$$

$$\| x \| = \sqrt{\sum_{i=1}^{d} x_i^2},$$

and we use the Epanechnikov kernel

$$K_\delta(t) = \begin{cases} c\delta^{-1}\left(1 - (t/\delta)^2\right) & t \le \delta \\ 0 & t > \delta \,. \end{cases}$$

The solution is

$$\begin{bmatrix} \widehat{\alpha} \\ \widehat{\beta} \end{bmatrix} = (S_s^T W_s S_s)^{-1} S_s^T W_s \Phi$$

where

$$\Phi = [\Phi_1, \cdots, \Phi_n]^T$$

$$W_s = \mathrm{diag}\{K_\delta(\| S_1 - s\|), \cdots, K_\delta(\| S_n - s\|)\}$$

$$S_s = \begin{bmatrix} 1 & (S_1 - s)^T \\ \vdots & \vdots \\ 1 & (S_n - s)^T \end{bmatrix}$$

Our best estimate of the posterior mean is then

$$\hat{\alpha} = e_1^T (S_s^T W_s S_s)^{-1} S_s^T W_s \Phi$$

where e_1 is a $d + 1$ length vector $(1, 0, \cdots, 0)$.

In order to estimate posterior densities, Beaumont *et al.* (2002), took a heuristic approach, in which they make an assumption that the errors are constant in the interval and adjust the parameter values as

$$\Phi_i^* = \Phi_i - (S_i - s)^T \hat{\beta}.$$

The posterior density for can be approximated as

$$\widehat{\pi}(\Phi \mid S = s) = \frac{\sum_i K_\Delta(\Phi_i - \Phi) K_\delta(\| S_i - s \|)}{\sum_i K_\delta(\| S_i - s \|)}$$

where $K_\Delta(t)$ is another Epanechnikov kernel with bandwidth Δ. Alternatively some other density method can be used, and in this paper the local-likelihood method of Loader (1996) is used, implemented in Locfit under R, weighting the points with $K_\delta(\| S_i - s \|)$ as above. In Beaumont *et al.* (2002) the 'tolerance' of the method was not measured directly in terms of the Epanechnikov bandwidth , but in terms of P_δ, the proportion of simulated points where $\| S_i - s \| \le \delta$.

Note

1. The final revision of this chapter was submitted 18/02/06. No attempt has been made to update at the proof stage the many developments in this area that have occurred in the last two years.

References

Beaumont, M.A. & R.A. Nichols, 1996. Evaluating loci for use in the genetic analysis of population structure. *Proceedings of the Royal Society of London*, Series B 263, 1619–26.

Beaumont, M.A., W. Zhang & D.J. Balding, 2002. Approximate Bayesian computation in population genetics. *Genetics* 162, 2025–35.

Cavalli-Sforza, L.L. & A.W.F. Edwards, 1967. Phylogenetic analysis: models and estimation procedures. *Evolution* 32, 550–70.

Cornuet, J.M., M.A. Beaumont, A. Estoup & M. Solignac, 2006. Inference on microsatellite mutation processes in the invasive mite, Varroa destructor, using reversible jump Markov chain Monte Carlo. *Theoretical Population Biology* 69, 129–44.

Excoffier, L., A. Estoup & J.M. Cornuet, 2005. Bayesian analysis of an admixture model with mutations and arbitrarily linked markers. *Genetics* 169, 1727–38.

Goldstein, D.B., A. Ruiz Linares, L.L. Cavalli-Sforza & M.W. Feldman, 1995. Genetic absolute dating based on microsatellites and the origin of modern humans. *Proceedings of the National Academy of Sciences of the USA* 92, 6723–7.

Goldstein, D.B., G.W. Roemer, D.A. Smith, D.E. Reich, A. Bergman & R.K. Wayne, 1999. The use of microsatellite variation to infer population structure and demographic history in a natural model system. *Genetics* 151, 797–801.

Green, P.J., 1995. Reversible jump Markov chain Monte Carlo computation and Bayesian model determination. *Biometrika* 82, 711–32.

Griffiths, R.C. & S. Tavaré, 1994. Simulating probability distributions in the coalescent. *Theoretical Population Biology* 46, 131–59.

Harpending, C., M.A. Batzer, M. Gurven, L.B. Jorde, A.R. Rogers & S.T. Sherry, 1998. Genetic traces of ancient demography. *Proceedings of the National Academy of Sciences of the USA* 95, 1961–7.

Hey, J. & R. Nielsen, 2004. Multilocus methods for estimating population sizes, migration rates and divergence time, with applications to the divergence of *Drosophila pseudoobscura* and *D. persimilis*. *Genetics* 167, 747–60.

Hudson, R.R., 2001. Two-locus sampling distribution and their application. *Genetics* 159, 1805–17.

Jennings, W.B. & S.V. Edwards, 2005. Speciational history of Australian grass finches (*Poephila*) inferred from thirty gene trees. *Evolution* 59, 2033–47.

King, J.P., M. Kimmel & R. Chakraborty, 2000. A power analysis of microsatellite based statistics for inferring past population growth. *Molecular Biology and Evolution* 17, 1859–68.

Kuhner, M.K., J. Yamato & J. Felsenstein, 1995. Estimating effective population size and mutation rate from sequence data using Metropolis-Hastings sampling. *Genetics* 140, 1421–30.

Li, N. & M. Stephens, 2003. Modelling linkage disequilibrium and identifying recombination hotspots using single-nucleotide polymorphism data. *Genetics* 165, 2213–33.

Loader, C.R., 1996. Local likelihood density estimation. *Annals of Statistics* 24, 1602–18.

Marjoram, P., J. Molitor, V. Plagnol & S. Tavaré, 2003. Markov chain Monte Carlo without likelihoods. *Proceedings of the National Academy of Sciences of the USA* 100, 15,324–8.

McVean, G., P. Awadalla & P. Fearnhead, 2002. A coalescent based method for detecting and estimating recombination from gene sequences. *Genetics* 160, 1231–41.

Nielsen, R. & J. Wakeley, 2001. Distinguishing migration from isolation: a Markov chain Monte Carlo approach. *Genetics* 158, 885–96.

Pritchard, J.K., M.T. Seielstad, A. Perez-Lezaun & M.W. Feldman, 1999. Population growth of human Y chromosomes: a study of Y chromosome microsatellites. *Molecular Biology and Evolution* 16, 1791–8.

Rosenberg, N.A., J.K. Pritchard, J.L. Weber, *et al.*, 2002. Genetic structure of human populations. *Science* 298, 2981–5.

Ruppert, D. & M.P. Wand, 1994. Multivariate locally weighted least squares regression. *Annals of Statistics* 22, 1346–70.

Saitou, N. & M. Nei, 1987. The neighbor-joining method: a new method for reconstructing phylogenetic trees. *Molecular Biology and Evolution* 4, 406–25.

Storz, J.F. & M.A. Beaumont, 2002. Testing for genetic evidence of population expansion and contraction: an empirical analysis of microsatellite DNA variation using a hierarchical Bayesian model. *Evolution* 56, 154–66.

Takezaki, N. & M. Nei, 1996. Genetic distances and reconstruction of phylogenetic trees from microsatellite data. *Genetics* 144, 389–99.

Wilson, I.J. & D.J. Balding, 1998. Genealogical inference from microsatellite data. *Genetics* 150, 499–510.

Wilson, I.J., M.E. Weale & D.J. Balding, 2003. Inferences from DNA data: population histories, evolutionary processes and forensic match probabilities. *Journal of the Royal Statistical Society* A 166, 155–88.

Wright, S., 1931. Evolution in Mendelian populations. *Genetics* 16, 97–159.

Wright, S., 1937. The distribution of gene frequencies in populations. *Proceedings of the National Academy of Sciences of the USA* 23, 307–20.

Chapter 15

Estimating Human Demographic Parameters from Genomic SNP Data

Rasmus Nielsen

Large Single Nucleotide Polymorphism (SNP) genotyping data sets are becoming available for a number of human populations. Such data may provide much information about present and past human demographic processes. However, analyses of such data are often challenged by the complicated ascertainment schemes used in selecting and discovering SNPs. In this paper we discuss some methods for estimating demographic parameters using SNPs, which can take ascertainment biases into account. In particular, we discuss Composite Likelihood approaches, which often may have desirable statistical properties, and are highly computationally tractable.

Single Nucleotide Polymorphism (SNP) data are to an increasing degree being used in human population genetics. Currently, several large-scale SNP genotyping projects are under way, such as the HapMap project (The International HapMap Consortium, 2003). Unfortunately, many of the current large-scale data sets may not be the best sources for estimation of parameters in complex demographic models, because admixed populations, such as African-Americans have been used, and because the available information regarding ethnicities of the sampled individuals is sparse. However, given the reduced cost of genotyping, large-scale human SNP data sets, based on carefully sampled ethnicities, will most likely see the light over the next few years. SNP data analyses of demographic models have a potential advantage over single marker analyses in that they may be more robust in the presence of selection because they average over many loci. In addition they may be cost-effective and have high statistical power because of the many markers typically involved. Over the next decade SNP analyses will likely replace mtDNA as the primary tool for demographic inferences in human evolutionary genetics. It is, therefore, now important to consider which statistical methods should be used in the analysis of such data.

One obvious statistical approach is to calculate the likelihood function in each SNP independently to form an equation used for estimation, based on the product of these individual marginal likelihood functions. If the SNPs are independent (roughly speaking when they are not tightly linked) this equation will form a true likelihood function. In the cases where the SNPs are linked, the equation forms a composite likelihood function (Lindsey 1988), that may also be used for estimation. In the case of a composite likelihood function, as defined here, there is no general theory that guarantees that the estimator will have desirable statistical properties, or theory that will help establish confidence intervals and hypothesis tests. However, in applications in population genetics, it is possible to show that the composite estimators in many cases have reasonable statistical properties (e.g. Nielsen & Wiuf 2005). However, confidence intervals and hypothesis tests must be done using simulation approaches. This approach has been used for demographic inference to estimate population growth rates by Nielsen (2000), Wooding & Rogers (2002), Polanski & Kimmel (2003), Adams & Hudson (2004) and Marth *et al.* (2004).

In this paper I will outline and review some results regarding likelihood estimation, and composite likelihood estimation of demographic parameters, based on genomic SNP data. Three approaches for calculating the likelihood, one based on coalescent simulations, one using analytical theory within the coalescent framework, and one using diffusion theory will first be reviewed. Then I will discuss issues relating to ascertainment biases produced by the SNP selection procedures, and the statistical properties of composite likelihood estimators. Familiarity with basic population genetic theory, such as coalescent theory, will be assumed throughout and will not be reviewed.

The composite likelihood function

In the following, we will refer to the product of individual likelihoods calculated for multiple SNP sites as a composite likelihood function, although this function in some cases will be a true likelihood function. The higher the recombination rates between SNP sites, the closer the product will become to being a true likelihood function. Mathematically we can define the function as

$$CL(\gamma) \equiv \prod_{j=1}^{n-1} \left(p_j(\gamma) \right)^{n_j},$$ (1)

where γ is a vector of parameters and $p_j(\gamma)$ is the probability of observing a SNP of type j under γ, n is the number of gene copies in the sample and n_j is the number of SNPs in the sample of type j, i.e. where the derived allele is of type j. This equation assumes that only variable sites (SNP sites) are included in the sample, but it could also be applied to the case where all sites are included in the sample by letting the product run for 0 to n. Equation (1) also assumes that the ancestral state of the mutation is known (or inferred using an outgroup). If it is not possible to make such assumptions the product should run from 1 to $[n/2]$, and n_j then indicates the number of SNPs with minor allele frequency j.

The values of $p_j(\gamma)$, $j = 1, 2,..,n-1$, are given by the expected frequency spectrum, where $p_j(\gamma)$ is sometimes called the frequency of mutations of size j. Analytical results for the standard coalescent model were first derived by Tajima (1989) under the infinite sites model. For more general demographic models, $p_j(\gamma)$ can be calculated or approximated by a consideration of the expected coalescence times in the tree (e.g. Fu 1995; Griffiths & Tavaré 1998). Using the notation of Nielsen (2000), the likelihood function can be written as

$$p_j(\gamma) = \frac{E_\gamma(t_j)}{E_\gamma(T)}$$ (2)

where t_j is the sum of branch-lengths in the tree in which a single mutation would cause a polymorphism

of size j, and T is the total tree length. This result can be derived both by considering a single variable site under the infinite sites model, or by assuming low mutation rates in the finite sites model with symmetric mutation rates or in an infinite alleles model. The latter two types of models become identical to an infinite sites model, at least with respect to the frequency spectrum, when conditioning on variability in the site and considering the limit of small mutation rates. Using the limit of small mutation rates, corresponding to the infinite sites model, implies assuming all SNPs are caused by a single mutation. The expression is valid for any demographic model for which the expectations in Equation (2) exist.

The coalescent simulation approach

The coalescent simulation approach for estimating the likelihood function is based on simulating independent genealogies, and then evaluating Equation (2) based on these simulated genealogies (Nielsen 2000). In brief, B coalescent genealogies are simulated under γ using standard methods (e.g. Hudson 2002). For genealogy i, the total tree length (T_i) and sum of the length of all edges in which a single mutation would cause a mutation of frequency j in the sample (t_{ij}) is calculated. Then $p_j(\gamma)$ is approximated as

$$\sum_{i=1}^{B} t_{ij} \left(\sum_{i=1}^{B} T_i \right)^{-1}$$ (3)

Parameters are then estimated by finding the value of γ that maximizes $CL_d(\gamma)$.

In some cases, it may be computationally advantageous to use an importance sampling scheme to help the estimation of the likelihood surface. Simulations are done under one value of γ, say γ_0, and the sampling probabilities for other values of γ can then be approximated by

$$\left(\sum_{i=1}^{B} \frac{t_{ij} p_\gamma(G_i)}{p_{\gamma_0}(G_i)} \right) \left(\sum_{i=1}^{B} \frac{T_i p_\gamma(G_i)}{p_{\gamma_0}(G_i)} \right)^{-1}$$ (4)

where $p_\gamma(G_i)$ is the density (with respect to a multidimensional Lebesgue measure) of genealogies under γ, and G_i is the ith simulated genealogy. In general, this method will work well when the distance between γ and γ_0 is very small, and poorly when the distance is large.

An example of the method is shown in Figure 15.1. The method was applied to 12,839 SNPs from the Seattle SNP project (SeattleSNPs. NHLBI Program for Genomic Applications, SeattleSNPs, Seattle, WA (URL: http://pga.gs.washington.edu) [Feb. 2004]) for 24 African-American individuals and 23 Europeans.

Although these samples are far from ideal for the purpose of estimating human demographic parameters, they can be used as an illustration of the methodology. A model which includes different population size, a bottleneck in Europeans, gene flow between the two populations and divergence of the populations from a common ancestral population, was fitted to the data. The profile likelihood for the migration parameter (m) and the divergence time (t) is shown in Figure 15.1. The joint maximum likelihood estimates for m and t are approx. 3.5 and 0.6, respectively. Both parameters are scaled in terms of the effective population size of Europeans. Assuming an effective population size of approx. 10,000 and a generation time of 25 years, the estimate of the divergence time translates into 150,000 years. The considerable amount of the gene-flow inferred is presumably due to recent introgression between Europeans and Africans in America.

The strength of this method is that demographic inferences can be made for any model which can be simulated. The disadvantage is that the simulation variance in some cases can be so high that optimization of the likelihood surface in multi-dimensional parameter spaces can be difficult.

Numerical coalescent methods

For some models, the expected site frequency spectrum can be evaluated without the use of simulations. Tajima (1989) derived results for the standard neutral equilibrium model and Fu (1995) extended and generalized the results. Wooding & Rogers (2002), Polanski & Kimmel (2003), Adams & Hudson (2004) and Marth *et al.* (2004) showed how the frequency spectrum could be calculated numerically for models with population growth. Equation (2) is evaluated in Wooding & Rogers (2002) by defining a matrix of time-dependent transition probabilities of the coalescent process. The probability of k ancestors at time t in the past can then be expressed in a system of differential equations defined in terms of this matrix. The system can be solved numerically and the expected time in the coalescent tree with k ancestors can then be found by integrating over the time-dependent probability of having k ancestors. Because of the computational problems involved, Wooding & Rogers (2002) also suggested how to approximate the history using models in which the population size is piece-wise constant. Marth *et al.* (2004) also used models with piece-wise constant population sizes. They furthermore showed how this approach can be used to model the divergence of multiple populations, and they fitted data from Europeans, Asians and African-Americans to estimate population size changes in a model with fixed

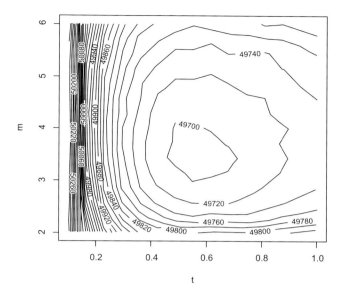

Figure 15.1. *The joint profile likelihood surface for the migration parameter* (m) *and the divergence time parameter* (t) *based on 12,839 SNPs from the Seattle SNP project from Europeans and African-Americans.*

divergence times between the populations. Adams & Hudson (2004) explored the properties of likelihood estimators in models of changing population size in more detail. They found that there, in general, is very little power to make inferences about recent growth in population size, but that ancient changes in population sizes could be inferred more accurately. Polanski & Kimmel (2003) developed a more computationally efficient method for evaluating Equation (2) for models with exponential population growth.

These approaches are in general computationally superior to approaches based on simulations. However, they may not be easily extendable to models with population structure that allow gene-flow between populations. Care must also be given to numerical problems that easily arise in the implementation of these models.

The diffusion equation approach

While the two previous approaches were based on a coalescent representation, it is also possible to derive the expected frequency spectrum using diffusion theory. This is done by calculating the density of mutation frequencies in the population, and then assuming binomial sampling to obtain the sample frequencies. If the density of the allele frequency, x, is given by $f(x)$, the expected frequency spectrum is given by (e.g. Sawyer & Hartl 1992; Griffiths 2003)

$$p_j(\gamma) = \frac{\int_0^1 \binom{n}{j} x^i (1-x)^{n-j} f(x) dx}{\int_0^1 (1 - x^n - (1-x)^n) f(x) dx} \quad (5)$$

The expression $(1 - x^n - (1-x)^n)$ in the denominator appears because we, as in the previous approaches, condition on variability in the sample. Inferences based on this type of approach were introduced by Sawyer & Hartl (1992) and Bustamante et al. (2001) in relation to models with natural selection. Such models are generally intractable in the coalescent framework. Sawyer & Hartl (1992) used the term Poisson Random Field (PRF) for these models.

Griffiths (2003) shows how the frequency spectrum quite generally can be calculated on the basis of the transition function of the diffusion process. Let the $f(x; p, t)$ be the density function for the population allele frequency (x), given that it was at frequency p, t generations ago. The sample frequency is then obtained by considering new mutations (taking the limit of $p \to 0$) and integrating over the time since the mutation arose, i.e. (Griffiths 2003):

$$p_j(\gamma) = \lim_{p \to 0} \frac{\int_0^\infty \int_0^1 \binom{n}{j} x^i (1-x)^{n-j} f(x;p,t) dx dt}{\int_0^\infty \int_0^1 (1 - x^n - (1-x)^n) f(x;p,t) dx dt} \quad (6)$$

Griffiths (2003) also discussed how this method could be used in the context of changing population sizes.

Williamson et al. (2005) used a similar method to simultaneously estimate population growth (piecewise linear) and selection. They assumed equilibrium population allele frequencies T generations ago, and then a single discrete change in population size. The density of population allele frequencies was then evaluated numerically, and the integral in (4) was solved using numeric integration.

The major advantage of these approaches is their flexibility. They can incorporate changing population sizes, selection (which the coalescent approaches have a very hard time incorporating), migration between multiple populations, etc. However, as with the previous approaches, evaluation of Equations (5, 6) may in many instances require numerical methods which can be unstable.

Ascertainment bias correction

A fundamental problem in the analysis of most human SNP data is that the SNPs have been discovered using a SNP ascertainment process that may severely bias any demographic inferences. Typically, the SNPs have

first been ascertained in a small sample (the ascertainment sample). The SNPs discovered in this sample have then subsequently been typed in a sample containing many more individuals (the typed sample). This procedure creates biases towards the inclusion of relatively more SNPs of high allele frequency, typically biasing estimates towards less population growth. Estimates of levels of gene flow, divergence times and relative effective populations sizes among different populations, may also be biased, particularly if the ascertainment samples do not have the same ethnic makeup as the typed sample. Fortunately, it is possible to correct the ascertainment biases in most cases. Such corrections have, for SNP data, been considered by Wakeley et al. (2001), Nielsen & Signorovitch (2003), Polanski & Kimmel (2003), Marth et al. (2004), Nielsen (2004), Nielsen et al. (2004) and others. The effect of ascertainment biases on RFLP or Alu variation has also been discussed extensively in the human genetics literature before SNP data emerged (e.g. Mountain & Cavalli-Sforza 1994; Rogers & Jorde 1996; Urbanek et al. 1996; Sherry et al. 1997; Eller 2001).

The correction for ascertainment bias usually proceeds in a likelihood framework where the likelihood function is modified to be defined conditionally on the ascertainment condition, e.g. variability in the ascertainment sample. The likelihood function is then defined as

$$\Pr(Data \mid \gamma; Ascertainment)$$
$$= \frac{\Pr(Data, Ascertainment \mid \gamma)}{\Pr(Ascertainment \mid \gamma)}. \quad (7)$$

In general, the expressions to the right-hand side of the equation can be calculated quite easily if information regarding the procedures used to obtain the SNPs is available and complete.

By letting γ be the vector of frequencies of the different classes in the frequency spectrum (i.e. $\gamma_j = p_j(\gamma) = p_j, j = 1, 2, ..., n-1$), the ascertainment corrected frequency spectrum can be estimated (Nielsen et al. 2004). For simple ascertainment schemes, where the ascertainment sample is a subset of the typed sample, and the ascertainment sample size is the same for all SNPs (Nielsen et al. 2004)

$$\hat{p}_k = \frac{n_k}{\Pr(\text{Ascer. of type } k)} \left[\sum_{j=1}^{n-1} \frac{n_j}{\Pr(\text{Ascer. of type } j)} \right]^{-1},$$
$$k = 1, ..., n-1, \quad (8)$$

where $\Pr(\text{Ascer. of type } j)$ is the probability that a SNP of frequency j/n will end up in the typed sample. This expression also generalizes to models with population subdivisions (where the multidimensional frequency spectrum is of interest). For the simple models this method provides a maximum likelihood estimate of the 'corrected' frequency spectrum. For more complex ascertainment schemes, it is no longer a maximum likelihood estimate, but a method of moments estimate. Use of this method may lead to a loss of information in cases where the ascertainment condition varies among SNPs and detailed information for each SNP is available.

In cases where information regarding the ascertainment data is available for all the SNPs that do not appear in the typed sample, the likelihood function for the typed sample and the ascertainment can be combined.

In general, while the ascertainment correction procedures mathematically are very simple, there are considerable problems associated with their application to real data because the ascertainment information typically is not publicly available.

Properties of composite likelihood

The composite maximum likelihood estimator is a statistically consistent estimator of demographic parameters under most demographic models. It provides a convenient and computationally tractable method for estimation of demographic parameters from large SNP data sets. A simple example is the case of estimation of θ ($= 4N\mu$) in the standard neutral equilibrium model. In a well-behaved exchangeable model, the composite likelihood function for θ (per site) is given by (Nielsen & Wiuf 2005)

$$\theta \left(1 - \frac{\theta E_\gamma(T)}{2} \right)^{k-S} \qquad (9)$$

where S is the number of variable sites and k is the total number of sites. This result can be derived for a symmetric finite sites model in the limit of small mutation rates. The maximum likelihood estimate of θ is then

$$\frac{2S}{E_\gamma(T)k} \qquad (10)$$

For the standard neutral model, this estimator is identical to the classical Watterson (1975) estimator. It was originally derived as a method of moments estimator, but it is also the composite maximum likelihood estimator. It is known to have good statistical properties, in that it is unbiased and consistent. The consistency property of the maximum composite likelihood estimators seem to be general and it also extends to

demographic models (Wiuf & Nielsen, unpublished results). If this holds true in general, it may provide a theoretical justification for the use of the composite likelihood methods. Nonetheless, it is important to be aware that the construction of confidence intervals, and hypothesis testing, in most cases must rely on simulations in the composite likelihood framework. The classical likelihood theory is not applicable to these estimators.

Conclusion

While most of the SNP data currently available are not very suitable for demographic inferences, more appropriate data sets will become available in the near future. It is, therefore, important to consider the different possible methods for making demographic inferences based on SNP data. The composite likelihood methods discussed in this paper provide an attractive framework for such inferences. In most cases, the numerical methods based either on the coalescent or the diffusion theory approach, are computationally superior to the coalescent simulation approaches. The diffusion theory approach in particular is attractive because it may be applicable to a larger set of models, (e.g. models with gene flow) than the coalescent methods. However, there may be very complex demographic models that are analytically and numerically intractable, even in the diffusion theory framework, where the coalescent simulation approaches may find good use.

References

Adams, M. & R.R. Hudson, 2004. Maximum-likelihood estimation of demographic parameters using the frequency spectrum of unlinked single-nucleotide polymorphisms. *Genetics* 168, 1699–1712.

Bustamante, C.D., J. Wakeley, S.A. Sawyer & D.L. Hartl, 2001. Directional selection and the site-frequency spectrum. *Genetics* 159(4), 1779–88.

Clark, A.G., R. Nielsen, J. Signorovitch, *et al.*, 2003. Linkage disequilibrium and inference of ancestral recombination in 538 single-nucleotide polymorphism clusters across the human genome. *American Journal of Human Genetics* 73, 285–300.

Eller, E., 2001. Effects of ascertainment bias on recovering human demographic history. *Human Biology* 73, 411–28.

Fu, X.-Y., 1995. Statistical properties of segregating sites. *Theoretical Population Biology* 48, 172–97.

Griffiths, R.C., 2003. The frequency spectrum of a mutation, and its age, in a general diffusion model. *Theoretical Population Biology* 64, 241–51.

Griffiths, R.C. & S. Tavaré, 1998. The age of a mutation in a general coalescent tree. *Stochastic Models* 14, 273–95.

Hudson, R., 2002. Generating samples under a Wright-Fisher neutral model. *Bioinformatics* 18, 337–8.

Lindsay, B.G., 1988. Composite likelihood methods. *Contemporary Mathematics* 80, 221–39.

Marth, G., E. Czabarka, J. Murvai & S.T. Sherry, 2004. The allele frequency spectrum in genome-wide human variation data reveals signals of differential demographic history in three large world populations. *Genetics* 166, 351–72.

Mountain, J.L. & L.L. Cavalli-Sforza, 1994. Inference of human evolution through cladistic analysis of nuclear DNA restriction polymorphisms. *Proceedings of the National Academy of Sciences of the USA* 91, 6515–19.

Nielsen, R., 2000. Estimation of population parameters and recombination rates using single nucleotide polymorphisms. *Genetics* 154, 931–42.

Nielsen, R., 2004. Population genetic analysis of ascertained SNP data. *Human Genomics* 3, 218–24.

Nielsen , R. & J. Signorovitch, 2003. Correcting for ascertainment biases when analyzing SNP data: applications to the estimation of linkage disequilibrium. *Theoretical Population Biology* 63, 245–55.

Nielsen, R. & C. Wiuf, 2005. Composite likelihood estimation in population genetics. *Proceedings of the 55th Sessions of the ISI.*

Nielsen, R., M.J. Todd & A.G. Clark, 2004. Reconstituting the frequency spectrum of ascertained SNP data. *Genetics* 168, 2373–82.

Polanski, A. & M. Kimmel, 2003. New explicit expressions for relative frequencies of single-nucleotide polymorphisms with application to statistical inference on population growth. *Genetics* 165, 427–36.

Rogers, A.R. & L.B. Jorde, 1996. Ascertainment bias in estimates of average heterozygosity. *American Journal of Human Genetics* 58, 1033–41.

Sawyer, S. & D.L. Hartl, 1992. Population genetics of polymorphism and divergence. *Genetics* 132, 1161–76.

Sherry, S.T., H.C. Harpending, M.A. Batzer & M. Stoneking, 1997. Alu evolution in human populations: using the coalescent to estimate effective population size. *Genetics* 147, 1977–82.

Tajima, F., 1989. Statistical method for testing the neutral mutation hypothesis by DNA polymorphism. *Genetics* 123, 585–95.

The International HapMap Consortium, 2003. The International HapMap Project. *Nature* 426, 789–96.

Urbanek, M., D. Goldman & J.C. Long, 1996. The apportionment of dinucleotide repeat diversity in Native Americans and Europeans: a new approach to measuring gene identity reveals asymmetric patterns of divergence. *Molecular Biology and Evolution* 13, 943–53.

Wakeley, J., R. Nielsen, S.N. Liu-Cordero & K. Ardlie, 2001. The discovery of single-nucleotide polymorphisms — and inferences about human demographic history. *American Journal of Human Genetics* 69, 1332–47.

Watterson, G.A., 1975. On the number of segregating sites in genetical models without recombination. *Theoretical Population Biology* 7, 256–76.

Williamson, S.H., R. Hernandez, A. Fledel-Alon, L. Zhu, R. Nielsen & C.D. Bustamante, 2005. Simultaneous inference of selection and population growth from patterns of variation in the human genome. *Proceedings of the National Academy of Sciences of the USA* 102, 7882–7.

Wooding, S. & A. Rogers. 2002. The matrix coalescent and an application to human single-nucleotide polymorphisms. *Genetics* 161, 1641–50.

Chapter 16

Demography, Ascertainment and the Genealogy of Haplotype Blocks

Ian Wilson

The search for genetic influences on human diseases has resulted in huge data bases of genetic variation in autosomal DNA. These data bases do not provide a complete picture of variation, are sequenced in a limited number of sites, and have properties that make them far from ideal for genetic anthropological studies. Nevertheless, the resource is huge and, if used correctly, likely to be useful for the study of ancient human history. Patterns of variation seen in human populations are the result of the interplay between shared ancestry and mutation in the history of the sample. This history is of direct interest for anthropological studies. Even without recombination, these data have a complex dependency structure. When we consider variability at a genome level in data sets such as the HapMap (The International HapMap Consortium 2005), the levels of complexity increase as recombinations become important. An exciting possibility is to use patterns of recombination within and between populations to learn about human demography, provided we can develop tools to visualize and to draw inferences from data. This work investigates how one might utilize genomic data to learn about human evolution, using simple summary statistics.

Background and motivation

The hunt for genes that influence human disease has driven the development of new technologies for discovering and measuring genetic variation in humans. Recent large studies have produced data bases of genomic variation like the HapMap (The International HapMap Consortium 2003; 2005), the SNP Map (The International SNP Map Working Group 2001) and the Perlegen data base (Hinds *et al.* 2005). While the gold standard of genetics studies of human history is likely to remain DNA sequence data, the general availability of technologies and data sets with published allele frequencies in known populations opens new possibilities for describing the patterns seen in human genetic variation. These data are not ideal for human historical studies and have some problems — most importantly the variation within them is not a random sample of variation in the genome — but they are an important resource and their potential for studies of human history should be investigated.

One aim of the HapMap is to divide the human genome into regions — 'haplotype blocks' — within which there has been limited recombination, and between which markers can be assumed to be independent. This is unlikely to be true, nevertheless it is useful for disease studies and we may expect that some of these blocks could act as population markers, and be useful for anthropological genetics. This data is of particular relevance as:

- The data covers the human genome with a coverage of about one Single Nucleotide Polymorphism (SNP) per 3 kB of DNA — see Table 16.1.
- These SNPs have been typed in four populations: Yoruba in Ibadan, Nigeria (YRI); Japanese in Tokyo; Han Chinese in Beijing; and CEPH (Utah residents with ancestry from northern and western Europe: CEU).
- The YRI and CEU data sets each consist of the genotypes of 30 parent–offspring trios so that the phase may be correctly inferred for the parental haplotypes (except for those positions where both

Table 16.1. *The number and median gaps between markers (in bases) for all SNPs that are in both YRI and CEU data bases for HAPMAP data base release #16.*

Chromo-some	No. of markers	Median distance	Chromo-some	No. of markers	Median distance
1	77,301	2410	12	42,665	2487
2	83,573	2531	13	34,460	2411
3	63,149	2587	14	27,674	2659
4	54,903	2986	15	25,044	2607
5	54,403	2764	16	23,816	2670
6	63,030	2176	17	23,591	2784
7	44,951	2819	18	37,104	1407
8	67,409	1545	19	16,771	2772
9	53,403	1642	20	19,739	2595
10	47,162	2307	21	18,364	1488
11	42,046	2690	22	17,642	1406
Overall				938,200	2310

Table 16.2. *Means (with standard deviation) of summary statistics for the whole of chromosome 3 for CEU and YRI samples. Analyses were performed on both samples from together.*

	MNP_{12}	MNP_8	MNP_4
n	31,569	31,571	31,573
Total alleles	37.81 (32.15)	16.33 (11.15)	6.07 (2.19)
CEU alleles	16.94 (15.31)	8.74 (5.82)	4.37 (1.8)
YRI alleles	26.54 (20.26)	12.76 (8.17)	5.3 (1.99)
Maximum relative frequency	0.3 (0.13)	0.37 (0.14)	0.5 (0.15)
P(Shared)	0.23 (0.14)	0.37 (0.15)	0.62 (0.19)
P(Singleton)	0.48 (0.21)	0.31 (0.16)	0.13 (0.14)
Estimated F	0.12 (0.08)	0.14 (0.09)	0.15 (0.12)
P(Only CEU)	0.25 (0.14)	0.19 (0.14)	0.12 (0.14)
P(Only YRI)	0.53 (0.15)	0.44 (0.17)	0.27 (0.19)
Expected H CEU	0.71 (0.17)	0.64 (0.17)	0.53 (0.18)
Expected H YRI	0.83 (0.1)	0.76 (0.12)	0.6 (0.16)

parents and the offspring in a triplet are heterozygous, or where there is missing data). The Han Chinese data set consists of 45, and the Japanese of 44 unrelated individuals.

These data provide an unrivalled resource for investigating patterns of variation in two populations in the human genome as haplotypes can be inferred accurately from freely available, good-quality data. Summaries of marker density for those markers present in both CEU and YRI data bases for HapMap public release #16 are given in Table 16.1. Close to one million variable markers have been typed in both the Yoruban and CEPH populations and, for the majority of these markers, phase is known giving 120 haplotypes from each population. The analyses following are done only on Yoruban and CEPH samples, as haplotypes can be inferred more accurately with this data from parent-offspring trios.

Fully linked data, such as Y-chromosome data and mtDNA, have a single gene genealogy underlying the data, and in theory all information in the data can be used with full probability modelling — although this may be slow — using programs such as MIGRATE (Beerli & Felsenstein 1999) and BATWING (Wilson et al. 2003). When we have recombination within a sequence the inferential problem becomes much more difficult, and for large samples, practically impossible.

Approximate Bayesian Computation (ABC) may provide a partial solution. ABC methods are more scaleable, can use multiprocessor computers easily and do not have the same convergence problems with extremely large data sets. Additionally, Beaumont et al. (2002) show that, for one problem, the precision of a full likelihood BATWING analysis outperforms an ABC by a factor of only about 10 per cent. ABC meth-

ods try to match summary statistics from simulations to those calculated from data; this allows us to proceed directly from simulation to inference, provided we choose appropriate summaries of the data.

Other methods with less explicit modelling assumptions can be put under the umbrella of *phylogeography*. Such methods typically define haplogroups (or clades which are groups of haplotypes labelled by ancient mutations) and look at geographic patterns of within haplogroup diversity (Templeton 1998). These techniques are restricted to non-recombining markers as the methods are critically dependent on accurately reconstructed trees, and will not work on autosomal sequences. However, haplotypes population markers should be useful to track population movements. Among the first results from the HapMap project is the considerable variation seen in recombination rates and diversity statistics in autosomal DNA (Fearnhead et al. 2004). Any survey using autosomal data should use the information available in the HapMap to design the appropriate markers, in the appropriate parts of the genome.

The work presented here develops visualization and statistical techniques by which the effort expended by the HapMap project may be utilized for the study of human history and evolution. I investigate how simple statistics calculated from simulated ascertained haplotype data behave under different models for population history and demography.

Simple data summaries

Using data from these libraries is not completely straightforward. Marker discovery mechanisms may be unknown, and can be of a form that is difficult to model (e.g. a marker may be included in the study if it is seen to be variable in two studies). Work has been done in trying to estimate human demographic parameters from SNPs taking account of this ascertainment (Nielsen 2000; Nielsen *et al.* 2004). Here I investigate an alternative approach: instead of considering each SNP independently, neighbouring SNPs are taken together to create a 'haplotype allele' that is used as a highly variable marker. I expect to gain useful information from these data. Balding (2003) observed that the precision of estimates of F_{ST} are strongly affected by the number of alleles in a sample and much less affected by the sample size. Using haplotypes as single loci allows us to have as many alleles as we want at an individual locus, and so to increase the precision of estimates of population structure. These multiple nucleotide polymorphisms may be considered as highly variable alleles, with the low mutation rates seen at individual nucleotides enhanced by recombinations between sites. Pluzhnikov & Donnelly (1996) showed that recombination can act to reduce the variability of estimators of diversity from sequence data.

To give a flavour of the patterns seen in the HapMap data, Figures 16.1, 16.2 and 16.3 show very simple summaries of small parts of chromosome three for the YRI and CEU data sets, considering just those SNPs that have been scored in both data sets and marked as non-problematic in HapMap data base release #16. I have based my summaries on 'haplotype blocks' by reconstructing the phase of the 120 parental genotypes in each population (an MCMC method with a Dirichlet prior on block frequencies was used to reconstruct phase and missing data where the data were ambiguous). The blocks used to infer phase can then be thought of as a single Multiple Nucleotide Polymorphism (MNP). Note that in my analysis the length of the blocks is fixed (as a number of SNPs), I am not considering the usual definitions of haplotype blocks (reviewed in Wall & Pritchard (2003)) which are determined based on an heuristic for allocating variability along the genome, with block lengths allowed to vary. As a shorthand, I will use MNP_n for haplotype polymorphisms made from *n* consecutive SNPs. The method I have used for phasing data, similar to meth-

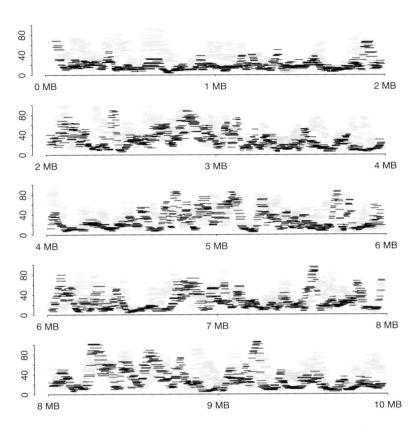

Figure 16.1. *Number of alleles for overlapping MNP_{16}'s from the first ten MB of chromosome three. Thick grey lines from Yoruba individuals, black lines for individuals of European origin. Unknown phases inferred by choosing the maximum posterior for each site using a Dirichlet prior and MCMC updates. The length of lines indicates the span of the underlying SNPs.*

ods listed in Stephens & Donnelly (2003), gave results almost completely in agreement with the phasing published on the HapMap web site.

Figure 16.1 gives a graphical summary of the number of MNP_{16} alleles for the first ten MB of chromosome three. The length of the lines indicates the span of the underlying SNPs. The MNP_{16}'s are overlapped to make the plot clearer. There is a huge variability in the number of MNP_{16} alleles in this section of DNA, and while for most positions there are more YRI alleles, in some positions, the CEU data are more polymorphic. It appears that levels of diversity are correlated as we look along the genome. Figure 16.2 confirms this for eight MN_8 alleles. This plot shows autocorrelation functions for the probability that an MNP_8 allele is shared between populations, an estimate of F_{ST}, and the probabilities of identity within the CEU and YRI populations. This figure also shows one of the features of the HapMap data: the correlation between sites is much less in the YRI sample.

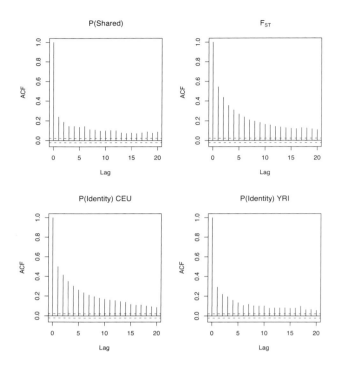

Figure 16.2. *Autocorrelation for summaries of non-overlapping MNP8s for HAPMAP data from human chromosome three. Unknown phases inferred by choosing the maximum posterior for each site using a Dirichlet prior and MCMC updates.*

Table 16.3. *Timings for simulations from the coalescent with recombination. All timings are for five samples of size 100, for 1000 loci.*

Recombination rate, ρ between sites	Time (seconds)
0	0.17
0.0001	0.17
0.001	0.19
0.01	0.28
0.1	0.97
1.0	13.6
10	790

More summaries are given in Table 16.2 which gives the mean and standard deviation of summary statistics of chromosome three for MNP_i's of lengths four, eight and twelve. A singleton is an MNP allele with only one copy in the sample and P(only YRI) is the probability that an MNP allele is seen only in the YRI sample. The maximum relative frequency is the relative frequency of the most common MNP allele. The last two lines give the expected heterozygosity for both samples. As expected, the YRI sample shows higher diversity, more rare alleles and higher expected heterozygosity.

Figure 16.3 shows trace plots of these statistics for a two MB section of DNA, approximately 1% of chromosome three. These summaries provide an easily understood snapshot of the data and can pick out areas of particular interest. In the next section I investigate how these summaries are affected by demography and ascertainment.

Simulations

The basis of inference from data that are in complete linkage disequilibrium (LD) is (in theory) straightfor-

ward. The coalescent, described in Hein *et al.* (2005), provides a basis. A single genealogy underlies the data, and we try to make inferences about history and population demography, by averaging over the genealogies that could have produced the observed data in some way. In a full Bayesian analysis, such as BATWING, we sample from genealogies proportional to their probability of giving the data under the coalescent. For ABC analyses (Beaumont 2003; Estoup *et al.* 2001) we sample lots of genealogies (using coalescent simulations) and throw away those that do not produce patterns like our data, although ABC within an MCMC framework is also possible (Marjoram *et al.* 2003).

The coalescent with recombination
When there is recombination, we can use the coalescent with recombination (Hein *et al.* 2005) for simulations and inference. The most basic problem, that of estimating the recombination rate, is hard and, while possible for small data sets, is computationally very intensive and various approximate schemes have been proposed (Li & Stephens 2003; Fearnhead & Donnelly 2001). The coalescent with recombination is far more difficult to work with for full likelihood analyses, and extensions to investigate other demographic parameters are not feasible. I shall use recombination to mean crossover here, and ignore recombinations that result in gene conversions, although this can be incorporated without too much difficulty.

Simulating from this process is simpler, but we must keep track of all sections of DNA that are *ancestral* to the sample (Hudson 1983), and which sections of DNA are on the same chromosome. This is far more computer intensive than the standard coalescent. Table 16.3 gives relative timings with increasing recombination rate. Chromosome three is 200 MB long, and the HapMap has about 60,000 markers common to the YRI and CEU samples on this chromosome. An average recombination rate for humans is thought to be approximately $10^{-2}\,MB^{-1}$ per generation. With an effective human population size of 10^5, this gives a average scaled recombination rate of about 1 between markers or a rate of between 10^5 and 10^6 for an entire human chromosome of length 200 MB. With the memory available in current desktop computers, we cannot simulate whole chromosomes at the density of the HapMap shown in Table 16.1, but we can simulate large sections of the genome.

There is evidence of large variations in recombination rate over small scales (Fearnhead *et al.* 2004), and the distance between markers is far from uniform. Ignoring this further difficulty, simulations of about 4000 variable sites are feasible, simulating about 100,000 potential variable sites with $\rho = 0.04$ between them, equivalent to a reasonable part of the genome.

Mutation and ascertainment
I use a very simple model for SNP mutations. I assume that only one mutation can occur at a site, and that it occurs uniformly on all the branches of the genealogy at that site. For simulating sequence data this would not be suitable, but for SNPs, we conditioning on a site being variable.

There is an additional complicating factor with SNPs, that of ascertainment (Nielsen *et al.* 2004). All SNPs in the HapMap are known to be variable from two different panel studies.

This means that they are likely to be at a high frequency than for DNA sequence data, where all variants in a sample are found. For the HapMap, where a stated aim is to get a SNP every 5 KB, the ascertainment may take on a more complex form — where there is low diversity then people have to search harder for SNPs, and allele frequency spectra are likely to be affected. This ascertainment bias affects the allele frequency spectrum of sampled data (Nielsen *et al.* 2004).

My models for ascertainment are:

Random More sites than required are sampled and the positions of SNPs are chosen uniformly at random from the pool of potential sites.

Length With this scheme the positions of SNPs are chosen at random proportional to the length of the genealogy underlying a site. This ap-

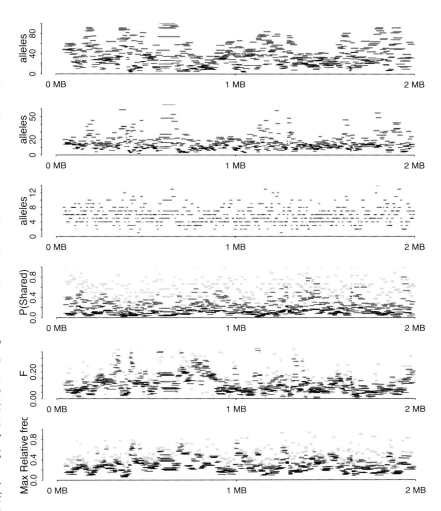

Figure 16.3. *Summary statistics for the first two MB of chromosome 3 for YRI and CEU data. Top three plots are the number of alleles for YRI (thick grey lines) and CEU (thin back lines) for MNP_{12}, MNP_8 and MNP_4 respectively. Bottom three plots are the estimated probability of a shared allele, estimated F_{ST} and maximum allele frequency for MNP_4 (thick light grey line), MNP_8 (grey line) and MNP_{12} (thin black line).*

proach keeps the property that mutations are more likely to occur on parts of the tree with long branches, but does not include the panel effect. This is similar to the marker ascertainment scheme of (Wang & Rannala 2004). Nielsen & Signorov (2003) discuss how this relates to the limiting distribution with small Θ. This is equivalent to the mechanism in the ms software (Hudson 2002).

Panel This approach extends the *Length* ascertainment to incorporate the fact that variable loci are discovered in some small *panel*, and then the loci screened over the rest of the sample.

The panel consists of a small number of individuals. This is done by selecting potential SNPs using the *Length* scheme and then simulating a mutation at that site. If SNP is polymorphic in the panel sample then the SNP is accepted, otherwise it is rejected and we sample again until we have the correct number of variable sites. This process means that there are fewer alleles than expected at low frequencies. A more extreme effect seen with double panels where a gene has to be variable in two different panels before it is accepted into a study and screened in larger samples.

A second effect is on the location and the density of markers. The Length ascertainment scheme detailed above leads to the density of markers being proportional to the relative length of the tree. Since this can vary by an order of magnitude along the genome for some combinations of growth and migration models, the density of potential markers is likely to vary hugely along the genome without needing selective explanations.

Recombination between markers within a MNP allele acts like mutation, and I hope that taking multiple markers together will reduce the effect of ascertainment — in fact I hope that because the markers are expected to be at a higher frequency than on average, that this will cause more recombinations to be 'visible' and increase the effective mutation rate of these markers. These properties of the data mean that we have to be very careful when drawing inferences. Before we look at the data I shall simulate some 'idealized' data to see what information we could consider extracting.

Population subdivision and demography

A variety of models have been suggested for population structure and demography in human populations. Beaumont (2004) describes and illustrates a number of these models. Much work on human populations involved the inference of subdivision and demography from population genetic data. Here I shall investigate what effects demography has on the patterns seen in lengths of DNA and in the observable variation.

I shall consider two classes of population subdivision. In the first, generally called the structured coalescent we have a migration matrix **M** where element m_{ij}, $i, j = 1, \ldots, K$ is the rate of movement from population i to population j, and K is the number of subpopulations. In the second model, the structure in current populations occurs through past population splittings (this is the population supertree

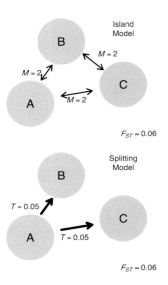

Figure 16.4. *Schematic for the migration and splitting models. In the island model migration occurs between all populations at a rate* M = 2Nm *where* N *is the diploid population size and* m *is the proportion of migrants per population. In the splitting model a single population splits into three populations at a time* T, *in the past.* T *is in units of* N *generations.*

model in Wilson *et al.* (2003)), allowing for different relative population sizes in every branch and leaf of the tree. Nielsen & Wakeley (2001) proposed a model with two populations with both fission and subsequent gene flow. These authors found that there is sufficient power to detect these two effects if the scaled mutation rate is large enough. Population growth and decline, bottlenecks and more general population size distributions can be added to both models, by appropriate scaling if coalescence times. The standard models used are shown in Figure 16.4.

The computer program used for these simulations, simascert, is available from the author on request as source code or as a library for the R package.

Summary statistics for simulated data

In this section I give details of simulation experiments that look at the expected value of summary statistics for simulated data. Twenty replicate simulations were performed by simulating short chromosomes with 100, 000 potential variable sites and then picking 4000 variable sites with ascertainment that are a) random, b) length and c) single panel of size 3 individuals. A further set of simulations were performed by generating uniformly spaced markers. The scaled recombination rates between sites were $\rho = 0.001, 0.002, 0.005,$

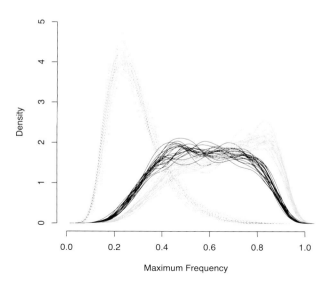

Figure 16.5. *Kernel density plots of the maximum MNP$_{12}$ frequency for all twenty replicates of the exponentially growing island populations (black lines) and fission models (grey lines) for models with panel ascertainment (solid lines) and length ascertainment (dotted lines).*

0.01, 0.02 and 0.04. Simulations were performed with island and splitting models and with constant population size and exponential growth.

Summary statistic means for exponentially growing and constant-sized populations without ascertainment were calculated (data not shown). There are no surprises: the number of alleles increases with the recombination rate , much more in constant sized population than for exponential growth. Levels of F_{ST} are unaffected by ρ — but the standard deviation decreases as ρ increases. The behaviour of statistics does not seem to depend too much on the number of markers.

We consider ascertained data in Figures 16.5, 16.6 and 16.7, now just for exponential growth, as these summary statistics show smaller differences for this model. Figure 16.5 compares the empirical density for the maximum frequency of alleles for ascertained data for MNP$_{12}$. It is striking that the main difference in the densities comes from the method of ascertainment, rather than the model from which the data were simulated — although there are differences for the two models.

Summary statistics calculated from MNP$_{12}$ (Fig. 16.6) are highly dependent on ascertainment scheme, which effects the mean values much more than the model for population subdivision. For random and length ascertainment, the mean summary statistics are relatively independent of ρ. For MNP$_{12}$ the curves for

random and length ascertainment overlie each other for most statistics, although for constant population sized models they do show differences. Panel ascertainment means that the recombination rate ρ has a strong influence on some statistics — which could be misinterpreted as a signal of a constant population size. For these statistics there is less signal from the model (except for F_{ST} where the two models have different means.)

The effects of the numbers of SNPs in the polymorphism can be seen in Figure 16.7. The amount of polymorphism increases with the length, this can be seen from the increases in the number of alleles and the decrease in frequency of the most common allele. The F_{ST} measure decreases as we increase the length. Some difference in behaviour of the probability of rare alleles can be seen as we increase the length for island and fission models.

If we compare these means values with the values observed from the chromosome three data shown in Figure 16.7 we see that the patterns are qualitatively the same, with some evidence that the human data look more like data from populations that have undergone a fission event. It is clear that the patterns are more consistent with a panel ascertainment model than random ascertainment, as expected.

Discussion

Most analyses of this type of data have concentrated on one of two areas: estimation of recombination rate and identification of recombination hot spots (Li & Stephens 2003; Fearnhead *et al.* 2004), and the analysis of association studies (Morris *et al.* 2002). These studies considered population histories as noise. The aims of genetic anthropology are different, and interest is the history of populations. I have shown that it is possible to use data of this form to make inferences about population history and demography despite the problems of ascertainment. While the power seen in any individual locus is small, when these haplotypes are combined then I expect that much more accurate inferences can be drawn. However, we must take account of the ascertainment scheme for our simulated data to look anything like the real HapMap data.

The HapMap data should prove to be a valuable resource for inference about early human evolution. In this paper I have demonstrated a graphical method for describing the patterns of variation along chromosomes, and shown that by carefully modelling the ascertainment process we can get simulated data that has the same properties as the HapMap data.

Much phylogeographical analysis depends on being able to look at geographic patterns of variation

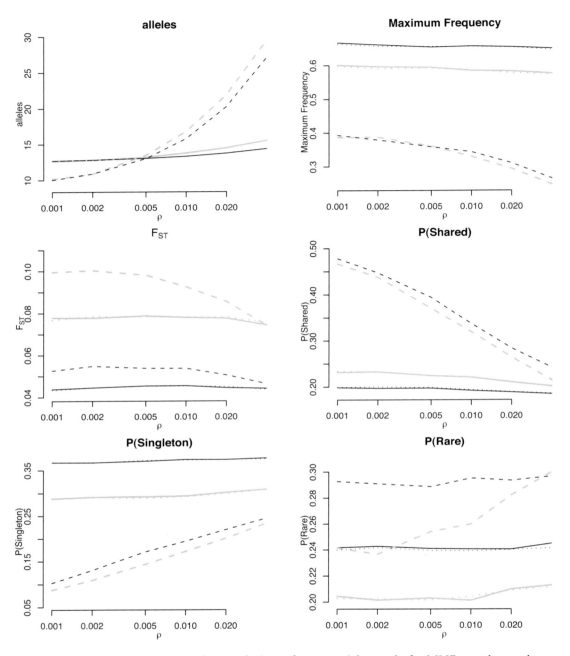

Figure 16.6. *Means for various statistics for simulations of exponential growth, for MNP$_{12}$ under random ascertainment (solid lines), length ascertainment (dotted lines) and panel ascertainment (dashed lines) for island model (thick grey lines) and fission model (black lines). Standard errors are small relative to the mean for all except P(rare). Where dotted lines are not visible they are below solid lines.*

Chapter 17

Archaeology, Genes and Demographic Histories

Stephen Shennan

It has long been apparent that the key common interest shared by those who study gene distributions in present-day populations and archaeologists studying the often prehistoric past is a concern with demographic histories at different scales. Demographic histories are central to many of the things that archaeologists want to know about the past, since many models of culture change are based on arguments about the importance of population fluctuations and range expansions and contractions; the Bellwood–Renfrew model of the implications of agricultural dispersals is a classic example of this. Archaeologists have always had problems in using the material evidence available to them to construct decisive tests of demographic hypotheses, in particular where these concern demic versus cultural diffusion, but even the tracing of patterns of population expansion and contraction is sometimes problematical, especially in earlier periods.

In present-day gene distributions modern genetics has given us access to a novel source of data about demographic histories and a complex and constantly developing mathematical toolkit for extracting relevant information from it. However, some of the things that both archaeologists and geneticists are interested in finding out about demographic processes seem very difficult to get at through the information available from present-day gene distributions — good dates for example. Moreover, it is clearly not straightforward to go from information about gene histories based on present-day gene distributions to inferences about population histories, which is what archaeologists at least are usually interested in. It has become increasingly apparent, and is very clearly demonstrated by the papers presented at the conference, that this always involves some sort of modelling process. Thus, the belief held at least by archaeologists until very recently that present-day proportional frequencies of genes of different geographical origins translate directly into demographic contributions of different origins to past populations now appears very naive,

as does the assumption that present-day geographical distributions of genes necessarily tell us anything very much about the absolute location of past populations as opposed to their relative proximity.

The question of scale is central to the linking of archaeological and genetic interests and inferences. Major advances in the reconstruction of global-scale demographic histories have been achieved on the basis of inferences from genetic data; reconstructions of small-scale histories have played a much lesser role. Such large-scale inferences could never have been made on the basis of archaeological data, which in many respects have a converse set of strengths and weaknesses to present-day gene distributions. They are very point specific. Even collecting point data is expensive, very large-scale data prohibitively so; regional and larger patterns can take decades to build up. The specificity of the data tells us most straightforwardly about local phenomena, but those phenomena can be localized in time in a way that genetic data cannot. However, the endless inconclusive debates about the links between pottery and peoples show how difficult it is very often to be confident about inferences from material culture about population processes. Even the present-day availability of Sr isotope evidence from ancient skeletons is only a very partial solution to the problem of tracking prehistoric populations using archaeological evidence.

From an archaeological perspective there are three different ways of bring archaeologists and geneticists onto a similar wavelength: the use of ancient DNA; the introduction of social/cultural anthropological and historical ideas and evidence into explanations of genetic patterns; and the use of spatial computer simulations of population processes and their genetic consequences, because they have implications for particular places and specific times. I will comment more briefly on the first two of these and concentrate on the last.

In the case of ancient DNA the recently published study of mtDNA results from skeletons of the

LBK first farmers of central Europe (Haak *et al.* 2005) shows some of the issues involved. The main focus of the genetic aspect of the debate about whether farming spread to Europe as a result of demic or cultural diffusion has been on the extent to which immigrant Neolithic farmers contributed to the present-day European gene pool, unsurprisingly given that the data have been present-day gene distributions; Haak *et al.*'s study maintains this emphasis. Their finding that a significant proportion of the LBK skeletons were characterized by an mtDNA haplotype which is very rare in present-day populations and that the decrease in frequency between 7500 years ago and the present cannot be accounted for by any plausible drift model is important in suggesting that female Neolithic farmers may not have contributed much to the present-day mitochondrial gene pool (whether this is also the case for the present-day Y-chromosome gene pool is, of course, another matter). However, this is not the question of interest to archaeologists, which concerns the extent to which farming spread by a process of demographic expansion. For archaeology the importance of their results is the indication they give us of the potential importance of past (virtual) extinction processes of a more structured nature than drift. In fact, there is evidence from some areas (see e.g. Zimmermann 2002) that, however successful the LBK was to start with, it finally went demographically extinct and the areas it had occupied were re-colonized by later groups. The extent of this process is the issue that now needs to be addressed. In other words, the present-day gene distributions can tell us about expansions but very little about subsequent extinctions and contractions, except to the extent that they can be encapsulated in simulations of drift models; to find out about these we need ancient DNA and archaeological evidence.

The importance of introducing specific social processes and the evidence for them into models that attempt to use modern genetic data to address questions about the past is well illustrated by Thomas's paper in this volume. Another good example is Hage & Marck's (2003) study of the apparently conflicting lines of evidence relating to the colonization of the Pacific. The linguistic and mtDNA evidence point to a relatively rapid expansion of Austronesian-speaking groups from the area of Taiwan starting about 4500 years ago, while the Y-chromosome data indicate a substantial contribution from indigenous non-Austronesian-speaking populations who had been in Melanesia for thousands of years. Hage & Marck (2003) account for the apparent contradiction by postulating that proto-Oceanic society was characterized by matrilocal residence and matrilineal descent. They cite a variety of evidence for the importance of matri-centred institutions in Oceanic societies. Such expanding and fissioning colonizing groups would have interacted with long-standing local Papuan populations and recruited males from them. In this study a huge range of lines of evidence, including archaeology, is brought together.

Perhaps the most important area for developing convergent genetic and archaeological approaches to demographic histories lies in the development of spatial predictive demographic modelling on a regional scale. Here too, in my view, papers at the conference showed important ways forward.

The starting point for such models is the natural selection-based assumption that human populations will quickly grow to their local carrying capacities. When there are adjacent areas not occupied to the same density, population will automatically flow from the high density to the low density area so long as the high-density adaptation is viable in the latter area. As Ray *et al.* showed at the conference, the construction of maps showing predicted population density in relation to vegetation patterns which are climatically controlled, and therefore change over time, provides the basis for making predictions about this, since high-quality climatic histories, based on both modelling and evidence, are becoming increasingly available. To these we need to add the archaeological evidence of innovations that increase local carrying capacities, like cereal agriculture or the introduction of the sweet potato.

These demographic processes have potentially recognizable archaeological signatures as well as genetic ones. Thus, archaeologists have had some success at recognizing expansions. One reason for this is that site densities increase, and in favourable circumstances it may even be possible to suggest population growth rates, e.g. for the spread of LBK farmers into central Europe (Petrasch 2001). Another is that expansions often produce contacts between cultural traditions that have had independent histories for very long periods and the result is that the boundaries between them when they come together are likely to be recognizable.

In any event, expansion processes produce splitting, which produces regional differentiation in material culture, as initial uniformity breaks down. Subsequently, those splits, or at least their visibility, will potentially be gradually eroded by interaction processes. In some circumstances, as noted above, expansions may be followed by contraction and/or abandonment processes, which again can potentially be archaeologically observed, for example by identifying breaks in local sequences. However, these are much less easy to pick up in the archaeological record because the detection of such breaks and gaps in local occupation requires high-resolution absolute chronological data that are only very gradually becoming available.

When we are not dealing with times and places where expansion/contraction processes are going on then we are in a more or less equilibrium situation, dealing with metapopulations made up of demes linked by relatively small amounts of gene flow. We can also make archaeologically testable predictions here — for example, where populations are denser then interactions will tend to be shorter in distance than when they are thinly distributed. While it is extremely difficult for archaeologists studying prehistoric periods to reconstruct the histories of specific social or political groups, at least beyond individual settlement micro areas, and there is every reason to believe that such entities would have been relatively short-lived anyway, we can provide information about the lengths of specific cultural traditions and their spatial extent. Some of those traditions represent domestic social learning traditions, which in my view tell us about population continuities. Moreover, some of their spatial patterns give us measures of interaction, for example if we can show that the trait in question is neutral, as opposed to being subject to some kind of social selection, then inter-site similarity is telling us about interaction frequency (Neiman 1995; Shennan & Bentley 2008). In addition, we have direct evidence on patterns in the movement of artefacts and raw materials.

Thus, the predictions of spatial demographic models of the kind presented by Ray *et al.* have consequences which can be tested with both archaeological and genetic data. Moreover, these processes are fractal in the sense that you can see the same processes operating at different scales. In other words, it's not simply a matter of distinguishing macro-scale from micro-scale evolution, important though this is; depending on the scale on which we focus there will be corresponding macro and micro processes. It may be that the most productive interactions between archaeology and genetics will remain focussed on the larger-scale end of the spectrum, or at least that at the more local scale they will depend on the availability of ancient DNA. However, as Haak *et al.*'s (2005) recent results show, the availability of this source of information does not solve all our problems; explanations come from well-founded model building.

References

Haak, W., P. Forster, B. Bramanti, *et al.*, 2005. Ancient DNA from the first European farmers in 7500-year-old Neolithic Sites. *Science* 310, 1016–18.

Hage, P. & J. Marck, 2003. Matrilineality and the Melanesian origin of Polynesian Y chromosomes. *Current Anthropology* 44, S121–7.

Neiman, F.D., 1995. Stylistic variation in evolutionary perspective. *American Antiquity* 60, 7–36.

Petrasch, J., 2001. Seid fruchtbar und mehret euch und fullet die Erde und.machet sie euch untertan. *Archaeologisches Korrespondenzblatt* 31, 13–25.

Shennan, S.J. & R.A. Bentley, 2008. Style, interaction, and demography among the earliest farmers of central Europe, in *Cultural Transmission and Archaeology: Issues and Case Studies*, ed. M. O'Brien. Washington (DC): SAA Press, 164–77.

Zimmermann, A., 2002. Landschaftsarchäologie I Die Bandkeramik auf der Aldenhovener Platte. *Bericht der Römisch-Germanischen Kommission* 2002, 17–38.

Chapter 18

Population Structure and Diversity Indices

James Steele

1. The interaction between archaeology and genetics

For an archaeologist this was an extremely constructive meeting. It is clear that genetic data have huge potential for elucidating major episodes in human population history. It is also clear that archaeogenetic inference is model-dependent, and that archaeogenetic reconstructions have intrinsic and often large error or uncertainty. There is therefore value in archaeology as a source of independent constraints on parameter values used in the models.

Quite how archaeology should be used to constrain genetic inference (and vice versa) is less clear. There are obvious risks of circular reasoning when the same archaeological data are used both to define a genetic hypothesis, and to constrain the subsequent interpretation of results. This can be avoided by independent archaeological and genetic inference, and subsequent examination of consistencies and inconsistencies in reconstructions. Where reconstructions differ, and we are able to rank the two sources in terms of directness of inference and level of uncertainty of estimation, the comparison will be instructive.

In some cases, the genetic data and inferences appear more direct and reliable indicators (in this case, of admixture) than the archaeology (cf. Thomas *et al.* this volume). This is not always the case. For interpreting divergence dates of mtDNA founder lineages, archaeology may be more precise and accurate. The peopling of the Americas has been estimated from genetic divergence dates to have taken place anywhere between 11,000 and 40,000 years ago, more precise estimates varying as a function of sample and methodology (Eshleman *et al.* 2003). Individually, these estimates often also have large error or uncertainty — there are fewer problems in converting archaeological radiocarbon determinations into calendar ages. Well-controlled sampling of early archaeological sites in the Americas yields a colonization time which constrains the mtDNA estimates to the younger end of their range (Kelly 2003).[1]

These cases illustrate the productive juxtaposition of independent analyses of the same events by archaeologists and by geneticists. One can also envisage a more subtle relationship in which the strengths of each discipline are used collaboratively. One could argue, for instance, that archaeological dating is more precise and accurate than molecular dating, for prehistoric events which need to be resolved on millennial or shorter timescales. If this were accepted, then the archaeological dates could be used in demographic parameter estimation by genetic modellers. They would provide a measure of fit in exploring the parameter space of the genetic model.

Conversely, one could argue that genetic data and models are better able to estimate admixture rates in two-population situations, and that these rates should be used to constrain archaeologists' interpretations of the demography of cultural transitions. It must be said, however, that the genetics of the Neolithic transition in Europe seem to be consistent with more than one interpretation, and here archaeologists would benefit from a concise exposition by geneticists, in non-technical language, of the basis of their internal disagreements.

Archaeology could be used to estimate not just dates, but also other demographic parameter values for genetic models. Attempts have been made to recover local values for fertility and intrinsic rate of increase (e.g. Bocquet-Appel 2002), for marriage distance (e.g. MacDonald 1998; MacDonald & Hewlett 1999), and for population density (e.g. Steele *et al.* 1998), all using archaeological data. Given a well-argued archaeogenetic rationale, these efforts could be augmented and new insights gained. However, we first need to develop a better shared understanding of the demographic parameters that are of relevance to genetic models. For example, the cumulative occupancy of a region over a given period of time (numbers of person-years) may be relevant to archaeologists estimating latency to visibility of a colonizing population in the archaeological record (Hazelwood & Steele 2004), but it is evidently not so relevant to geneticists (who need to know about structure as well as density, when estimating effective population size). In fact, archaeologists may not always fully understand either the nature of demographic parameters in genetic models (e.g. generation time, migration rate, effective *vs* census population sizes), or the sensitivity of these models' historical interpretation to variation in the parameter values estimated. A simple 'Idiot's Guide' would be most helpful.

2. The identification of common research questions in archaeology and genetics

The above observations are made in the belief that archaeology and genetics can be made to work together effectively to refine accuracy and precision when reconstructing human population history. How then should we identify the questions at which to direct our efforts? The examples discussed above relate primarily to the timing of primary dispersals, and to the admixture dynamics between two populations in secondary dispersals. These are very interesting and productive topics, but they are only a subset of the problems for which archaeologists and geneticists can and do make common cause.

Among these, one problem on which more attention might be focused relates to the cultural and genetic markers of population structure, which may also be applied when the system is near to equilibrium (i.e. there is approximate balance between birth and death rates, and between immigration and emigration rates). What are the effects on cultural and genetic diversity, in such a simplified model system, of varying rates of background migration (or of varying mean marriage distance)?

In cultural and linguistic studies, measures of diversity do exist, but they have usually been formulated to address other kinds of research problems. An example is Greenberg's (1956) index of linguistic diversity,

$$A = 1 - \sum_{i=1}^{k} (i^2),$$

where i is the fraction of the population speaking a given language X, and k is the total number of languages spoken.

A precisely similar index of concentration has been developed in economics to index the distribution of market share, Herfindahl's Concentration Index (H), with S_i the market share of the ith of n companies:

$$H = 1 - \sum_{i=1}^{n} (s_i^2).$$

Herfindahl's Index has been applied in cultural studies as the index of ethnolinguistic fractionalization (Bossert *et al.* 2005), and used to study effects of cultural and ethnic diversity on economic and social indicators in large-scale population comparisons.

These are of course direct analogues of the measure of expected heterozygosity in genetics (H_E), with p_i the frequency of the i-th of k alleles (in a single-locus case):

$$H_E = 1 - \sum_{i=1}^{k} (p_i^2).$$

It seems intuitive that such indices could be used to estimate historical population structure. In genetics, the F statistics of Sewall Wright (1931) include an inbreeding coefficient

$$F = \frac{(H_E - H_O)}{H_E}$$

where H_O is the observed heterozygosity. Positive values for a sub-population indicate above-average levels of inbreeding, and negative values indicate above-average levels of mixing. A related statistic is F_{ST}, a measure of the distance separating a descendant from a founder population:

$$F_{ST} = \frac{(H_T - H_S)}{H_T},$$

where H_T is the expected heterozygosity for a pooled sample of alleles and H_S is the average expected heterozygosity within each population. In genetics, the F_{ST} statistic is evidently used to estimate divergence in both time and space. The latter is by the inference from F_{ST} of N_e and m, the effective population size and the migration rate, assuming a simple island model (Wright 1931; cf. Whitlock & McCauley 1999):

$$F_{ST} \approx \frac{1}{4 N_e m + 1}.$$

It would be good to be able to generalize this approach to the study of linguistic variation, with a linguistic *F*-statistic used to predict effective population size and diffusion rate for an empirical cultural inheritance system. We might aspire to estimate mixing levels in cultural populations, for example comparing word lists from adjacent populations where cognates, loan words and unique occurrences all represent variants. This would give a focus contrasting with word-list analyses which are designed to recover trees (cf. Bryant *et al.* 2004), and it would also have the virtue of making use of all the data in such word-lists.

How might this work? At the level of a set of sub-populations, we might compare A_T (as the total linguistic diversity in the population as a whole), and then calculate A_S for each sub-population. This would apply in a situation where all variants were initially available, and present diversity reflects a population structure in which historical processes in different groups have led to different frequencies of these variants. This is unlikely to be relevant when studying language differences which are the product of mutation and selection, but it might be relevant when studying the initial fixation of dialect variants in colonization episodes (for example, in the divergence of American and British English pronunciation), or the rate of diffusion of loan-words.

A relevant attempt to address the issue of language diversity and population structure at a much larger scale is Nettle's use of a languages/stock index SL (number of stocks per thousand languages spoken), although the quantification is incomplete. The 'stock' (or phylum, or superfamily) is a level of aggregation of languages that represents 'the deepest level reconstructible by the standard comparative method of historical linguistics (the existence of deeper nodes frequently is hypothesized; in no case, however, have they been reconstructed)' (Nettle 1999, 3326). Nettle finds that globally, empirical stock diversity SL (number of stocks proportional to the number of communities, as indexed by number of actual languages) is negatively correlated with population age, when the latter is estimated archaeologically. This finding contrasts with Nichols's (e.g. 1990) model, which predicts a positive correlation between stock diversity and population age (cf. Nichols 2000; Nettle 2000). Nettle's interpretation is that the pattern of linguistic evolution associated with primary dispersals involves an initial diversification as a population radiates into small and spatially-segregated geographical niches, followed by a predominance of lineage extinction and loss of diversity as populations grow and smaller groups are assimilated, in a context of increasingly large-scale political and economic systems.

It is not immediately clear how SL, as a measure of cultural population structure, would relate mathematically to the F statistics discussed above. A, H and H_E are all entropy-like measures of diversity in different inheritance systems. Greenberg (1956) also added a weighting term to allow for the degree of similarity between languages in a polyglot population, giving:

$$B = 1 - \Sigma_{mn}(mn)(r_{MN})$$

where m and n are the fractions of the population

speaking languages M and N, and r is the measure of resemblance (based e.g. on the number of cognates and shared loanwords in a standard word list). Greenberg (1956) intended his B index to help distinguish between populations with high levels of isolation by distance (e.g. in small-scale subsistence agricultural societies, lower B) and populations with high levels of recent long-distance economic migration (e.g. industrializing societies, higher B). Nettle's stock diversity measure could readily be assimilated as a large-scale empirical approximation of r_{MN} where there are only two possible values for any language pairing (related or unrelated by common stock membership). We might then reformulate SL as:

$$SL = 1 - \Sigma_{mn}(mn)(r_{MN})$$

where r took an arbitrarily high value, say 0.75, for languages in a common stock, and an arbitarily low value, say 0.25, for languages not in a common stock. The term here missing from Nettle's (1999) analysis, mn, is based on the fraction (cf. p_i) of the population speaking each i-th language.

A high value of SL (high stock diversity) would equate to a high value of B, and *vice versa*. It is intuitive that the contrast between simple agricultural societies and urban industrial societies just outlined would also be reflected by variation in SL for cultural populations. It is less intuitive — as Nettle himself observes — why SL should be found to decrease with age of population in the absence of selection. It seems unlikely that the analogy should be with genetic drift in the absence of mutation and selection (i.e. when heterozygosity declines with age at a rate inversely proportional to the effective population size N_e). The effective cultural population sizes would surely have been too large for a noticeable effect of this kind to be expected, and furthermore mixing rates would have been structured by linguistic similarity. A selection process therefore seems implied.

Greenberg also developed a series of other indices of the social potential for communication, to allow for the possibility that individuals can speak and understand more than one of the languages which are current in their population. A moment's reflection suggests that word forms and structural language properties are not selectively neutral traits in language contact situations, since their being shared determines the potential for cultural exchange — unlike neutral markers in genetic systems and genetic exchange. In this case, any attempt to recover population structure from linguistic diversity must consider the horizontal effects of cultural selection, as well as the effects of a historical branching process of diversification.

In archaeological assemblages of material culture, much discussion of diversity indices has focused on the effects of sample size (e.g. Kintigh 1984; Meltzer *et al.* 1992). Neiman (1995), however, has attempted to model population structure as a function of empirical diversity measures. He proposes, following Crow & Kimura (1970), that in a cultural system with innovation and drift, the equilibrium level of homogeneity ($\hat{F}$) at a neutral cultural locus can be estimated as

$$\hat{F} \cong \frac{1}{2N_e\,\mu + 1}$$

where N_e is the effective population size and μ is the innovation rate, and can also be approximated by an empirical estimator of the number (k) and relative frequency (p) of variants

$$\widehat{F} = \sum_{i=1}^{k}\left(p_i^2\right).$$

The effective number of variants, n_e, is given by the reciprocal of $\hat{F}$ and the confounding effect of sample size on observed variation can be estimated using Ewens's (1972) formula. Neiman uses these results to reconstruct the dynamics of cultural systems (levels of transmission between groups) as these varied over time, based on diversity indices of pottery styles at a series of prehistoric sites in Woodland-period Illinois.

Neiman's approach is developed further by Shennan & Wilkinson (2001), and the same neutral model is used by Hahn & Bentley (2003) to estimate μ (given empirically known values for N_e) from the empirical frequency distribution of variants of twentieth century US baby names (see also Bentley *et al.* 2004).

There is clearly scope for further collaborative work on these and other cultural and genetic indices of population structure under a neutral model, as a direction to explore that would complement the existing collaborative focus on reconstruction of major dispersals and migrations. An extension which would enable us also to identify the pattern of cultural diversification associated with selection (as distinct from drift) would also be very valuable.

Note

1. Incidentally, the publication conventions of archaeological dating can easily mislead the unwary. I have heard geneticists suggest — as a piece of special pleading to justify a 'long' mtDNA settlement chronology — that the North American Clovis culture represents an episode of rapid population growth stimulated by climatic warming at the onset of the Holocene (and

that settlement may therefore substantially pre-date that culture). This is based on a mistaken correlation of uncalibrated radiocarbon determinations for the Clovis culture, which underestimate these sites' true age by about 2000 years, with true calendar ages for the end of the Younger Dryas cold period. If one compares like with like, one finds that the Clovis culture dates to before and in the early stages of the Younger Dryas (Steele *et al.* 2000) — and does not, therefore, correlate with climatic warming.

References

Bentley, R.A., M.W. Hahn & S.J. Shennan, 2004. Random drift and culture change. *Proceedings of the Royal Society (Biological Sciences)* 271, 1443–50.
Bocquet-Appel, J.-P., 2002. Paleoanthropological traces of a Neolithic transition. *Current Anthropology* 43, 637–50.
Bossert, W., C. D'Ambrosio & E. La Ferrara, 2005. *A Generalized Index of Ethno-linguistic Fractionalization.* http://www.iae.csic.es/konstanz/BossertDAmbrosioLaFerrara.pdf (link checked 26 January 2006).
Bryant, D., F. Filimon & R.D. Gray, 2004. Untangling our past: languages, trees, splits and networks, in *The Evolution of Cultural Diversity: Phylogenetic Approaches*, eds. R. Mace, C.J. Holden & S. Shennan. London: UCL Press, 69–85.
Crow, J.F. & M. Kimura, 1970. *An Introduction to Population Genetics Theory.* New York (NY): Harper Row.
Currat, M. & L. Excoffier, 2005. The effect of the Neolithic expansion on European molecular diversity. *Proceedings of the Royal Society (Biological Sciences)* 272, 679–88.
Eshleman, J.A., R.S. Malhi & D.G. Smith, 2003. Mitochondrial DNA studies of Native Americans: conceptions and misconceptions of the population prehistory of the Americas. *Evolutionary Anthropology* 12, 7–18.
Ewens, W.J., 1972. The sampling theory of selectively neutral alleles. *Theoretical Population Biology* 3, 87–112.
Greenberg, J., 1956. The measurement of linguistic diversity. *Language* 32, 109–15.
Hahn, M.W. & R.A. Bentley, 2003. Drift as a mechanism for cultural change: an example from baby names. *Proceedings of the Royal Society (Biological Sciences)* 270 (Suppl. 1), S120–S123.
Hazelwood, L. & J. Steele, 2004. Spatial dynamics of human dispersals: constraints on modelling and archaeological validation. *Journal of Archaeological Science* 31, 669–79.
Kelly, R.L., 2003. Maybe we do know when people first came to North America; and what does it mean if we do? *Quaternary International* 109–10, 133–45.
Kintigh, K.W., 1984. Measuring archaeological diversity by comparison with simulated assemblages. *American Antiquity* 49, 44–54.
Macdonald, D.H., 1998. Subsistence, sex, and cultural transmission in Folsom culture. *Journal of Anthropological Archaeology* 17, 217–39.

MacDonald, D.H. & B.S. Hewlett, 1999. Reproductive interests and forager mobility. *Current Anthropology* 40, 501–23.

Meltzer, D.J., R.D. Leonard & S.K. Stratton, 1992. The relationship between sample size and diversity in archaeological assemblages. *Journal of Archaeological Science* 19, 375–87.

Neiman, F.D., 1995. Stylistic variation in evolutionary perspective: inferences from decorative diversity and interassemblage distance in Illinois Woodland ceramic assemblages. *American Antiquity* 60, 7–36.

Nettle, D., 1999. Linguistic diversity of the Americas can be reconciled with a recent colonization. *Proceedings of the National Academy of Sciences of the USA* 96, 3325–9.

Nettle, D., 2000. Linguistic diversity, population spread and time depth, in *Time Depth in Historical Linguistics,* vol. 2, eds. C. Renfrew, A. McMahon & L. Trask. (Papers in the Prehistory of Languages.) Cambridge: McDonald Institute for Archaeological Research, 665–77.

Nichols, J., 1990. Linguistic diversity and the first settlement of the New World. *Language* 66, 475–521.

Nichols, J., 2000. Estimating dates of early American colonization events, in *Time Depth in Historical Linguistics,* vol. 2, eds. C. Renfrew, A. McMahon & L. Trask. (Papers in the Prehistory of Languages.) Cambridge: McDonald Institute for Archaeological Research, 643–54.

Ray, N., M. Currat, P. Berthier & L. Excoffier, 2005. Recovering the geographic origin of early modern humans by realistic and spatially explicit simulations. *Genome Research* 15, 1161–7.

Shennan, S.J. & J.R. Wilkinson, 2001. Ceramic style change and neutral evolution: a case study from Neolithic Europe. *American Antiquity* 66, 577–94.

Steele, J., J. Adams & T. Sluckin, 1998. Modelling Paleoindian dispersals. *World Archaeology* 30, 286–305.

Steele, J., G. Gamble & T. Sluckin, 2000. Estimating the rate of Paleoindian expansion into South America, in *People as Agents of Environmental Change*, eds. T. O'Connor & R. Nicholson. Oxford: Oxbow Books, 125–33.

Whitlock, M.C. & D.E. McCauley, 1999. Indirect measures of gene flow and migration: $F_{ST} \neq 1/(4Nm+1)$. *Heredity* 82, 117–25.

Wright, S., 1931. Evolution in Mendelian populations. *Genetics* 16, 97–159.

Chapter 19

Whither Archaeogenetics? A View from the Trenches

Charles Higham

Introduction: the genesis of a new discipline

Over the past two decades, we have lived through the genesis of the new discipline of archaeogenetics. I suspect that my role, and the only one that I am able to fulfill, is to assess critically its current contribution to the study of our past, and to ponder its future. I believe that we are now in the stage of identifying the doubts, the problems, the pitfalls, and its potential. We have passed the initial heady days, which distinguished, between the principal groups of modern humans based on haplotype phylogeny. This relied on the fact that a mutant allele represents a unique event, and that all those sharing it have a common ancestor. I recall hearing a paper by Peter Underhill as recently as 2001, in which he showed a diagram of the divisions into which humanity falls on this criterion, and the slight gasp in the audience when he assured as that these results are 'bullet proof' (Underhill 2005, 297).

This might well be the case. But the diagram, revealing as is does the fact that there is, in fact, relatively little genetic diversity in our species despite its burgeoning weight of numbers, is only a beginning. It is so because both mtDNA, inherited exclusively through the female line, and Y-chromosomal DNA passed down through male descent, mutate. A shared mutation indicates a common ancestry. By sampling modern populations, it is possible to generate the equivalent of an ancestral tree, where bifurcations based on such mutations indicate the branches. While we may never be precise, there are estimates of the mutation rate (for example, one mutation per 20,000 years: Heyer *et al.* 2001). It thus becomes possible to propose a temporal framework for the human family tree. These facts have revolutionized the study of human biology and prehistory.

In moving forward, the application of simulations to specific issues of human dispersal, mixing and demography takes centre stage. Many contributors share my view. We are, says one, 'still trudging in the foothills, the grand vistas have yet to open up'.

Another comments that we are 'still crawling'.

A simulation in this context, involves taking a particular issue illuminated by archaeological and linguistic data, such as the size of a founder population, or the degree with which an invaded population mixed with newcomers. New programs and increasingly powerful computers can then run thousands of simulations in which the range of inputs may comprise different points of origin, environmental variables, the number of elapsed generations, to generate statistical results necessarily linked with confidence limits. This is best undertaken at first in island situations, because islands are discrete, they are often isolated, they are less prone to multiple intrusions and mixing between different ethnic groups that often have different genetic signatures. Islands are thus more likely to have an uncomplicated genetic history.

Islands

The application of simulations to islands is not a new departure. Murray-McIntosh *et al.* (1998) considered the settlement of New Zealand on the basis of 54 sequences of the hypervariable 1 region of mtDNA sampled from Maori and East Polynesian respondents. In doing so, they stressed that Polynesian islands are well suited for such simulation studies, because there is no issue with sea-level changes, the population is unlikely to be affected by admixture, and the prehistoric sequence is relatively short. Maori are also intimately acquainted with their *whakapapa*, or genealogy, and their oral traditions relate initial settlement by few ocean-going craft. Their three-step simulation to the frequencies of the haplotypes in eastern Polynesia and New Zealand, repeated 20,000 times, found that the initial settlement probably involved between 40 and 90 women.

A related approach was taken in our meeting for the initial settlement of Malagasy, an island settled at a period defined archaeologically, linked with linguistic evidence for the origin of the settlers. Again, it was necessary to draw on independent information before the simulations were enacted. It was assumed that settlement took place about 1500 years ago; hence there has been a passage of 55 generations. One hundred thousand iterations were applied to the data, and the results suggested a founding population of between 60 and 200 people. Is this result of any value to a prehistorian?

I find it intriguing that the number of putative settlers matched that obtained for New Zealand. The small number of people hints that it would be highly unlikely that an archaeologist could pinpoint evidence for the actual earliest settlement sites; hence the founder date might be in error. However, this can be checked independently, and in the case of New Zealand, determinations relevant for any further simulations are being identified through the dating of seeds or nuts partially consumed by the rats that would have accompanied the first immigrants (Wilmshurst & Higham 2004).

Early Inuit settlement of Greenland is a second island case reviewed. A nagging feeling that assumed inputs will seriously affect results is confirmed, but the way forward from the foothills to the higher vistas is also laid out, in particular the reduction in confidence limits through incorporating increased sets of genetic data.

Two further presentations on island groups highlight the role of simulation statistics in analysing genetic variability to isolate population histories. In the case of the Japanese archipelago, while the material is intriguing, we learn only of differences between three long-defined groups, the Ainu, Okinawans and the Japanese majority with no attempt at simulations. More analysis of the Ainu would be very interesting, while the origin of the inhabitants of Honshu, Shikoku and Kyushu relative to the establishment of the Yayoi culture appeals. As it stands, this contribution appears one-dimensional in its lack of any application of simulations to time depth. Both geographically and culturally, the population history of Japan relative to the mainland of China and Korea could be considered profitably following the methods espoused by Amos *et al.* in their presentation on English population history (see Chapter 5 this volume). I found the latter profoundly stimulating and promising. As an untutored observer, I came to the meeting intrigued to find how archaeogeneticists cope with problems of mixing, particularly in a situation as in England, where there are so many documented invasions of new people. The gulf that separates studies in the early recognition of phylogenetic trees on a world scale, and the application of powerful exploratory analytical programs and computing techniques to actual and simulated data, is

widening dramatically. I was particularly impressed by the employment of non-combining markers in the Y chromosome, allowing for a very large data input, data that 'retain a marker of their origin indefinitely', since this source can characterize specifics for virtually each individual sampled. The metaphoric trees that are generated by identifying branches, linked with reasonable estimates of time depth through applying known or estimated mutation rates, whets the appetite for the in-depth analyses that are permitted.

The freedom to manipulate through the Markov Chain Monte Carlo technique, any number of plausible simulations to compare with actual data is further stressed in this paper. Having identified varying degrees of mixing between pairs of populations to be largely as expected, the authors sought to identify the implications of their results through comparing them with their simulation outputs. This initial exploration encourages optimism that even in the opposite of the ideal in an island situation, the reconstruction of trees with time depth will illuminate demographic histories.

With this in mind, one turns to think of other islands that would respond to such analyses other than Japan. Eastern Polynesia has the qualities described by Murray-McIntosh *et al.* (1998) for demographic study employing real and simulated data sets. The Tasmanians would have been a fascinating group had any survived their holocaust. The Andaman Islands are vital in any consideration of the early expansion from Africa of anatomically modern humans (AMH), but if experiments on the reality of multiple simulations in island situations were envisaged consider Pitcairn, settled on the 23 January 1790 by a group including ten Polynesian women. It would be salutary to take mtDNA samples from the present descendants and through the same simulations as were performed on Malagasy or Greenland, propose the initial number of settlers before testing the results against reality.

Out of Africa

Over the years, I have listened to conference debates by protagonists for and against a single African origin of AMH. This theme was the subject of simulations at the meeting, and resolving this conflict is arguably the most notable contribution made yet by archaeogeneticists. Setting realistic spatial and environmental parameters is part of the SPLATCHE simulation framework. Extending beyond a simple, subdivided world, the authors have added information for each of the spatial units to reflect the former environment, and the degree of friction inhibiting movement. Thus, a broad river or a coast is conducive to the spread of people, where mountain ranges or a tropical rainforest are not. Each geographic unit will have its own carrying capacity, and therefore population ceiling. Friction will influence the direction of movement, assuming that a human group will opt for the least difficult. Both carrying capacity and friction are in turn, influenced by vegetation, for which there are few data available for the period between the putative expansion of AMH from Africa, and the end of the last glacial period. This the authors compensate for by incorporating temperature change as a proxy for adjustments in the vegetation cover. Central to the SPLATCHE program, are values for the carrying capacity and friction, because they will directly influence the results of simulations for the degree of genetic diversity.

Listening to this paper, I was reminded of another concluding address, written by Edmund Leach (Leach 1973, 764). Following a meeting concerned with models of social change in prehistory, he warned that attempting to answer the question, 'how was the prehistoric game of social chess played out?' involved moving from 'verifiable facts to pure speculation'. He went on to warn participants, that the social organization of a prehistoric society is contained in a black box. While, he warns, an archaeologist can identity the work patterns that produced what he excavates, the contents of the black box, in Leach's words 'social organization as the social anthropologist understands the term, must for ever remain a mystery'. Pregnant with implications for SPLATCHE is his stricture that 'There are always an indefinitely large number of alternative ways in which particular human social systems might be adapted to meet particular ecological and demographic situations'.

I will not, however, be as pessimistic as Leach. Recent advances in molecular biology itself, and isotope studies, have the potential to provide a fleeting glimpse into the black box of prehistoric social systems. Moreover, the originators of SPLATCHE are keenly aware of their difficulties of marshalling appropriate inputs, signposting ways of honing them.

The simulation incorporating these environmental variables over time involved an assumed exodus from Africa, followed by 4000 generations. This witnessed 5000 coalescent simulations. The results for a uniform habitat, that is devoid of carrying capacity and friction, and those incorporating such estimates, reinforces the importance of beginning to formulate possible values for the latter. In the case of the uniform base, simulated human expansion pathways radiate out from East Africa in relatively straight lines following unlikely routes. When incorporating environments and time, however, we see a more realistic pattern emerge.

In a further study, this technique incorporating environmental heterogeneity is applied to a specific problem, which simulates two scenarios: the unique expansion from an African source of AMH, and the hydra-headed evolution of modern humans from many African and Eurasian *Homo erectus* ancestors. The power of simulation is immediately apparent. The results sustain the unique African source, and fail to provide support for multiple origins.

Neanderthals and Neolithic farmers

During the course of the meeting, I was questioning myself on the possible future of ancient DNA, a topic barely mentioned, save for a reference to the Neanderthal contribution to the European gene pool. In this context, there is a sharp methodological contrast between a situation in which there was expansion into an unoccupied region, as in the Pacific islands, and movement into an area with an entrenched population.

The sequencing of Neanderthal (HN) DNA has made it possible to examine possible genetic relationships between the two species. The HN genetic signature does not appear in modern humans, but that does not in itself, indicate lack of interbreeding. Hence, simulations anchored in archaeological observations, but with the freedom to vary vital inputs, such as population size, intrusion routes and rates of expansion, may be employed. Earlier simulations could not exclude the possibility that HN contributed to the early AMH gene pool, because the elapsed time since such events could have removed any surviving evidence. However, the refinement of simulation inputs has led to the very high probability indeed, that HN became extinct without any interbreeding.

A later expansion into Europe from the southeast, this time involving the spread of agriculture, offered a similar canvas for analysis. Here, we have been for some time familiar with a map of Europe showing progressive change of allele frequency clines, as one proceeds in the westward in the direction taken by the first farmers (Cavalli-Sforza *et al.* 1994). This map has been used to support the model of demic diffusion, that is, farmers progressively bringing their genes westward. To advance our understanding of this expansionary process, the authors model and simulate two alternatives: one saw a virtually complete replacement of hunter-gatherers with little inter-breeding, contrasting with random genetic admixture between established hunters and intrusive farmers. The results reveal that only a small degree of admixture between the two populations would be sufficient for hunter-gatherer genes to figure prominently. This finding contrasts markedly with the conclusions of Chikhi *et al.* (1998), who in their study of allele frequencies, found that the major contribution to genetic diversity originated in the invasive farmers. Significantly, the allele frequency clines need not necessarily reflect the Neolithic expansion at all, because AMH also spread into Europe along the same axis. The upshot is clear: the time depth of the nodes in the phylogenetic trees is required.

This returns us to the issue of ancient DNA. The Neanderthal case is unique, but could be matched if only mtDNA sequences could be teased out of the bones of *Homo floresiensis* (Brown *et al.* 2004). The question for a prehistorian, is whether sufficiently large, and acceptable sequences of ancient mtDNA will ever become available for testing simulations of demography, origins and movement, and contributing to the establishment of time depth.

Conclusions

If this volume is a way station in the development of simulation in archaeogenetics, where are we on the road? Most contributors are well aware of the raw nature of their discipline, no one more so than Daniel Falush. In an idiosyncratically stimulating review, he swims against the current others have taken by recommending that data derived from archaeology or palaeontology be set aside when seeking patterns in genetic variation in island situations. Rather than beginning with a settlement model based on archaeological information and then seeking to embellish or expand it, thus flirting dangerously with circularity, he urges a search for phylogeographic patterns only as a prelude to possible causes. The myriad of possible causes, as he notes, reflects the different paths leading to differentiation between populations. His results are in a sense, refreshingly realistic. 'Even if the data set is excellent…. It is unlikely to tell you the exact number of boats that arrived on a particular island'. It is vital in this context, that subscribers to a particular discipline take the greatest care when incorporating one of a number of possible alternatives furnished by another discipline into their own. Nevertheless, the results of phylogeographic analyses are now being woven into archaeological models. Foley (2002) for example, predicts that this integration will be prominent as palaeoanthropology gains further momentum. Renfrew likewise has explored the potential of employing modern DNA to sharpen our understanding of human population history (Renfrew 2002).

This volume is a further vehicle in a series designed to explore the limits of knowability. It illuminates a discipline in the springtime of its develop-ment. I am just an ordinary archaeologist, trying to understand a tiny segment of world prehistory in a remote part of Southeast Asia. I was detached from my study to spend four days listening to papers many of which might as well have been delivered in a foreign language for all I understood from them. But reading and re-reading them, defining in my own mind what is a Markov Chain, a pseudoautosomal region or single nucleotide polymorphism, has led me inevitably to this conclusion, that with the application of simulations in the field of archaeogenetics, the edges of knowability, about understanding our human past, are being extended, and will extend further.

Acknowledgements

I would like to thank Dr P. Forster, Professor Lord Renfrew and Shuichi Matsumura for inviting me to the Symposium 'Simulations, Genetics and Human Prehistory: a Focus on Islands' as a discussant. Shuichi Matsumura has been most helpful with subsequent advice and encouragement. I also wish to thank an anonymous reviewer for commenting on an early draft of this paper.

References

Brown, P., T. Sutikna, M.J. Morwood, *et al.*, 2004. A new small-bodied hominin from the Late Pleistocene of Flores, Indonesia. *Nature* 431, 1055–61.

Cavalli-Sforza, L.L., P. Menozzi & A. Piazza, 1994. *The History and Geography of Human Genes*. Princeton (NJ): Princeton University Press.

Chikhi, L., G. Destro-Bisol, G. Bertorelle, V. Pascali & G. Barbujani, 1998. Clines of nuclear DNA markers suggest a largely neolithic ancestry of the European gene pool. *Proceedings of the National Academy of Sciences of the USA* 95, 9053–8.

Foley, R., 2002. Parallel tracks in time: human evolution and archaeology, in *Archaeology: the Widening Debate*, eds. B.W. Cunliffe, W. Davies & C. Renfrew. Oxford: Oxford University Press, 3–43.

Heyer, E., E. Zietkiewicz, E. Rochowski, V. Yotova, J. Puymirat & D. Labuda, 2001. Phylogenetic and familial estimates of mitochondrial substitution rates: study of control region mutations in deep-rooting pedigrees. *American Journal of Human Genetics* 69, 1113–26.

Leach, E.R., 1973. Concluding address, in *The Explanation of Culture Change: Models in Prehistory*, ed. C. Renfrew. London: Duckworth, 761–71.

Murray-McIntosh, R.P., B.J. Scrimshaw, P. Hatfield & D. Penny, 1998. Testing migration patterns and estimating founding population size in Polynesia by using human mtDNA sequences. *Proceedings of the National Academy of Sciences of the USA* 95, 9047–52.

Renfrew, A.C., 2002. Genetics and language in contemporary archaeology, in *Archaeology: the Widening Debate*, eds. B.W. Cunliffe, W. Davies & C. Renfrew. Oxford: Oxford University Press, 43–77.

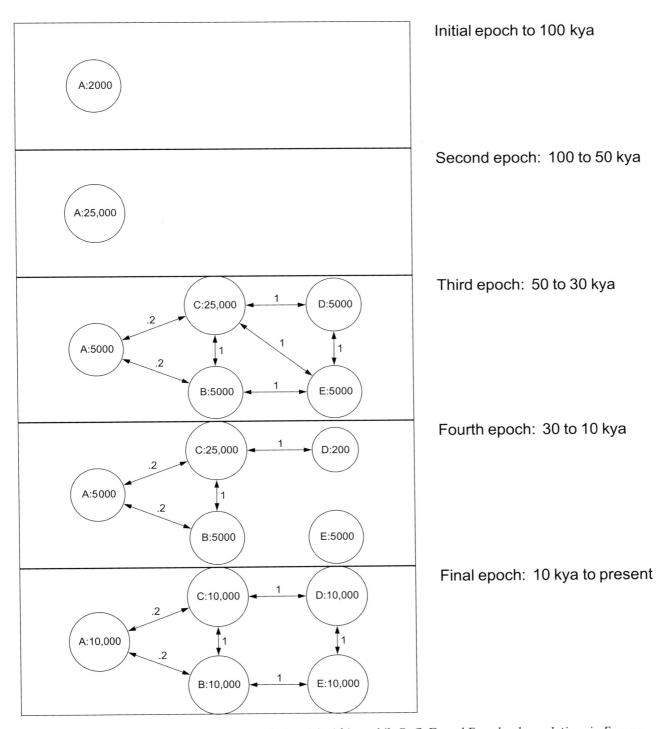

Figure 20.3. *Identify the LGM refugium. Population A is Africa, while B, C, D, and E are local populations in Europe. During the Last Glacial Maximum population E was isolated from the rest of Europe for twenty thousand years.*

Glossary

ABC (Approximate Bayesian Computation)

A method of Bayesian inference on the basis of population genetic summary statistics, such as the number of segregating sites or heterozygosity. In Bayesian inference based on the coalescent theory, a large amount of genealogies or data are generated by simulations first, then each generated genealogy or data set is evaluated on the basis of its probability of yielding genetic samples equivalent to the observed data. If full data agreement with the observed data is pursued, however, the probability is often so low that impractically long computation times are required to obtain reasonable estimates. In ABC, simulated genealogies are utilized more efficiently using summary statistics, together with local regression and weighting techniques. ABC is particularly useful for large data sets and/or for complex population models.

Allele

A stretch of DNA sequence found at a particular location (locus) of a chromosome. Historically, the term allele was first used to refer to a variant of a gene, however it has since become clear that most of our DNA does not consist of genes but is non-coding, and thus many DNA alleles (variable regions) are likewise non-coding.

Individual diploid organisms have two homologous chromosomes, so the genotype of an individual at a given locus is a combination of the individual's two alleles at that locus.

Analytical solution

A solution obtained by resolving or transforming equations. Some problems, for example, the classical three-body gravitational problem, cannot be solved analytically. Numerical methods, typically Monte Carlo methods, are used to obtain solutions for such analytically-unsolvable problems.

Likewise, problems in population genetics sometimes cannot be solved analytically. So they are approached numerically, by simulating population dynamics and changes in allele frequency over time.

Bayesian

Relating to a statistical approach which considers probability as a measure of belief or uncertainty. It is one of the two major schools in the statistical sciences (see also 'Frequentist'). In Bayesian inference, the person's degree of belief in a hypothesis can be updated by an observation or data. During the process of inference, Bayes's theorem is used as follows:

$$\Pr(\theta_1 \mid D) = \frac{\Pr(D \mid \theta_1)\Pr(\theta_1)}{\Pr(D)}$$

$\Pr(\theta_1)$ is a prior probability, which represents the degree of the belief in the hypothesis θ_1 before obtaining the data D. $\Pr(D \mid \theta_1)$ is the conditional probability that the data D is obtained when the hypothesis θ_1 is true. $\Pr(\theta_1 \mid D)$ is called the posterior probability, which represents the degree of his belief after observing the data D. $\Pr(D)$ is the probability of observing the data D.

Example
Assume that you know your genotype of the ABO blood type system is 'AO'. Let us infer your partner's ABO blood type by calculating the Bayesian posterior probability. There are six 'hypotheses' about your partner's type, i.e. {'AA', 'AO', 'BB', 'BO', 'AB', 'OO'}. First, you need prior probabilities. You may assume that all the six hypotheses are equally likely, i.e.

Pr('*AA*') = 0.167
Pr('*AO*') = 0.167
Pr('*BB*') = 0.167
Pr('*BO*') = 0.167
Pr('*AB*') = 0.167
Pr('*OO*') = 0.167.

If you know the proportions of the blood types in your region, however, it may be more reasonable to use these values as the prior probabilities: for example,

Pr('*AA*') = 0.25
Pr('*AO*') = 0.30
Pr('*BB*') = 0.04
Pr('*BO*') = 0.12
Pr('*AB*') = 0.20
Pr('*OO*')') = 0.09.

Now assume that you have a baby of 'AO'. If your partner's genotype is 'AA' (hypothesis 1), the conditional probability to having a 'AO' child is $\Pr(D = {}'AO' \mid \theta = {}'AA') = 0.5$. In other words, 50% of your children would be expected to have genotype 'AO'. Similarly, the other conditional probabilities are caluated as follows

Pr(D = '*AO*' | θ = '*AO*') = 0.5
Pr(D = '*AO*' | θ = '*BB*') = 0.0
Pr(D = '*AO*' | θ = '*BO*') = 0.25
Pr(D = '*AO*' | θ = '*AB*') = 0.25
Pr(D = '*AO*' | θ = '*OO*') = 0.5.

As the probability of observing the data (i.e. the probability that an 'AO' father has an 'AO' baby) would be $\Pr(D = 'AO') =$

$\Pr(D = 'AO' | \theta = 'AA')\Pr(\theta = 'AA')$
$\Pr(D = 'AO' | \theta = 'AO')\Pr(\theta = 'AO')$
$\Pr(D = 'AO' | \theta = 'BB')\Pr(\theta = 'BB')$
$\Pr(D = 'AO' | \theta = 'BO')\Pr(\theta = 'BO')$
$\Pr(D = 'AO' | \theta = 'AB')\Pr(\theta = 'AB')$
$\Pr(D = 'AO' | \theta = 'OO')\Pr(\theta = 'OO') =$

$(0.5 \times 0.25) + (0.5 \times 0.3) + (0.0 \times 0.04) + (0.25 \times 0.12) + (0.25 \times 0.20) + (0.5 \times 0.09) = 0.4$, you obtain the following posterior probabilities:

$$\Pr(\theta = "AA" | D = "AO") = \frac{\Pr(D = "AO" | \theta = "AA")\Pr(\theta = "AA")}{\Pr(D = "AO")} = \frac{0.5 \times 0.25}{0.4} = 0.3125$$

$$\Pr(\theta = "AO" | D = "AO") = \frac{\Pr(D = "AO" | \theta = "AO")\Pr(\theta = "AO")}{\Pr(D = "AO")} = \frac{0.5 \times 0.3}{0.4} = 0.375$$

$$\Pr(\theta = "BB" | D = "AO") = \frac{\Pr(D = "AO" | \theta = "BB")\Pr(\theta = "BB")}{\Pr(D = "AO")} = \frac{0.0 \times 0.04}{0.4} = 0$$

$$\Pr(\theta = "BO" | D = "AO") = \frac{\Pr(D = "AO" | \theta = "BO")\Pr(\theta = "BO")}{\Pr(D = "AO")} = \frac{0.25 \times 0.12}{0.4} = 0.075$$

$$\Pr(\theta = "AB" | D = "AO") = \frac{\Pr(D = "AO" | \theta = "AB")\Pr(\theta = "AB")}{\Pr(D = "AO")} = \frac{0.25 \times 0.20}{0.4} = 0.125$$

$$\Pr(\theta = "OO" | D = "AO") = \frac{\Pr(D = "AO" | \theta = "OO")\Pr(\theta = "OO")}{\Pr(D = "AO")} = \frac{0.5 \times 0.09}{0.4} = 0.1125.$$

Evidently, the most likely hypothesis is 'AO', which is five times more likely than the hypothesis 'BO' and three times more likely than 'AB'. Throughout the process of this Bayesian inference, the degree of belief in the hypothesis 'AO' has increased from 0.167 (no information), to 0.300 (with the genotype information in the region), and finally to 0.375 (with the child's genotype).

Coalescent theory
An approach in population genetics which is based on the calculation of genealogies backwards in time from existing samples. In comparison with traditional forward simulation approaches, coalescent theory provides efficient algorithms to simulate samples under various demographic models. (See Introduction for further details.)

Frequentist
Relating to a statistical approach which considers the probability of an event as the number of occurrences of such an event within all events considered. It is one of the two major schools in the statistical sciences (see also 'Bayesian'). Frequentists define the probability of a particular event A, $\Pr(A)$, on the basis of the frequency through experiment. If an experiment is repeated n times and the event A occurs m times, then m/n approaches $\Pr(A)$ given $n \to \infty$.

Frequentists assume the existence of the true parameter value, so the aim of the statistical inference is to obtain this true value. Results of the inference are often represented as point estimates with confidence intervals. The probability that the 95% confidence interval covers the fixed, true parameter value is 0.95.

Example
In contrast to Bayesians, Frequentists do not generally consider the probability of one's partner having a certain genotype unless some 'experimental situations' of having the genotype are defined. Let us assume that the proportions of the blood types in your country (which has a large number of residents) are as follows: 'AA' = 25%, 'AO' = 30%, 'BB' = 4%, 'BO' = 12%, 'AB' = 20%, and 'OO' = 9%. Then, the probability of your partner's having 'AO' is 0.30. This means if you have taken a large number of random samples from the residents in your country, 30% of the samples are 'AO'. Alternatively, let us consider the case where you know that the genotype of both parents of your partner was 'AO'. The probability of your partner's having 'AO' is 0.25. This means that if your partner's parents have a large number of children, 25% of their children are expected to be 'AO'.

F_{ST}
A measure of the degree of differentiation between sub-populations. It ranges between 0 (identical) and 1

(completely different). It is sometimes used as a kind of genetic distance.

$$F_{ST} = \frac{H_T - H_S}{H_T}$$

where H_T is the expected heterozygosity in the overall population and H_S is the mean of the expected heterozygosity across the sub-populations. F_{ST} is one of the 'fixation' indices proposed by Sewall Wright, whereby fixation in this case is the attainment of 100% of an allele in each sub-population.

HapMap project

The International HapMap Project aims to develop a haplotype map of human genome (the HapMap) which will be a useful resource for researchers to find genes affecting health, disease, and response to pharmaceuticals. The project was officially launched in October 2002, and involves scientists from Canada, China, Japan, Nigeria, the UK and the USA. In 2005, a compilation of more than one million SNPs of 269 DNA samples from four populations (China, Japan, Nigeria, and USA) was published.

IS (Importance Sampling)

A method implemented in the process of Monte Carlo simulation to reduce the variance of estimates. In coalescent simulations, a typical application of Monte Carlo simulations, genealogies $\{x_1, x_2, x_3, \ldots x_N\}$ are sampled from a distribution $P_\theta(x)$ determined by the parameters θ. By carefully choosing a distribution $Q_\theta(x)$ and sampling genealogies from it, the variance of the estimates are expected to become smaller.

Example
Consider the case of calculating the area of a circle relative to a square by throwing stones (see the example in 'Monte Carlo method'). This time the size of the circle is so small that the stones drop in the circle infrequently. Thus, the estimate of the area of the circle contains a large error. It will be more efficient if it is somehow possible to throw stones in a more concentrated manner on the circle (but still randomly).

IM (Isolation with Migration)

A population genetic model which assumes that two populations descend from an ancestral population and continue exchanging migrants since separation.

(a)   (b)   (c)

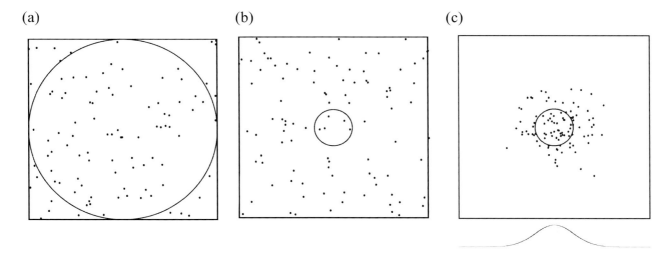

*Basic concept of **importance sampling**. (a) One hundred stones are distributed randomly in the square. Seventy-seven out of them are in the square. The square is estimated as 0.77 times as the area of the square, which is a good approximation of the true value (0.785). (b) The diameter of the circle is five times smaller than that in (a). Only five stones are in the circle, and the estimate of the size of the circle is 0.05. This is 60% larger than the true value (0.0314). The variance of the estimate is large because the expected number of stones in the circle is small. (c) One hundred stones are now thrown in a way that the realized distribution follows a normal distribution. Thirty-three stones are found in the circle. As the distribution of the stones is biased toward the centre, a weighting procedure is required. The adjusted value is 0.0254 in this example.*

Likelihood

Shorthand for 'likelihood function'. Likelihood functions tell us about unknown parameters when we have an observation or data. The likelihood that the value of an unknown parameter θ is θ_1, provided we know a particular event D_1 has occurred, is as follows:

$$L(\theta_1) = L(\theta = \theta_1 \mid D_1) = \alpha \Pr(D_1 \mid \theta = \theta_1)$$
$$(\alpha \text{ is a positive constant})$$

The conditional probability $\Pr(D_1 \mid \theta_1)$ usually describes the probability of occurrence of the event D_1 given a parameter value θ_1. We can also see it as a likelihood that the value of the unknown parameter is θ_1 when we have the event D_1. The absolute value $L(\theta_1)$ or $L(\theta_2)$ is of less practical value than the ratio of the likelihood of two parameter values $L(\theta_1)/L(\theta_2)$. If $L(\theta_1)/L(\theta_2) > 1$, θ_1 is more likely than θ_2.

Example

Assume that you know your genotype of the ABO blood system is 'AO'. If you marry a person with 'AB' (parameter θ), the probability of the blood type of your expected child (event D) is as follows:

$\Pr(D = 'AA' \mid \theta = 'AB') = 0.25$
$\Pr(D = 'AO' \mid \theta = 'AB') = 0.25$
$\Pr(D = 'BB' \mid \theta = 'AB') = 0$
$\Pr(D = 'BO' \mid \theta = 'AB') = 0.25$
$\Pr(D = 'AB' \mid \theta = 'AB') = 0.25$
$\Pr(D = 'OO' \mid \theta = 'AB') = 0.$

If you have an 'AO' child but you do not know your partner's blood type, the likelihood of his/her blood type $L(\theta)$ is as follows:

$L('AA') = L(\theta = 'AA' \mid D = 'AO') = 0.5$
$L('AO') = L(\theta = 'AO' \mid D = 'AO') = 0.5$
$L('BB') = L(\theta = 'BB' \mid D = 'AO') = 0.5$
$L('BO') = L(\theta = 'BO' \mid D = 'AO') = 0.25$
$L('AB') = L(\theta = 'AB' \mid D = 'AO') = 0.25$
$L('OO') = L(\theta = 'OO' \mid D = 'AO') = 0.5$

So 'AA', 'AO', and 'AO' are more likely than the other types. Note that the sum of the likelihood values is not equal to one.

Locus

The position of a gene (or of some specific DNA sequence) in a genome or a chromosome.

MCMC (Markov Chain Monte Carlo) method

Algorithm improving the efficiency of sampling in the Monte Carlo method. Owing to MCMC, Bayesian computation has become widely-used in many areas including genetics.

Example

Consider the case of calculating the area of a circle relative to a square by throwing stones (see the example in 'Monte Carlo method'). Imagine that the square is very large. In MCMC, each random throw is carried out from the point where the previous stone dropped. Using special algorithms, sampling can be done intensively around a relatively small circle (Fig. (b)). This makes computation more efficient.

(a)
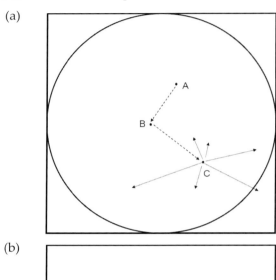

(b)
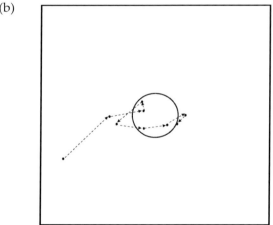

*Basic concept of **MCMC**. In normal Monte Carlo method, every throw of a stone (sampling) is carried out independently. In MCMC, each stone is thrown from the place where the previous stone dropped (A→B→C→...). In other words, two successive samplings are correlated with each other. This is why it is called a Markov Chain method. Special algorithms enable effective sampling even if the target is small (b).*

Monte Carlo method

A class of numerical approaches to collect information about a system by repeating experiments based on a large amount of random numbers. In a narrower sense, it is a mathematical method to obtain solutions for definite integrals of a function using random numbers. Using random numbers between a and b $\{x_1, x_2, x_3, \ldots x_N\}$, N samples $\{f(x_1), f(x_2), f(x_3), \ldots f(x_N)\}$ are obtained, then

$$\int_a^b f(x)dx \approx \frac{1}{N}\sum_{k=1}^N f(x_k)$$

if N is sufficiently large. In numerical simulations, the behaviour of a system which involves stochastic elements is often simulated using (pseudo-)random numbers generated by a computer, which distribute (almost) uniformly between 0 and 1 (see 'Stochasticity').

Example
π can be calculated using a Monte Carlo method. First, one draws a large regular square and an inscribed circle on the ground. Then one throws stones randomly on the square. After many trials, one counts the number of stones in the square (N_S) and the ones in the circle (N_C). If it is known that the area of the square is $A_S = a^2$, then the area of the circle is

$$A_C = \frac{N_C}{N_S}A_S = \frac{N_C}{N_S}a^2.$$

Using $A_C = \pi \times \left(\frac{a}{2}\right)^2$, one obtains $\pi = \frac{4N_C}{N_S}$.

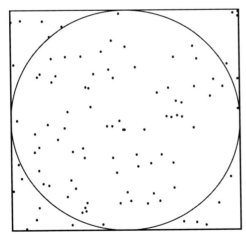

A result of random throwing of stones. One hundred stones are distributed randomly in the square. Seventy-seven out of them are in the square. The square is estimated as having 0.77 times the area of the square, which is a good approximation of the real value (0.785). In other words, the value of π is estimated as $4 \times 0.77 = 3.08$, which is close to 3.14.

Phase
Phase, or gametic phase, represents physical association of two alleles at different loci on a chromosome.

Polymorphism
Generally, the state where more than one type exists in a group. In population genetics, the term has been applied to phenotypic variability by Darwin since at least 1846. Individuals in a population sometimes are polymorphic in amino acid sequences for a protein. Since about 1990, population geneticists have shifted their focus to polymorphisms (i.e. nucleotide differences) between individuals in DNA sequences (see also 'SNP' and 'STR').

SNP (Single Nucleotide Polymorphism)
A variant nucleotide at one position in the DNA, which can be a substitution, insertion or deletion of a single nucleotide (see Introduction, Fig. I.4).

STR (Short Tandem Repeat)
Tandemly repeated DNA motifs, for example, (GT)(GT)(GT)...(GT). STRs are also known as microsatellites or SSRs (short simple repeats). STRs are prone to motif insertions and deletions (see Introduction, Fig. I.4). The mutation rates of STRs are generally much higher than other parts of the genome.

Stochasticity
The probabilistic or unpredictable nature of a system. In population genetics, for example, a stochastic fluctuation of population sizes arises when the number of offspring displays random variation among parents. Stochastic simulations incorporate this type of fluctuation, often by defining a probability distribution of the lifetime offspring number per parent.

System
An entire set of entities which are connected or interact with each other. The term also has discipline-specific meanings, for example, in forensics an 'STR system' is a synonym for an STR locus.

Index

205